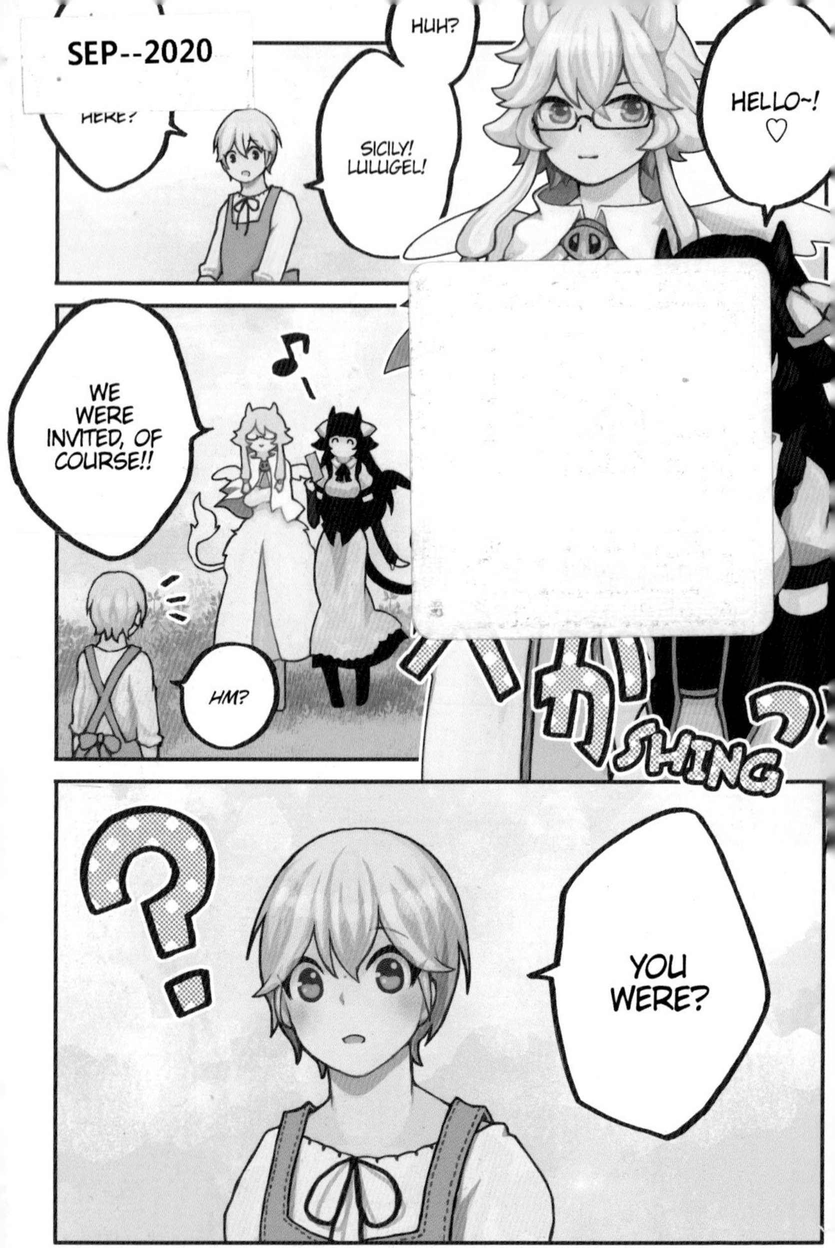
HELLO~! ♡
SHING
HUH?
SICILY! LULUGEL!
HERE?
WE WERE INVITED, OF COURSE!!
HM?
YOU WERE?

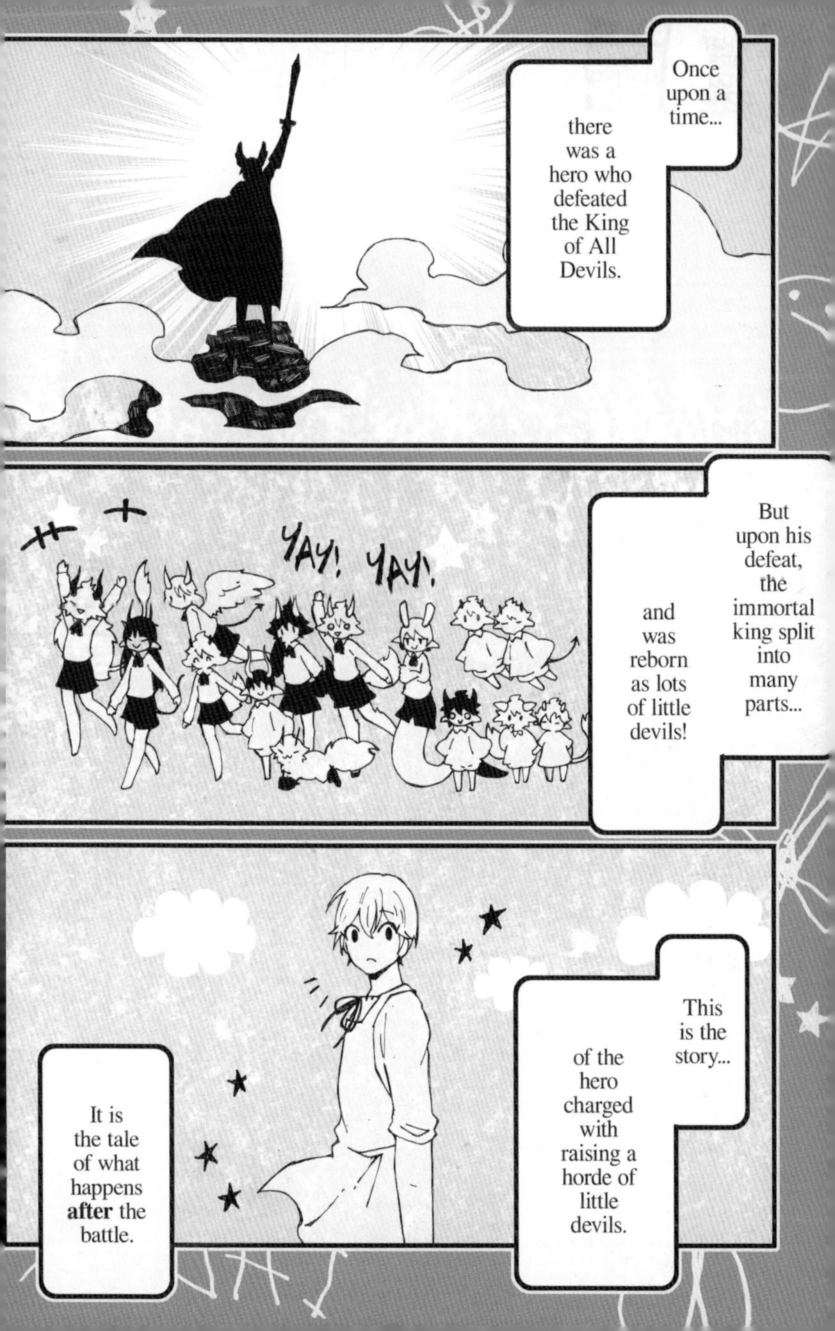
Once upon a time...
there was a hero who defeated the King of All Devils.
But upon his defeat, the immortal king split into many parts...
and was reborn as lots of little devils!
YAY! YAY!
This is the story...
of the hero charged with raising a horde of little devils.
It is the tale of what happens **after** the battle.

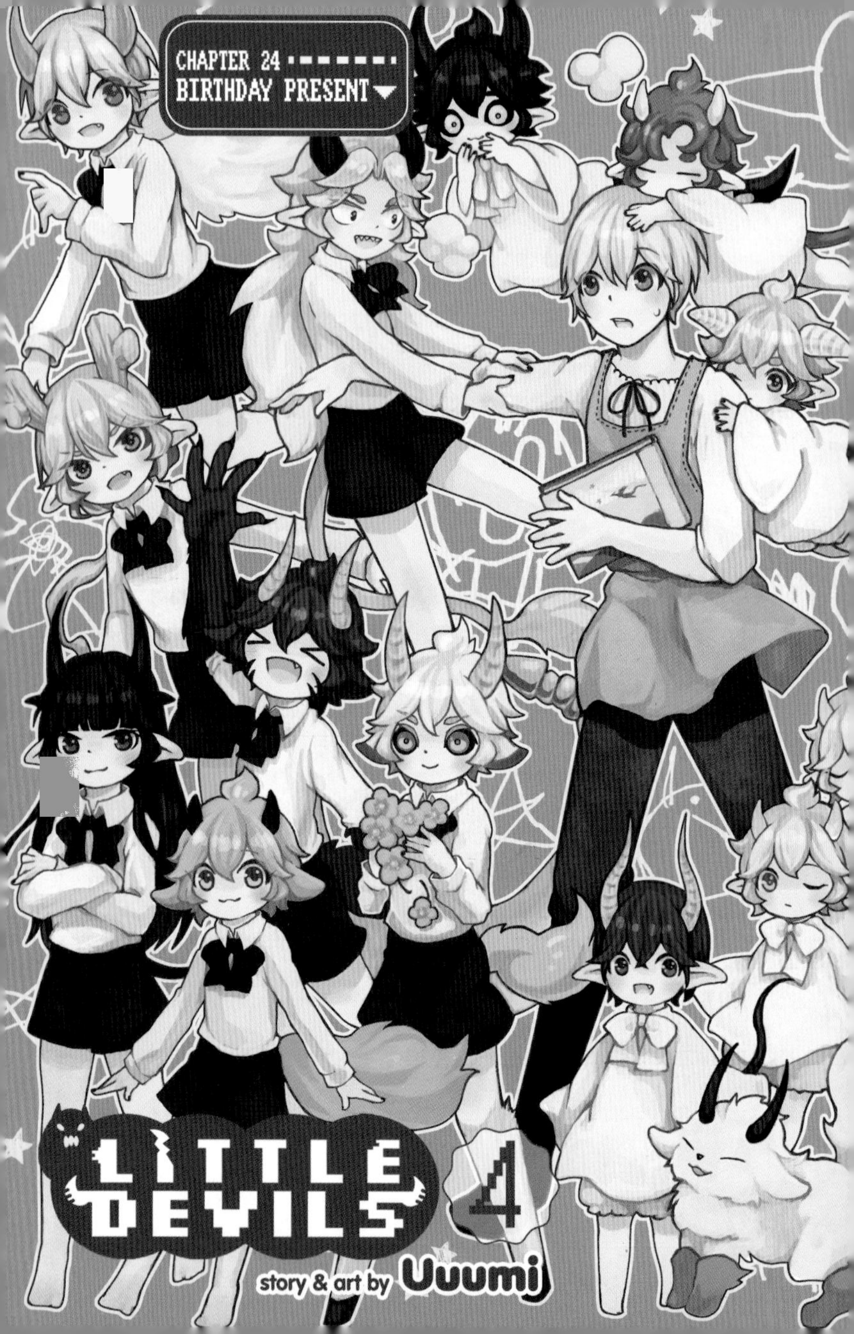
CHAPTER 24
BIRTHDAY PRESENT
LITTLE DEVILS
4
story & art by Uuumi

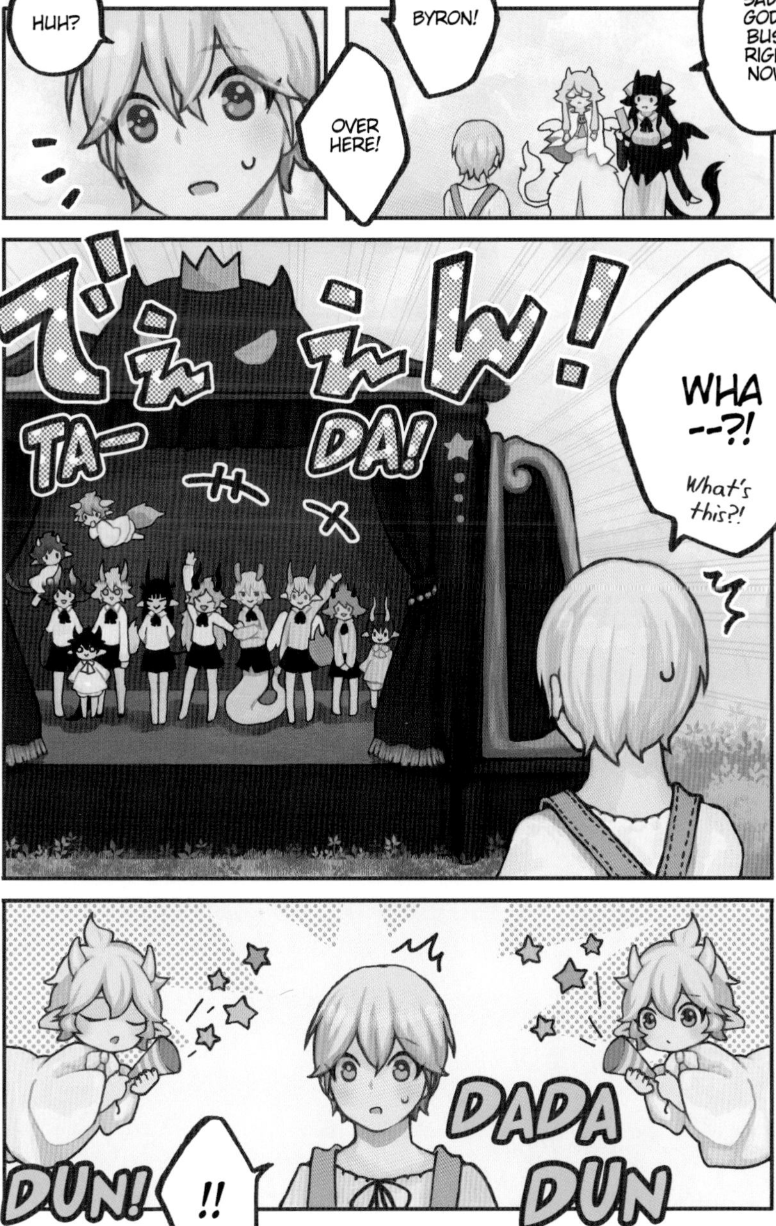
SADLY, GOD'S BUSY RIGHT NOW.
BYRON!
OVER HERE!
HUH?
でぇぇん!
TA— DA!
WHA--?!
What's this?!
DADA DUN
!!
DUN!

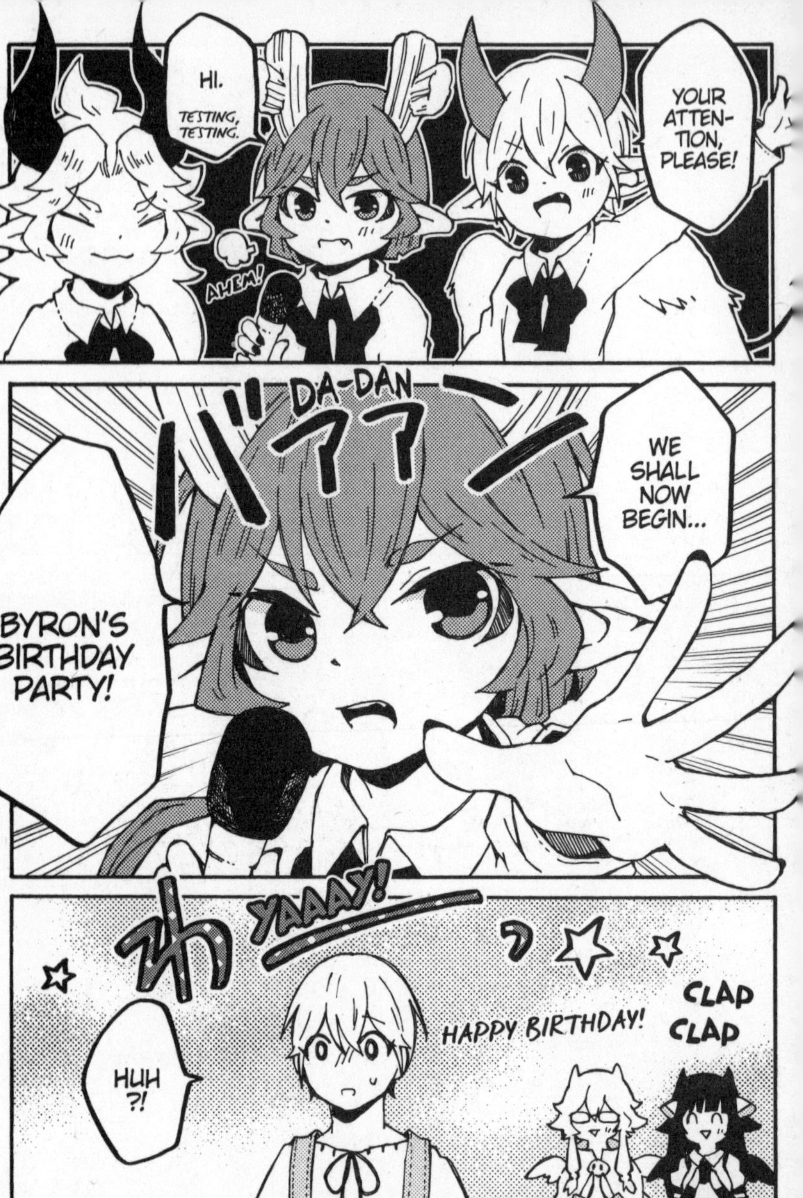
YOUR ATTENTION, PLEASE!
HI.
TESTING, TESTING.
AHEM!
DA-DAN
WE SHALL NOW BEGIN...
BYRON'S BIRTHDAY PARTY!
CLAP CLAP
YAAAAY!
HAPPY BIRTHDAY!
HUH ?!

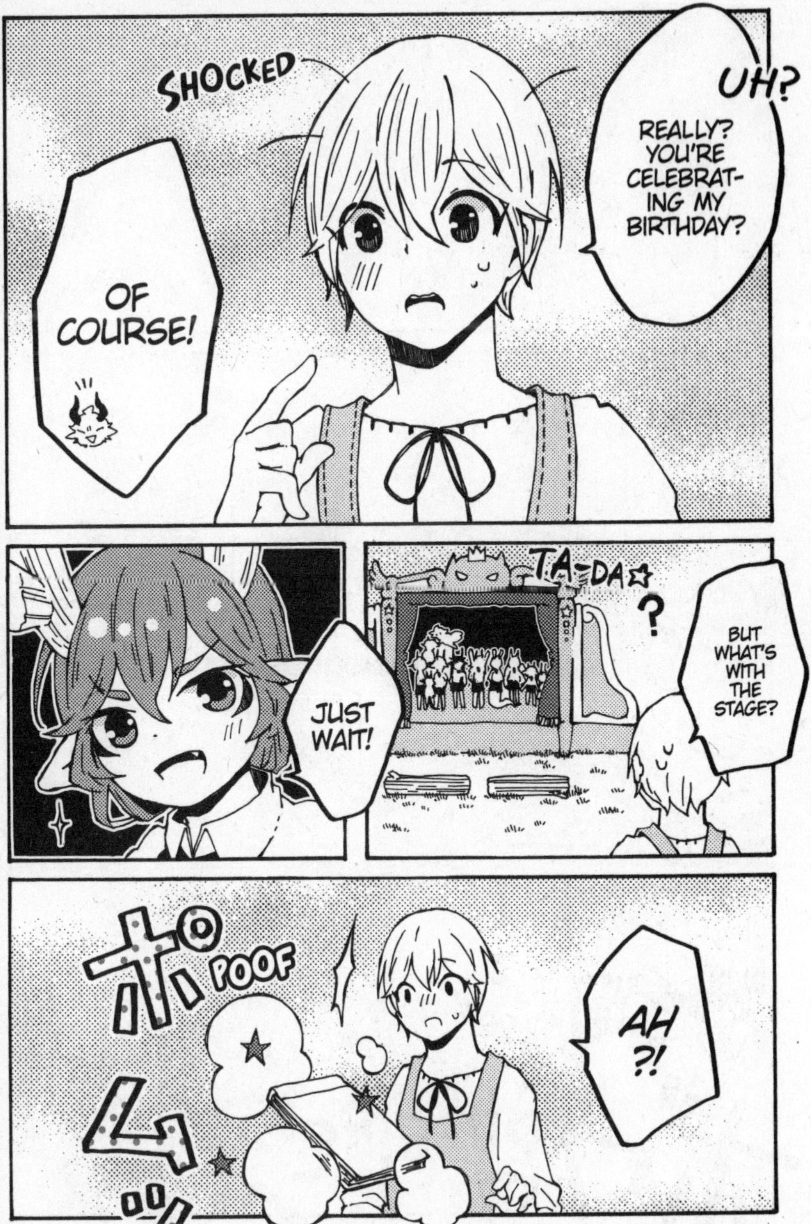
UH?
REALLY? YOU'RE CELEBRAT-ING MY BIRTHDAY?
SHOCKED
OF COURSE!
TA-DA☆
?
BUT WHAT'S WITH THE STAGE?
JUST WAIT!
AH?!
POOF

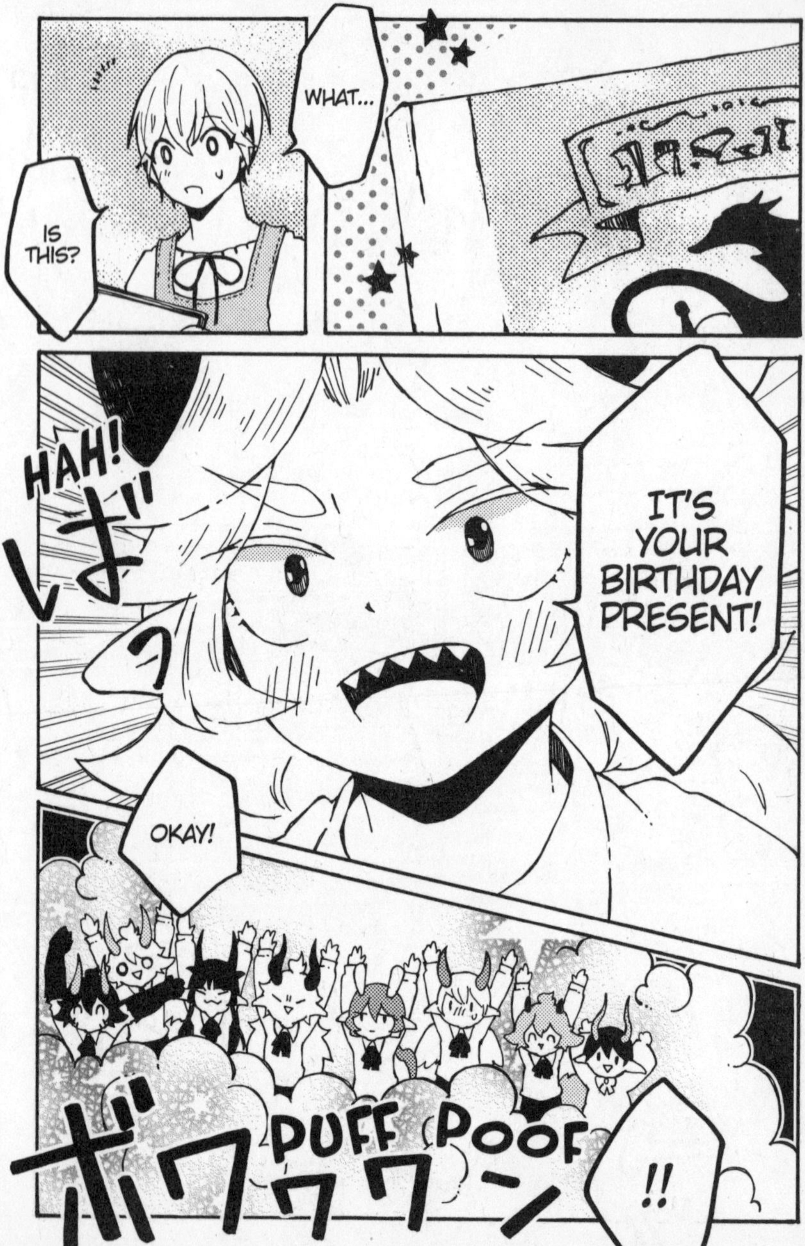
WHAT...
IS THIS?
IT'S YOUR BIRTHDAY PRESENT!
HAH!
OKAY!
PUFF
POOF
!!

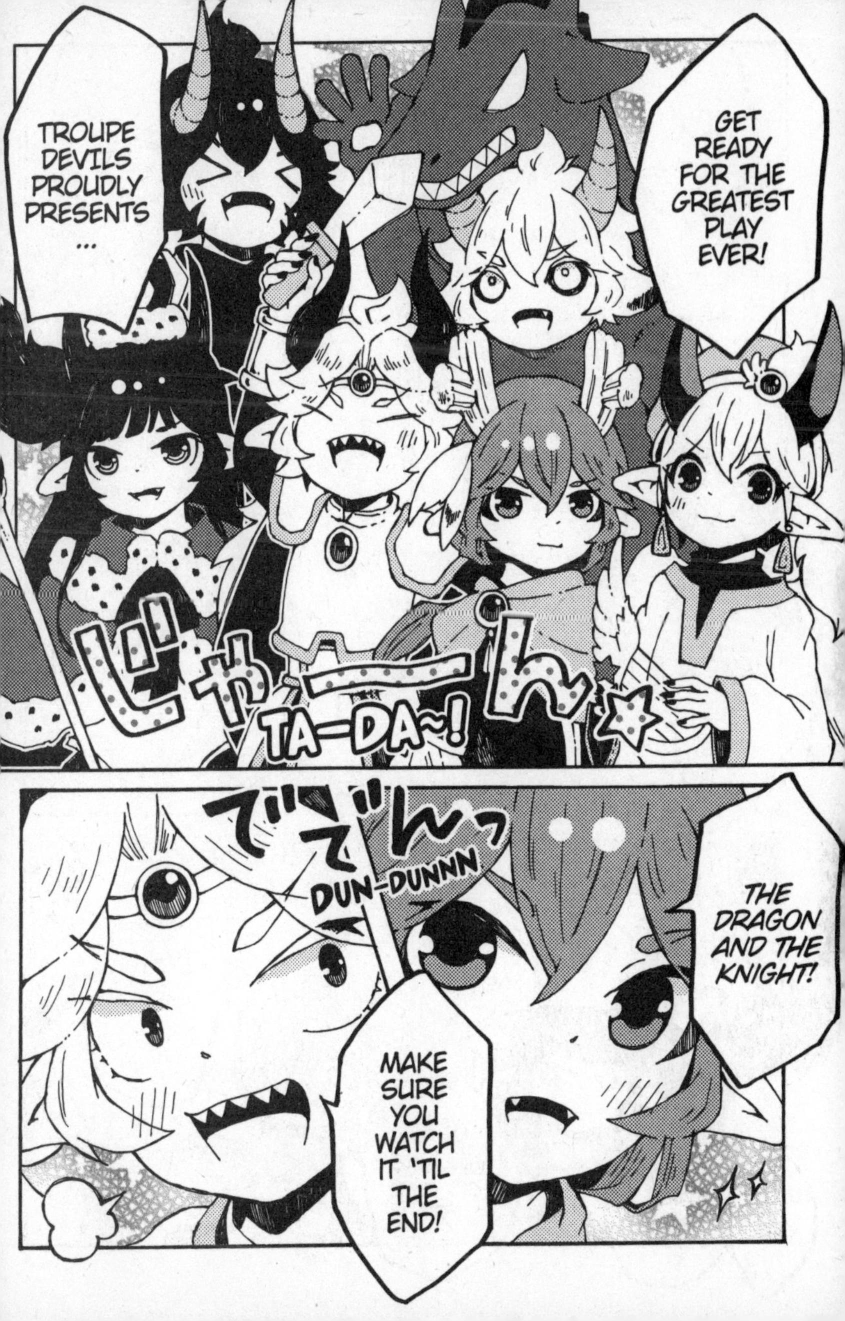
GET READY FOR THE GREATEST PLAY EVER!
TROUPE DEVILS PROUDLY PRESENTS ...
じゃーん☆
TA-DA~!
ででんっ
DUN-DUNNN
THE DRAGON AND THE KNIGHT!
MAKE SURE YOU WATCH IT 'TIL THE END!

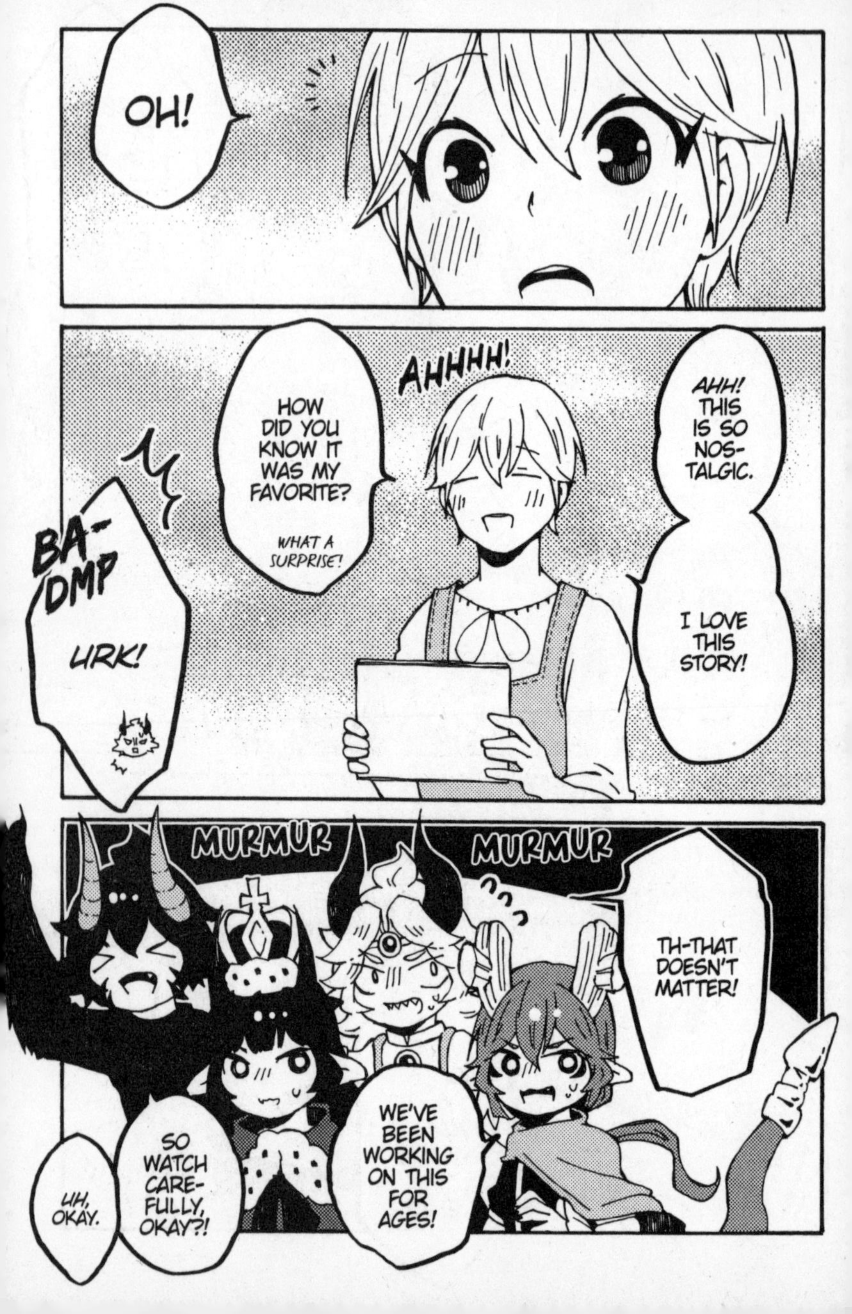
OH!
AHH! THIS IS SO NOS-TALGIC.
I LOVE THIS STORY!
AHHHH!
HOW DID YOU KNOW IT WAS MY FAVORITE?
WHAT A SURPRISE!
BA-DMP
URK!
MURMUR
MURMUR
TH-THAT DOESN'T MATTER!
WE'VE BEEN WORKING ON THIS FOR AGES!
SO WATCH CARE-FULLY, OKAY?!
UH, OKAY.

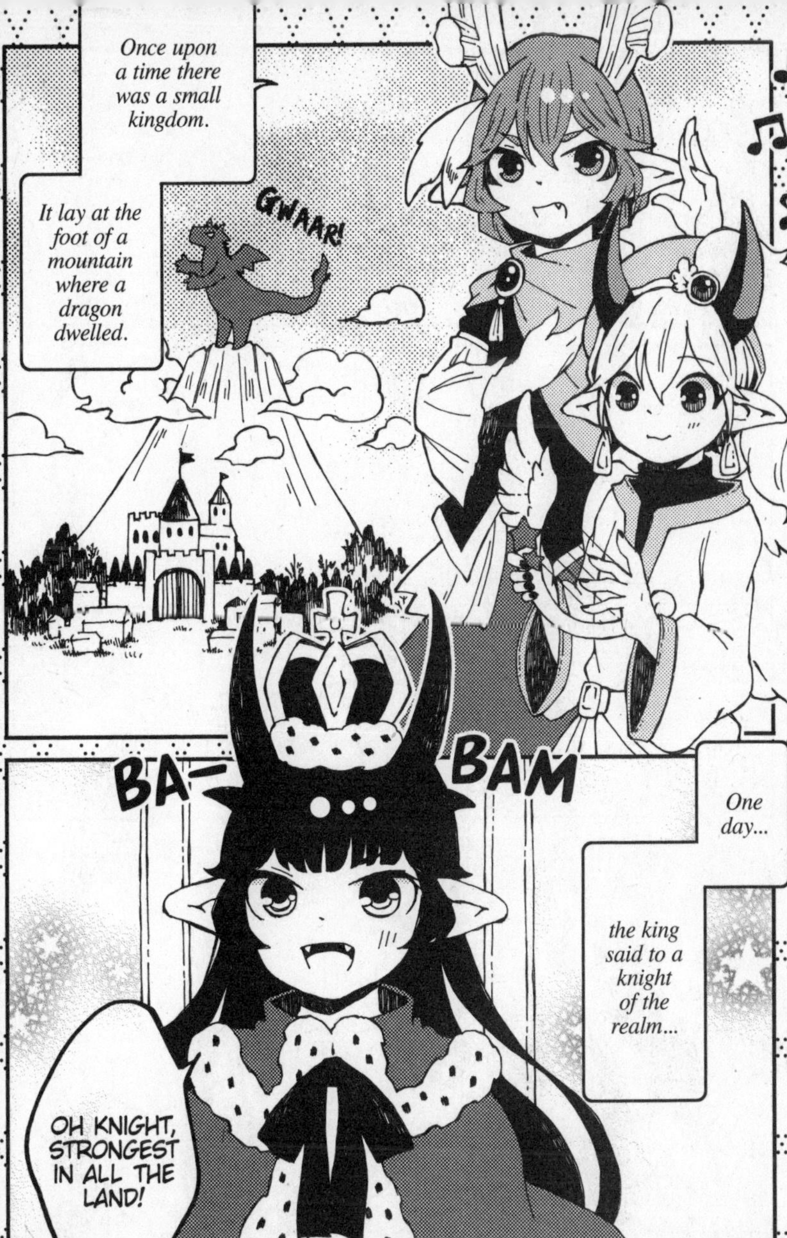
Once upon a time there was a small kingdom.
It lay at the foot of a mountain where a dragon dwelled.
GWAAR!
One day...
the king said to a knight of the realm...
BA— BAM
OH KNIGHT, STRONGEST IN ALL THE LAND!

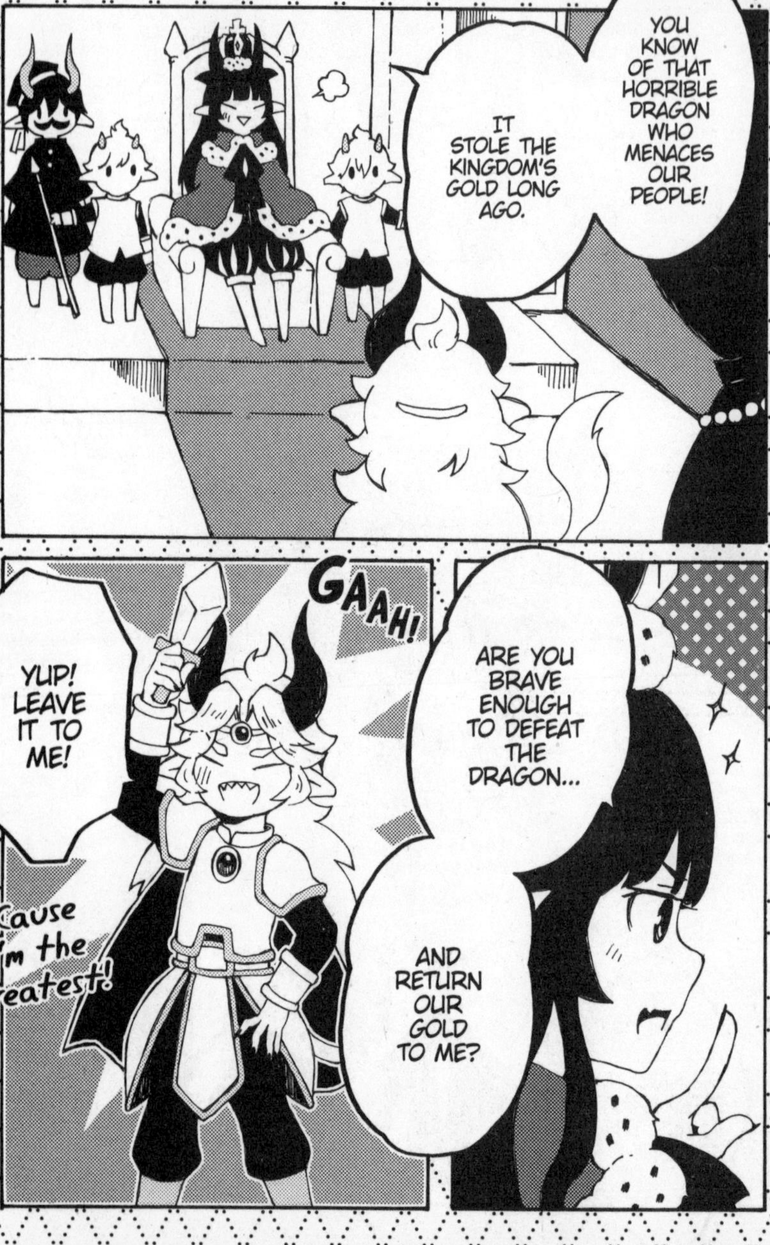
YOU KNOW OF THAT HORRIBLE DRAGON WHO MENACES OUR PEOPLE!
IT STOLE THE KINGDOM'S GOLD LONG AGO.
ARE YOU BRAVE ENOUGH TO DEFEAT THE DRAGON...
AND RETURN OUR GOLD TO ME?
GAAAH!
YUP! LEAVE IT TO ME!
'Cause I'm the greatest!

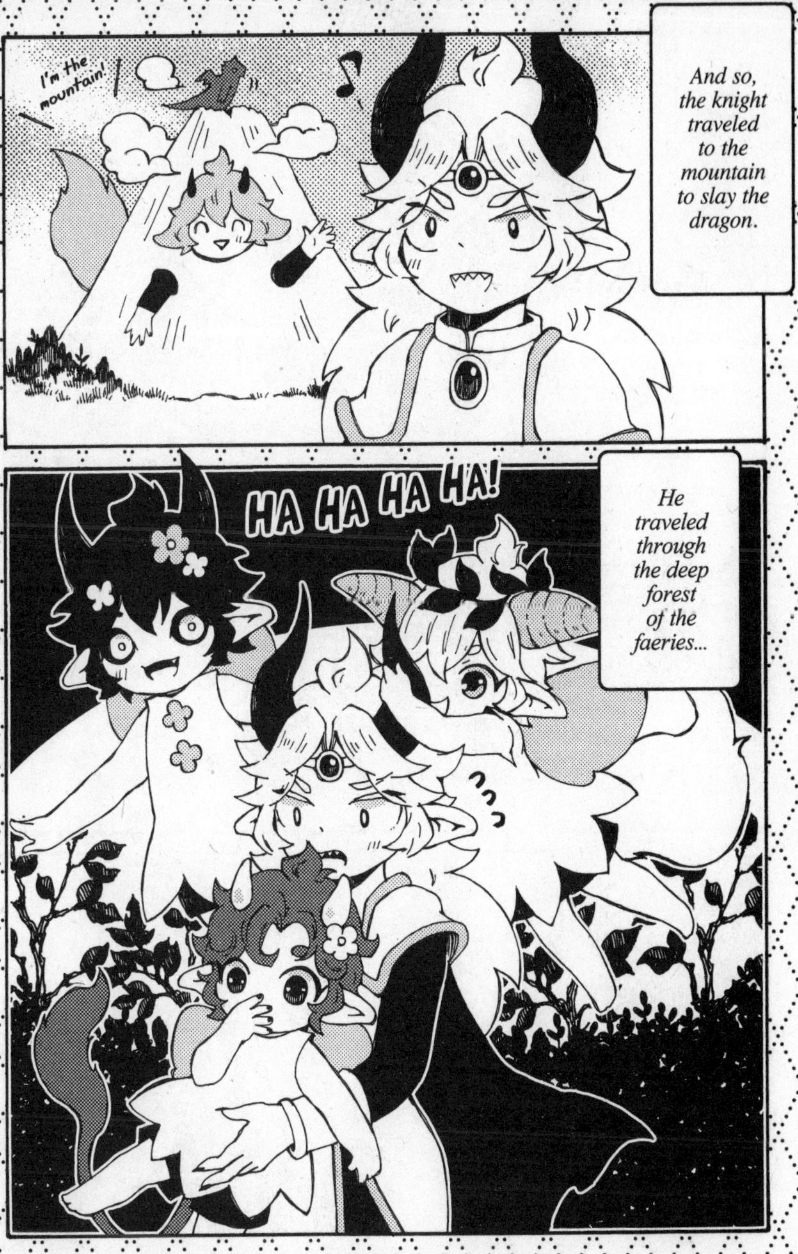
And so, the knight traveled to the mountain to slay the dragon.
I'm the mountain!
He traveled through the deep forest of the faeries...
HA HA HA HA HA!

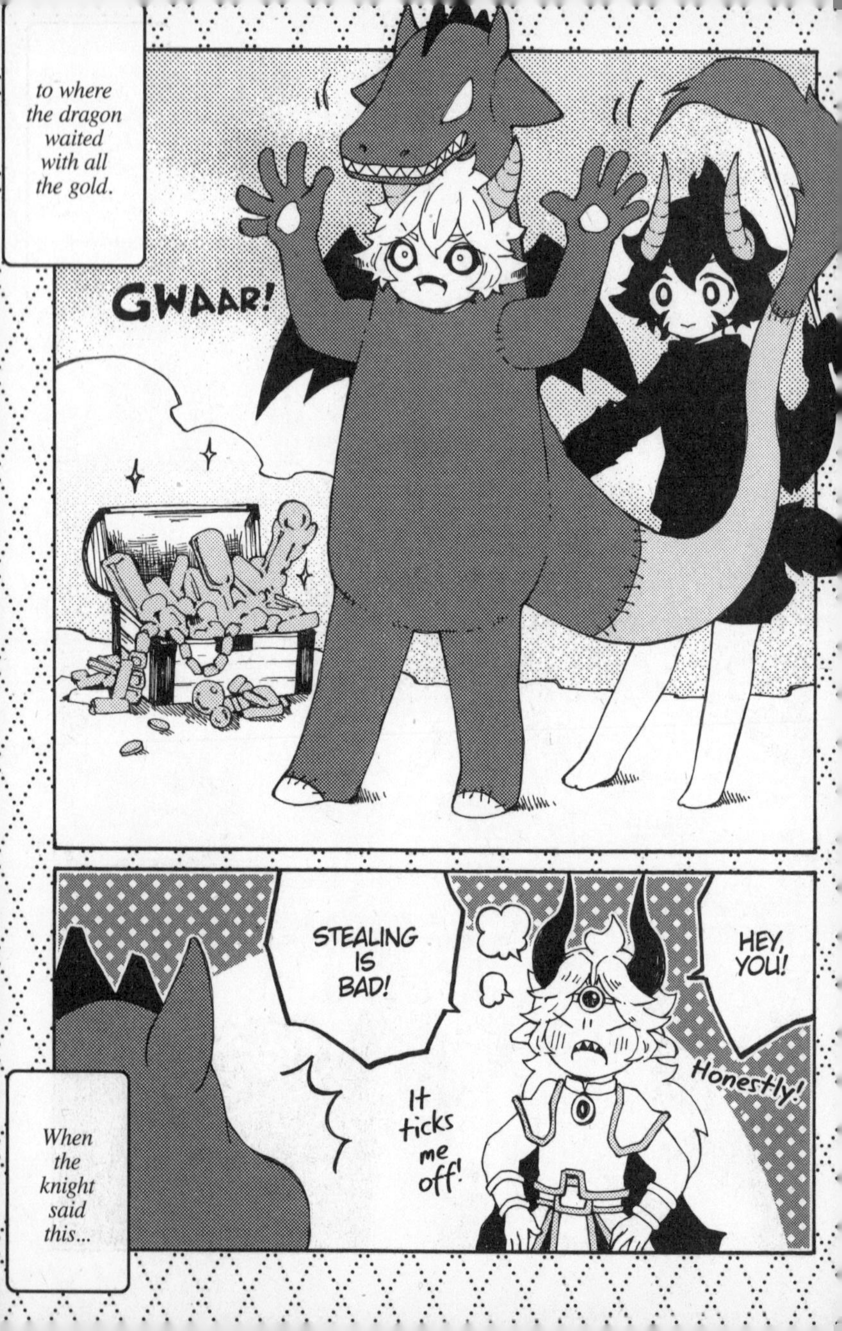
to where the dragon waited with all the gold.
GWAAR!
HEY, YOU!
Honestly!
STEALING IS BAD!
It ticks me off!
When the knight said this...

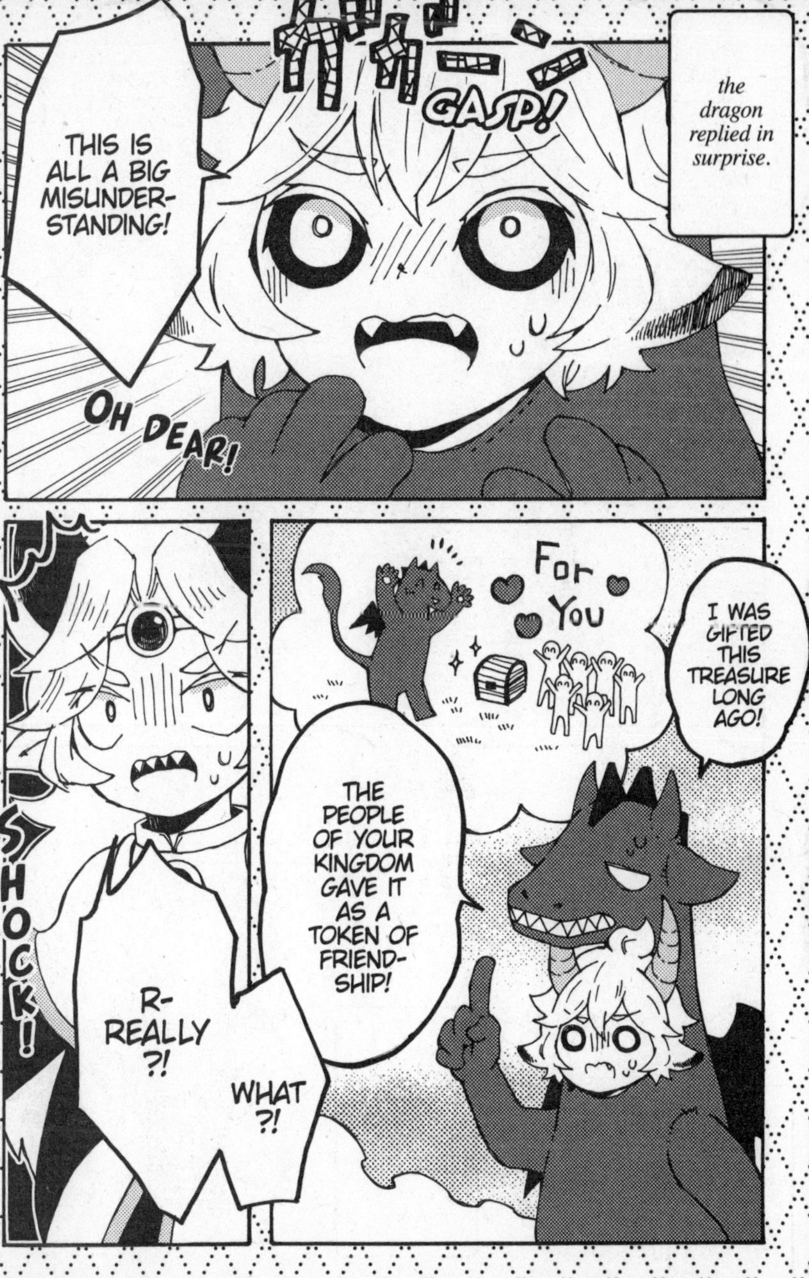
the dragon replied in surprise.
GASP!
THIS IS ALL A BIG MISUNDER-STANDING!
OH DEAR!
I WAS GIFTED THIS TREASURE LONG AGO!
For You
THE PEOPLE OF YOUR KINGDOM GAVE IT AS A TOKEN OF FRIEND-SHIP!
WHAT?!
SHOCK!
R-REALLY?!

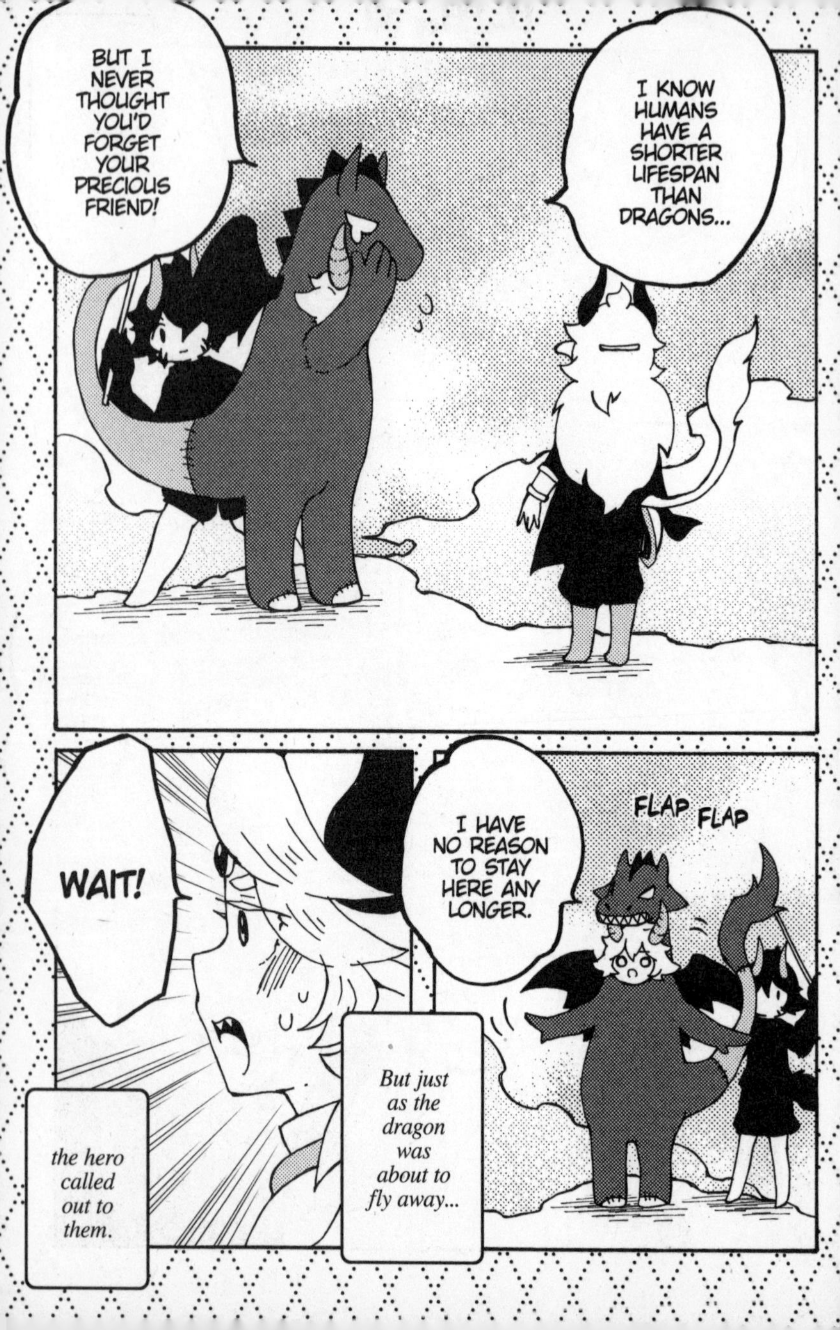
I KNOW HUMANS HAVE A SHORTER LIFESPAN THAN DRAGONS...
BUT I NEVER THOUGHT YOU'D FORGET YOUR PRECIOUS FRIEND!
FLAP FLAP
I HAVE NO REASON TO STAY HERE ANY LONGER.
But just as the dragon was about to fly away...
WAIT!
the hero called out to them.

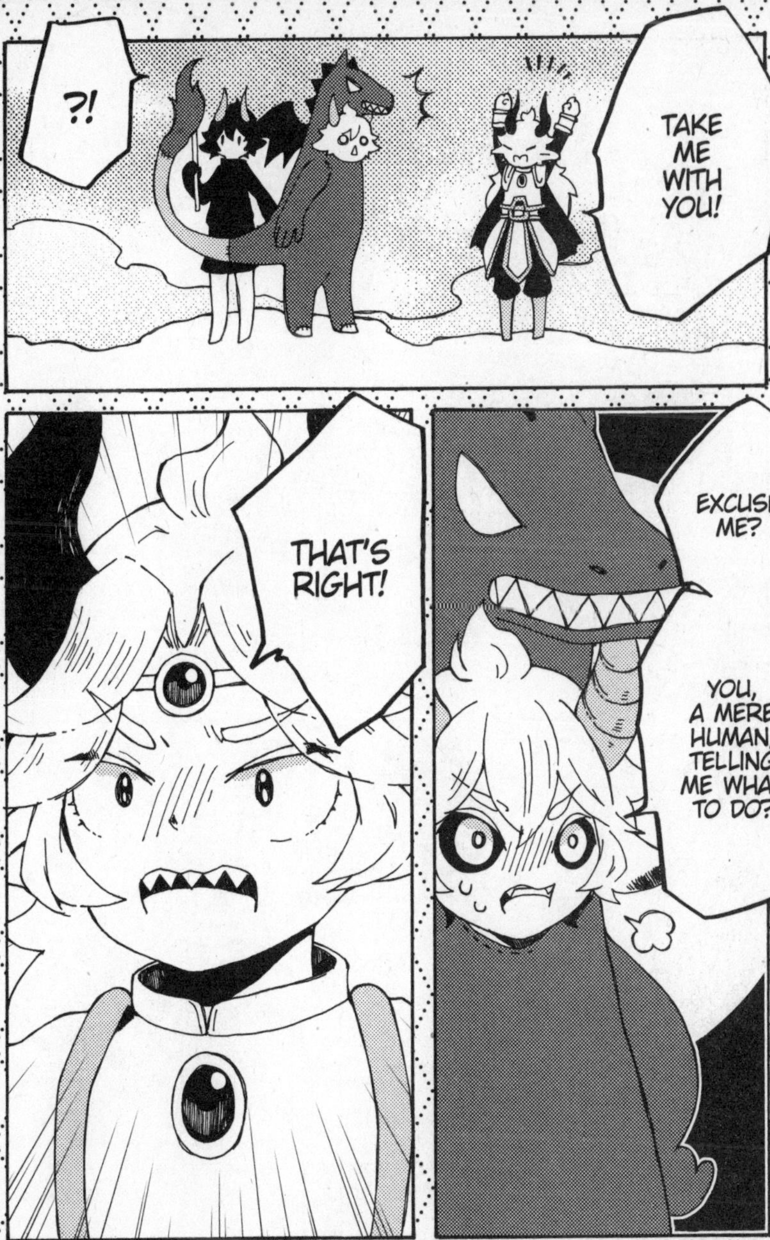
TAKE ME WITH YOU!
?!
EXCUSE ME?
YOU, A MERE HUMAN, TELLING ME WHAT TO DO?
THAT'S RIGHT!

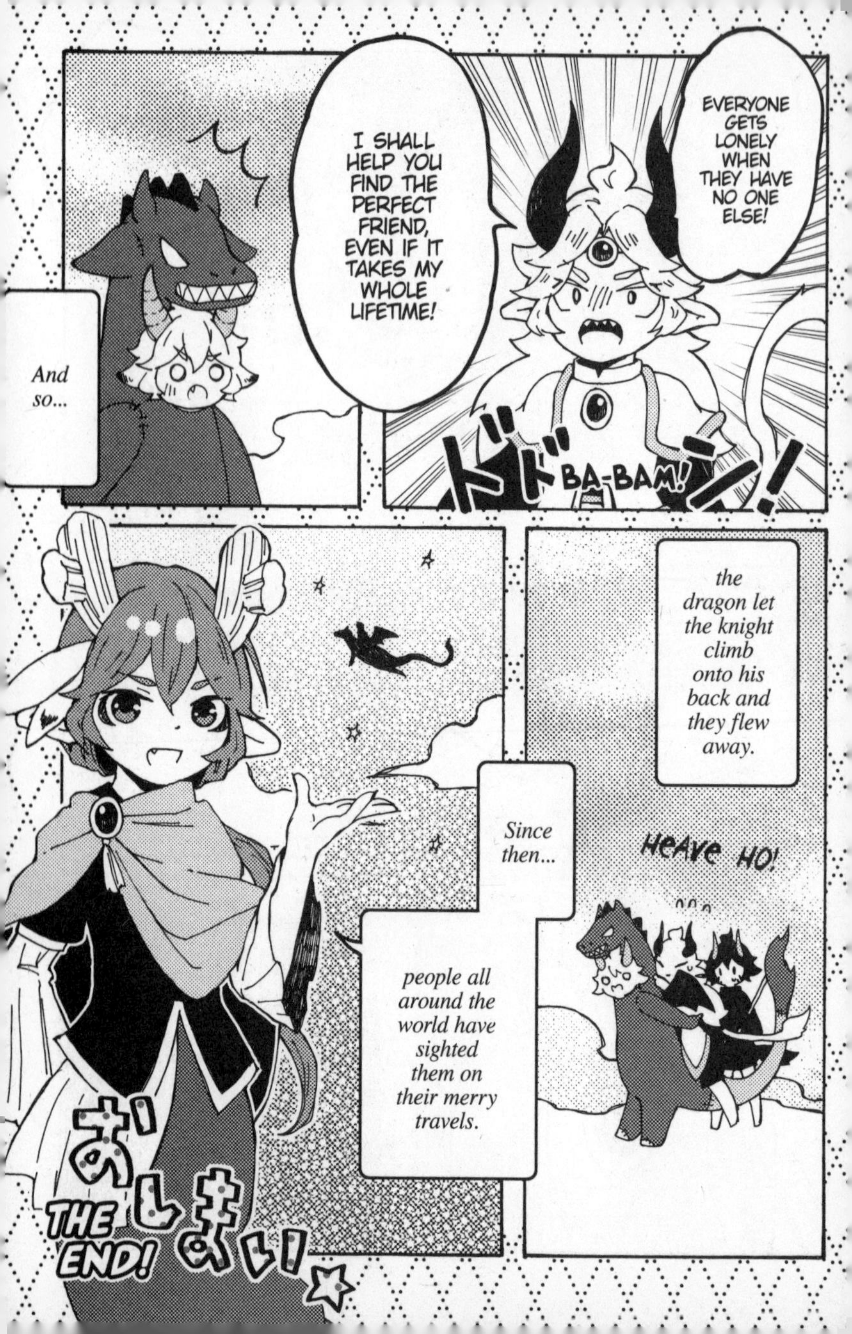
EVERYONE GETS LONELY WHEN THEY HAVE NO ONE ELSE!
I SHALL HELP YOU FIND THE PERFECT FRIEND, EVEN IF IT TAKES MY WHOLE LIFETIME!
BA-BAM!
And so...
the dragon let the knight climb onto his back and they flew away.
HEAVE HO!
Since then...
people all around the world have sighted them on their merry travels.
おしまい!
THE END!

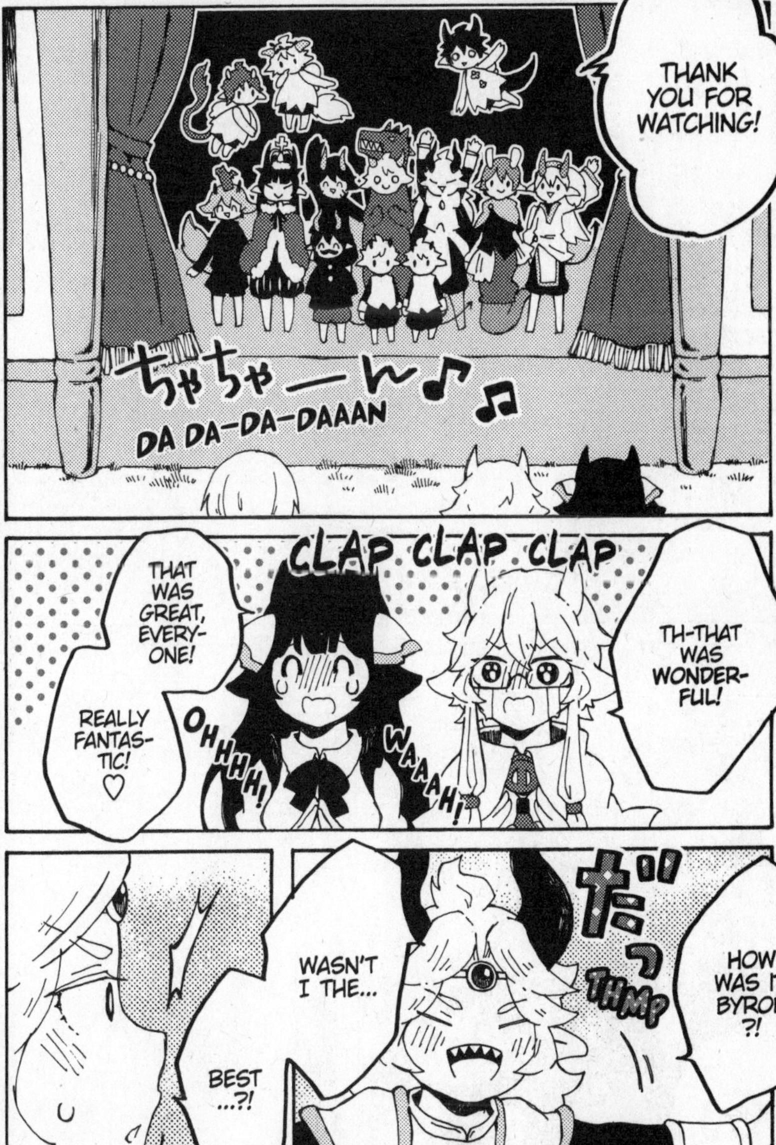
THANK YOU FOR WATCHING!
ちゃちゃーん♪♫
DA DA-DA-DAAAN
TH-THAT WAS WONDER-FUL!
CLAP CLAP CLAP
WAAAAH!
OHHHHH!
THAT WAS GREAT, EVERY-ONE!
REALLY FANTAS-TIC! ♡
だっ
THMP
HOW WAS IT, BYRON?!
WASN'T I THE...
BEST ...?!

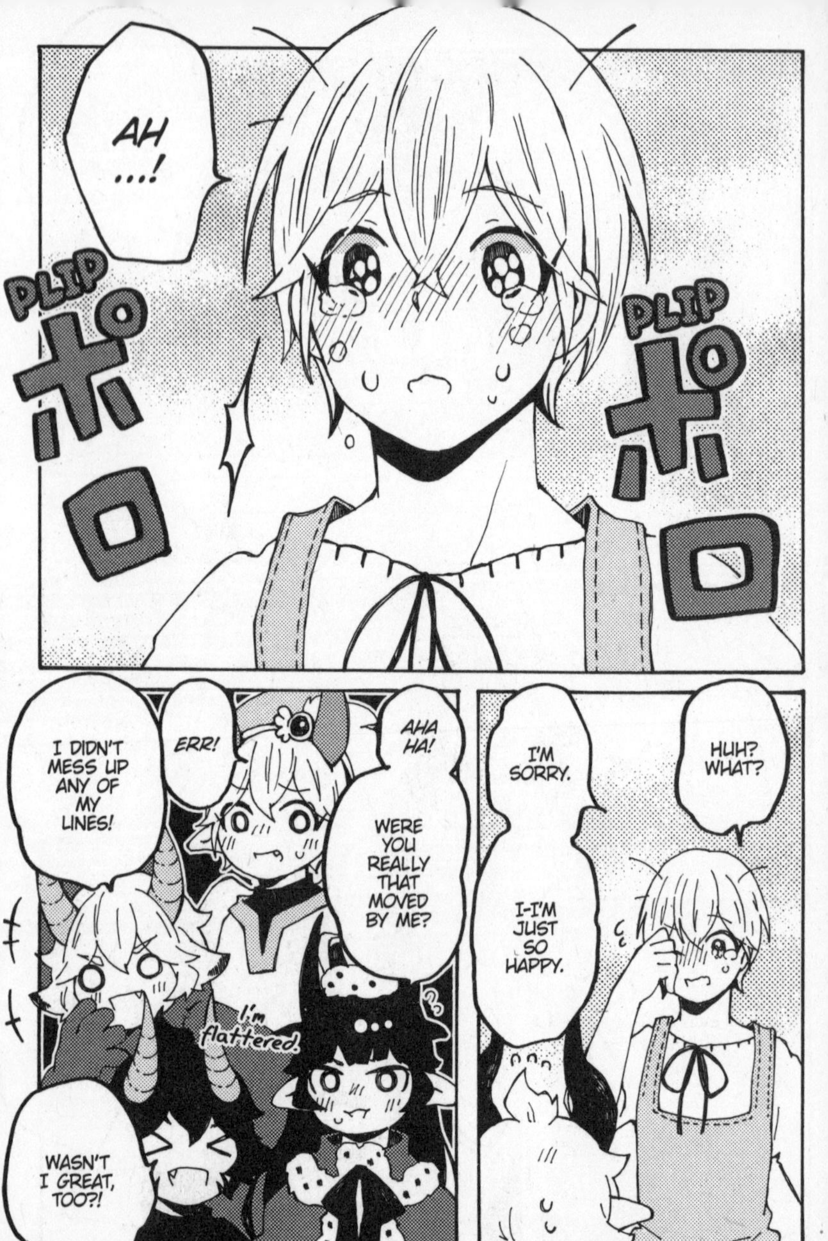
AH ...!
PLIP
ポロ
PLIP
ポロ
HUH? WHAT?
I'M SORRY.
I-I'M JUST SO HAPPY.
AHA HA!
WERE YOU REALLY THAT MOVED BY ME?
ERR!
I DIDN'T MESS UP ANY OF MY LINES!
I'm flattered.
WASN'T I GREAT, TOO?!

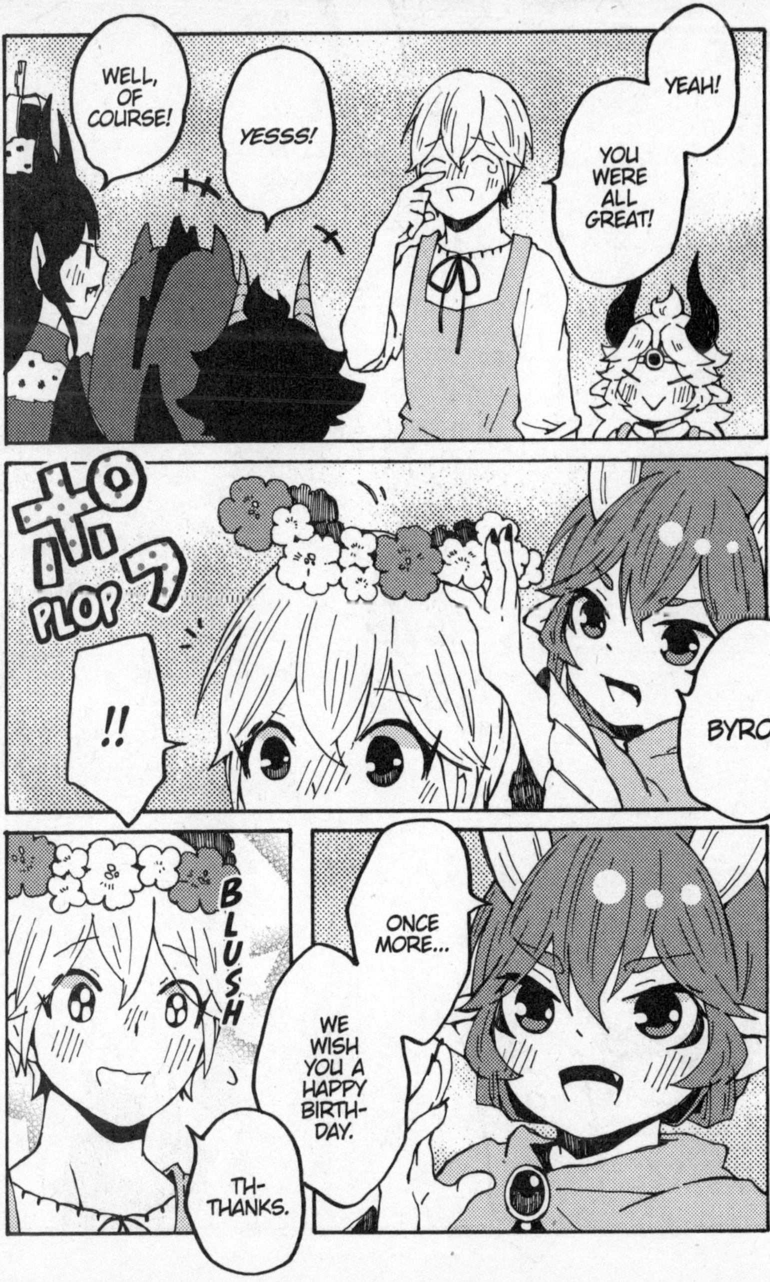
YEAH!
YOU WERE ALL GREAT!
YESSS!
WELL, OF COURSE!
BYRON.
ポフ PLOP
!!
ONCE MORE...
WE WISH YOU A HAPPY BIRTH-DAY.
BLUSH
TH-THANKS.

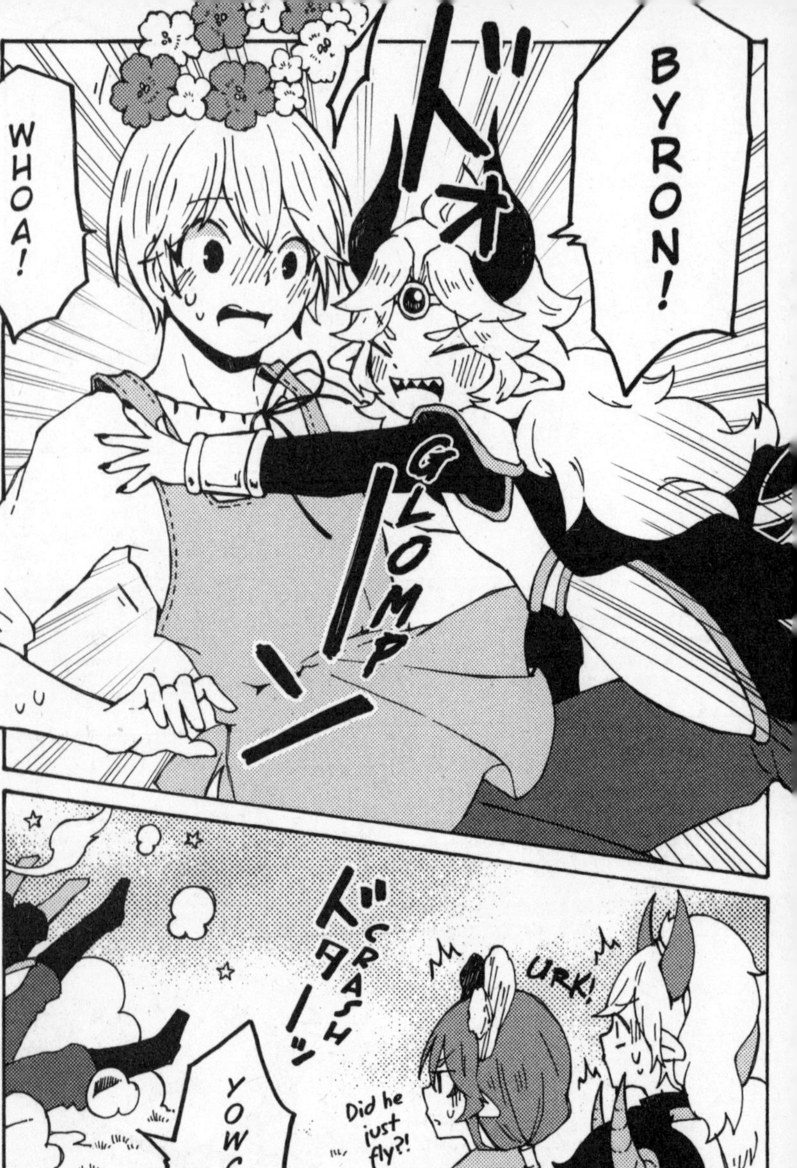
BYRON!
ドオ
GLOMP
WHOA!
URK!
Did he just fly?!
ドターッ
CRASH
YOWCH!

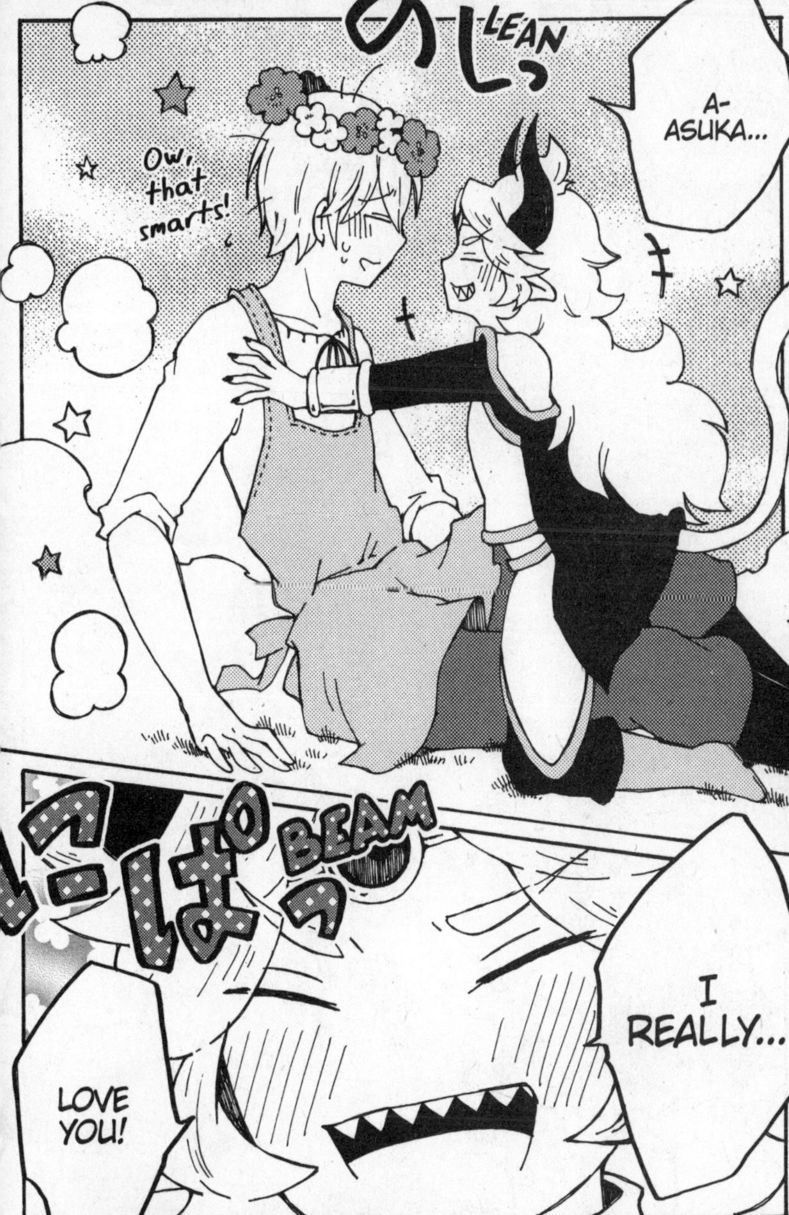
A- ASUKA...
のしっ LEAN
Ow, that smarts!
I REALLY...
BEAM
LOVE YOU!

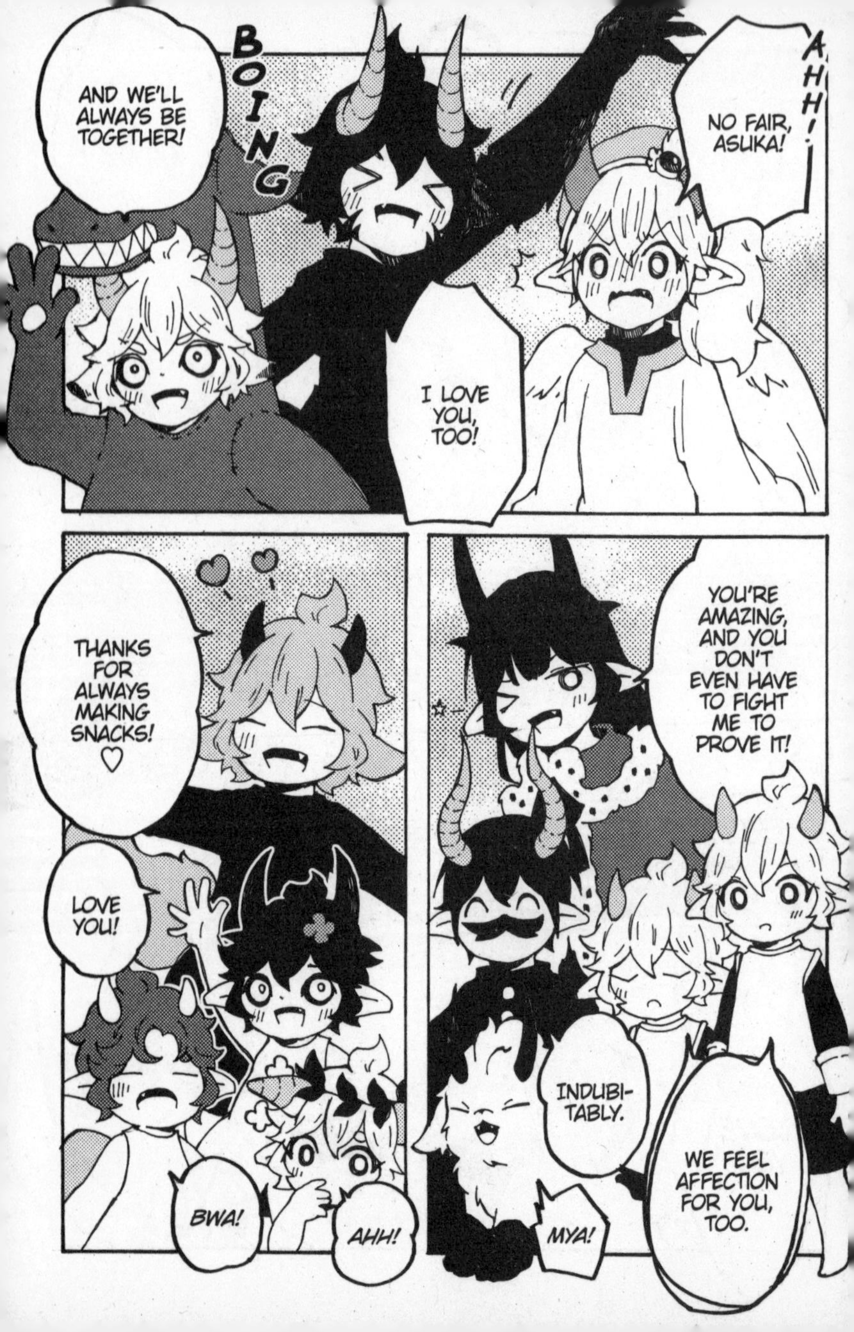
AHHH!
NO FAIR, ASUKA!
BOING
AND WE'LL ALWAYS BE TOGETHER!
I LOVE YOU, TOO!
YOU'RE AMAZING, AND YOU DON'T EVEN HAVE TO FIGHT ME TO PROVE IT!
INDUBITABLY.
WE FEEL AFFECTION FOR YOU, TOO.
MYA!
THANKS FOR ALWAYS MAKING SNACKS! ♡
LOVE YOU!
AHH!
BWA!

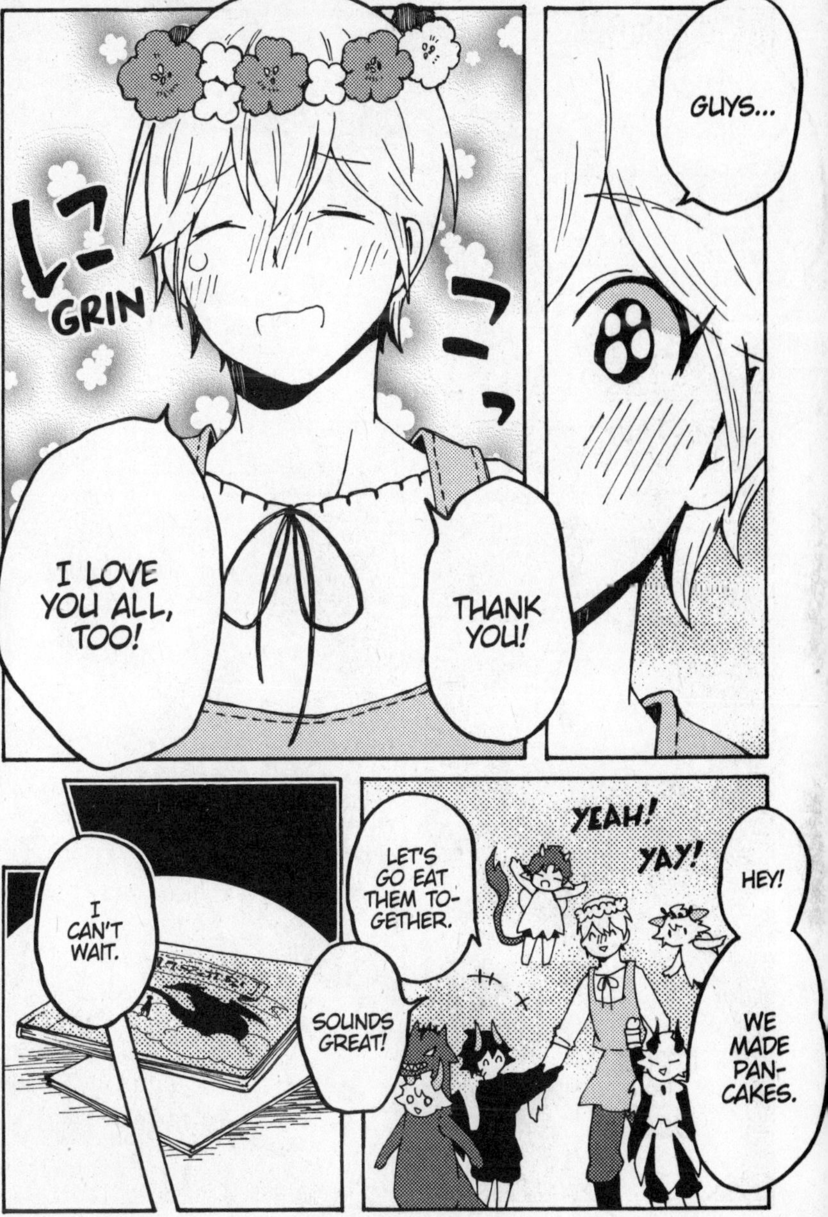
GUYS...
THANK YOU!
I LOVE YOU ALL, TOO!
GRIN
HEY!
WE MADE PANCAKES.
YAY!
YEAH!
LET'S GO EAT THEM TOGETHER.
SOUNDS GREAT!
I CAN'T WAIT.

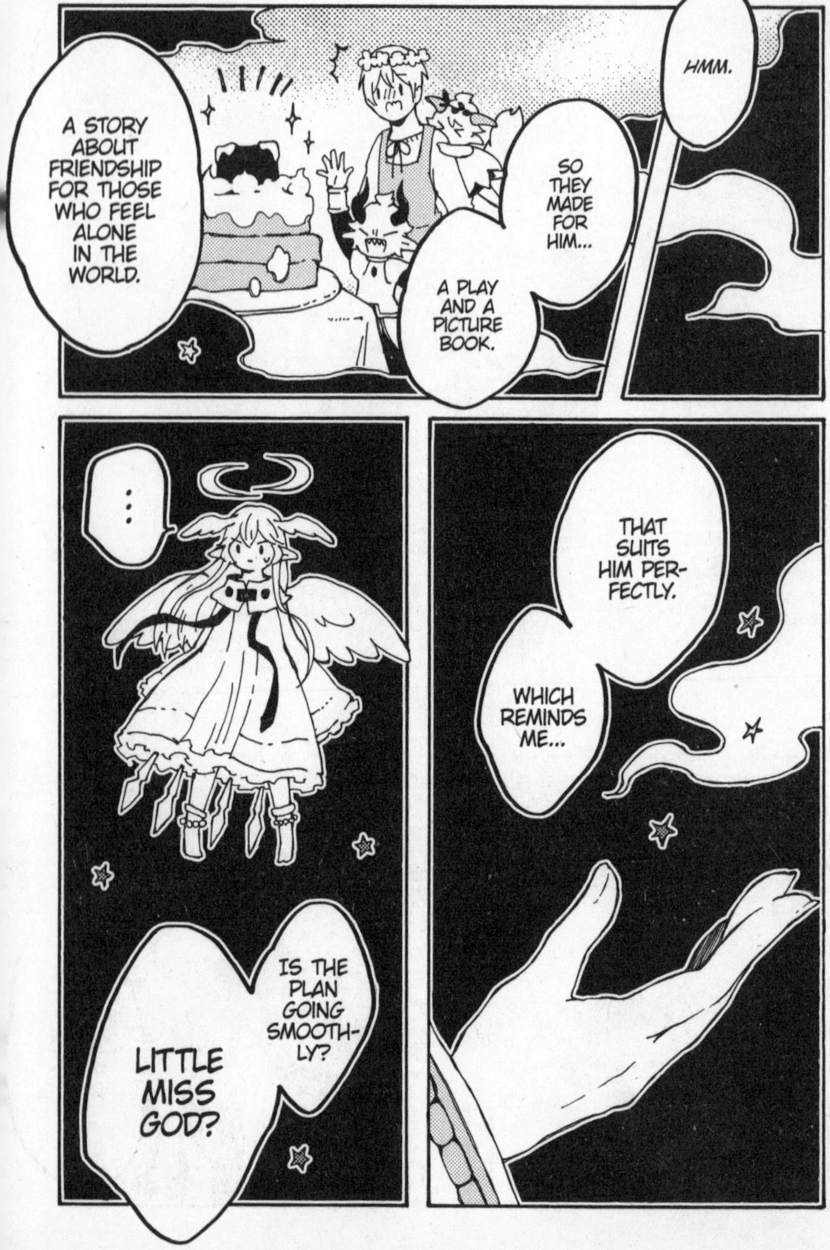
HMM.
SO THEY MADE FOR HIM...
A PLAY AND A PICTURE BOOK.
A STORY ABOUT FRIENDSHIP FOR THOSE WHO FEEL ALONE IN THE WORLD.
THAT SUITS HIM PER-FECTLY.
WHICH REMINDS ME...
...
IS THE PLAN GOING SMOOTH-LY?
LITTLE MISS GOD?

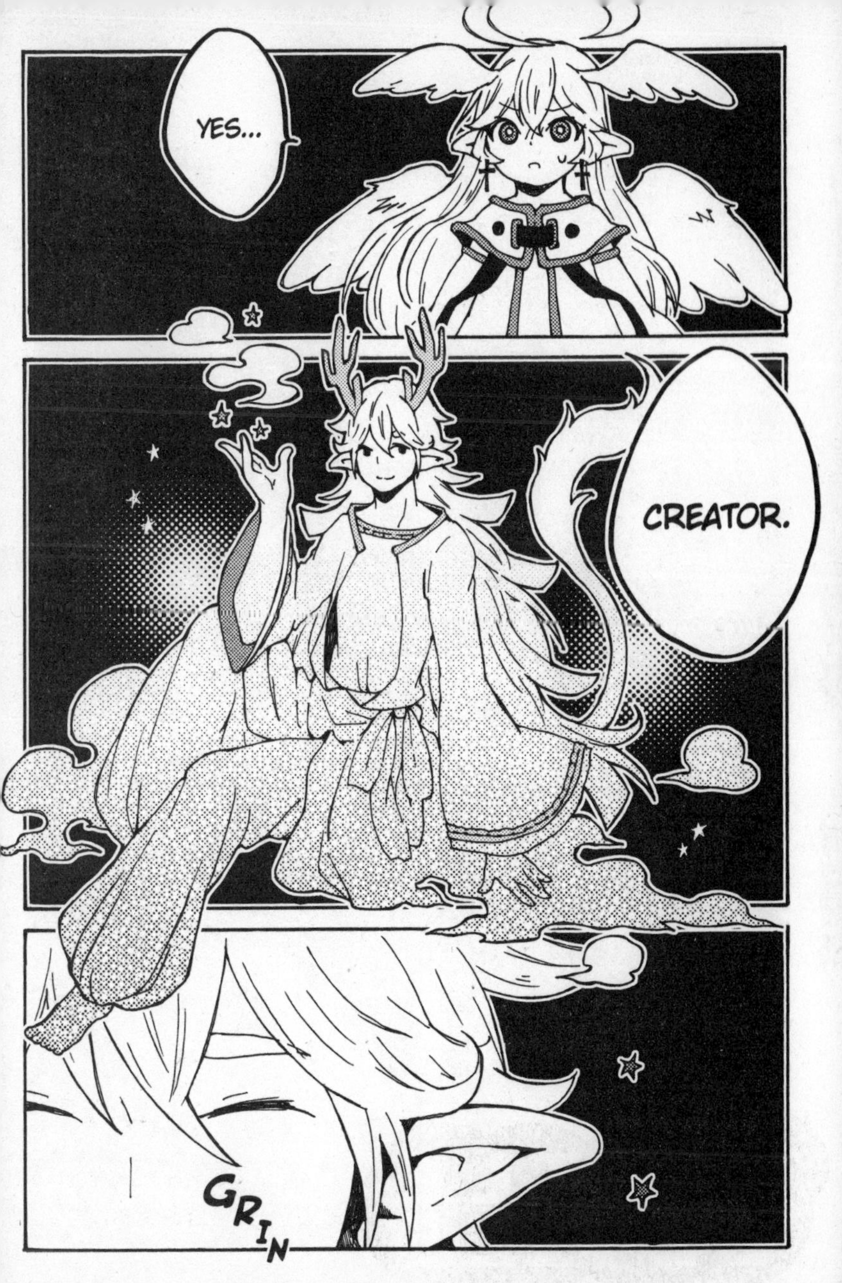
YES...
CREATOR.
GRIN

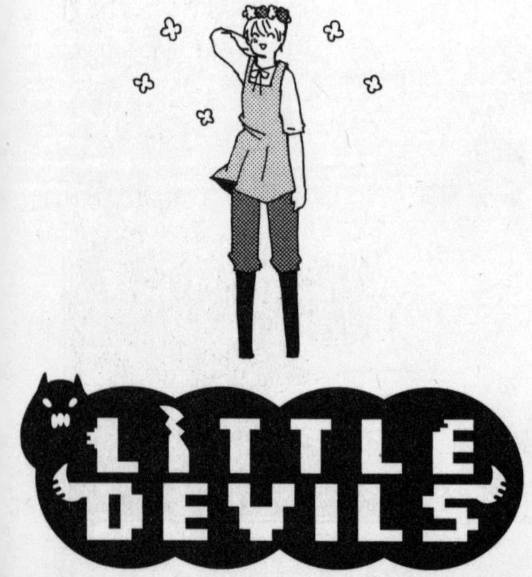

LITTLE DEVILS

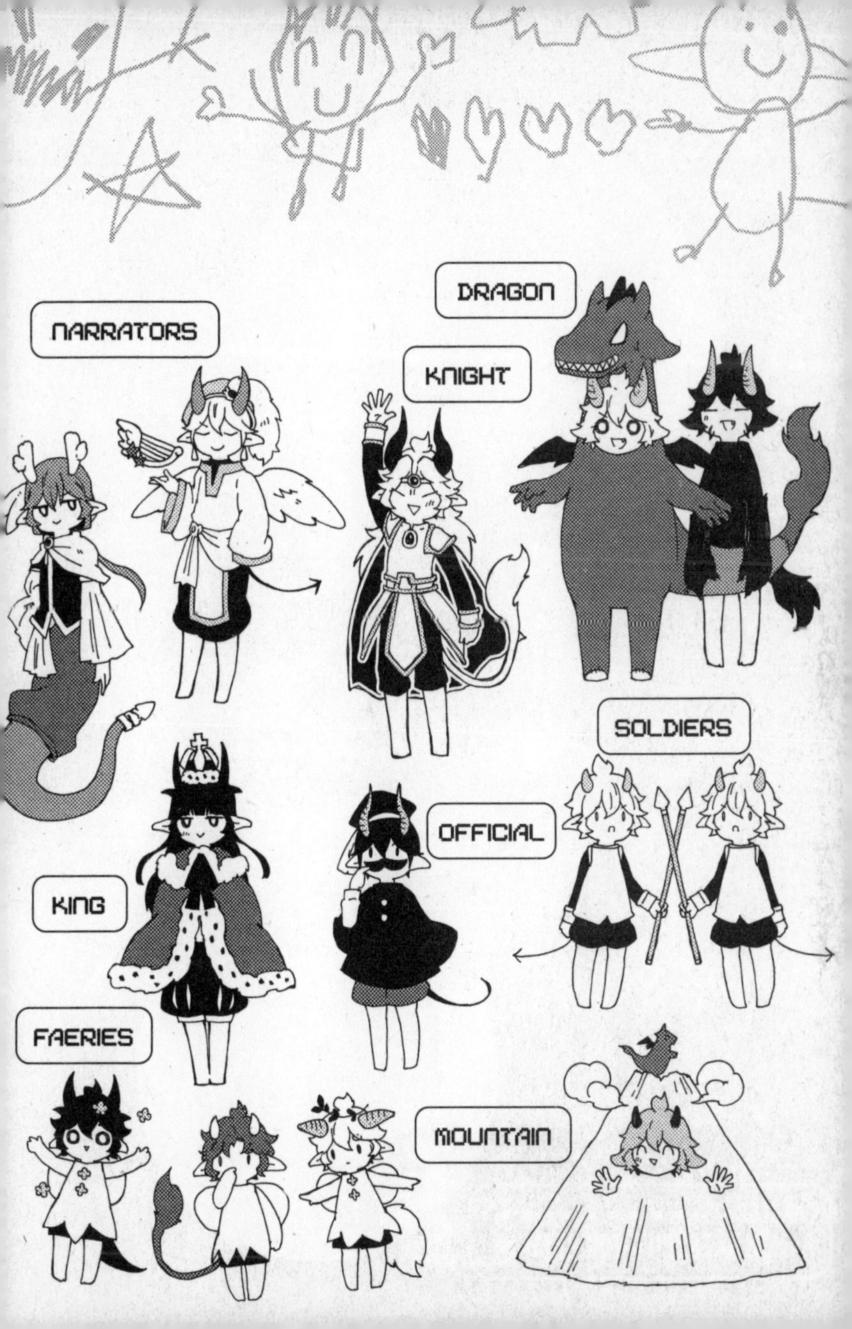
DRAGON
NARRATORS
KNIGHT
SOLDIERS
OFFICIAL
KING
FAERIES
MOUNTAIN

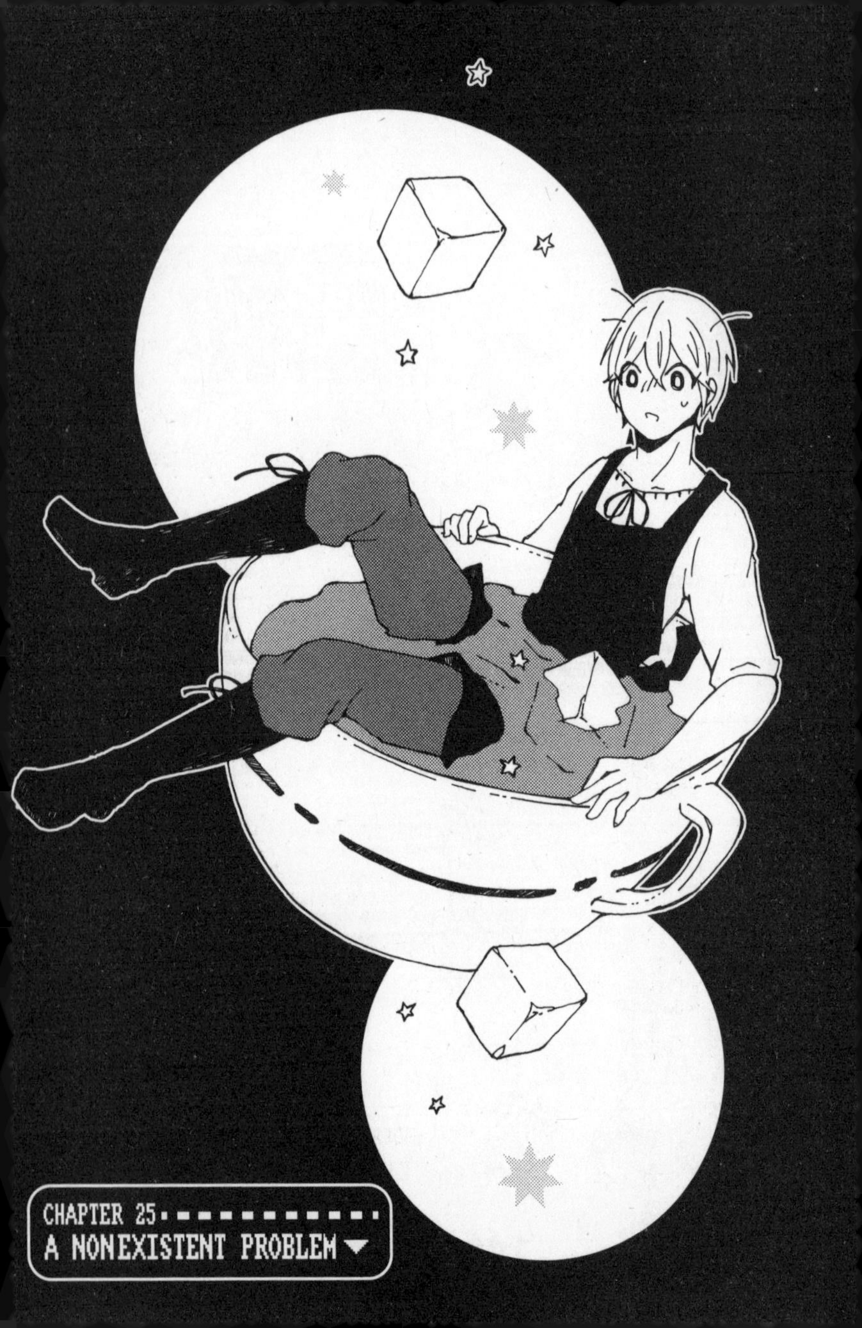

CHAPTER 25
A NONEXISTENT PROBLEM

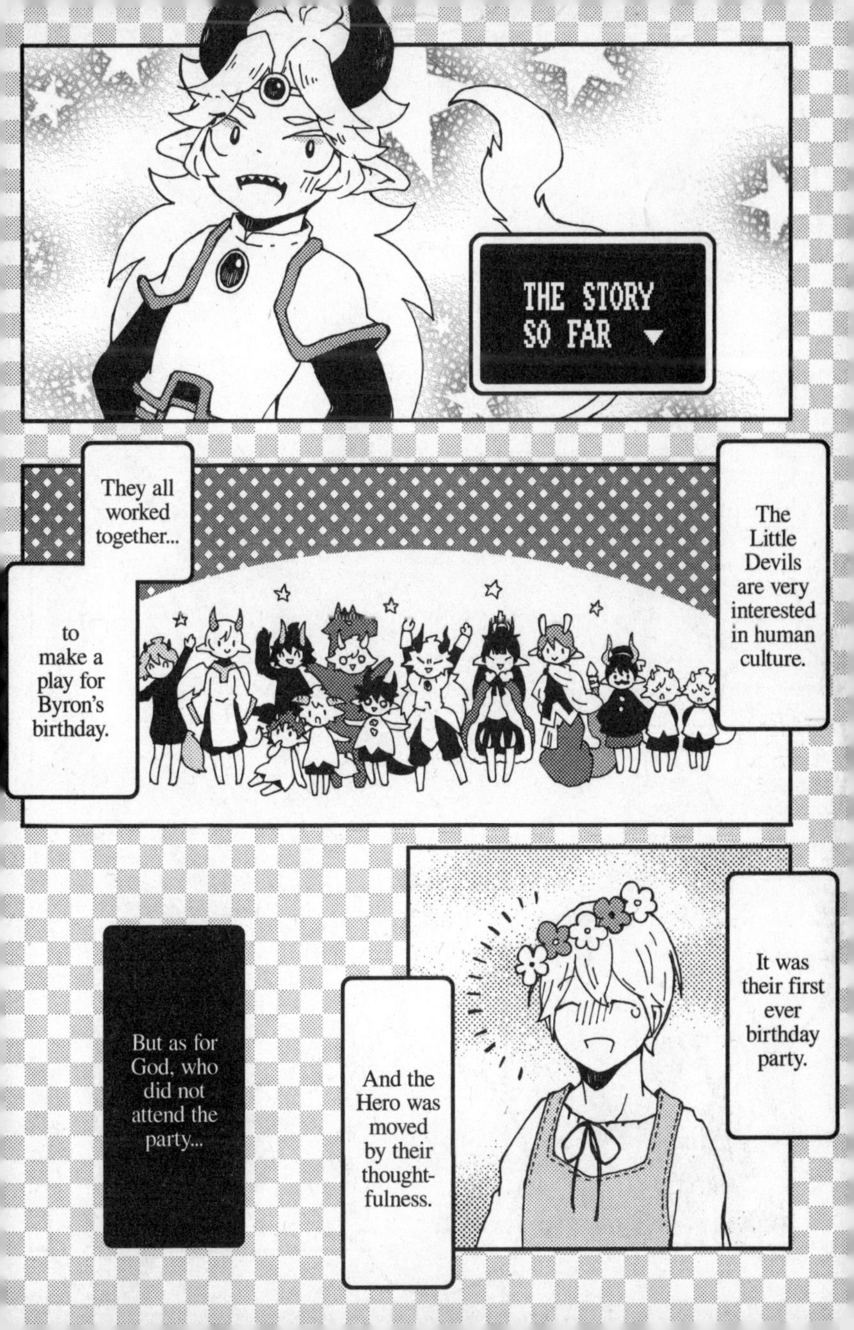
THE STORY SO FAR
The Little Devils are very interested in human culture.
They all worked together...
to make a play for Byron's birthday.
It was their first ever birthday party.
And the Hero was moved by their thoughtfulness.
But as for God, who did not attend the party...

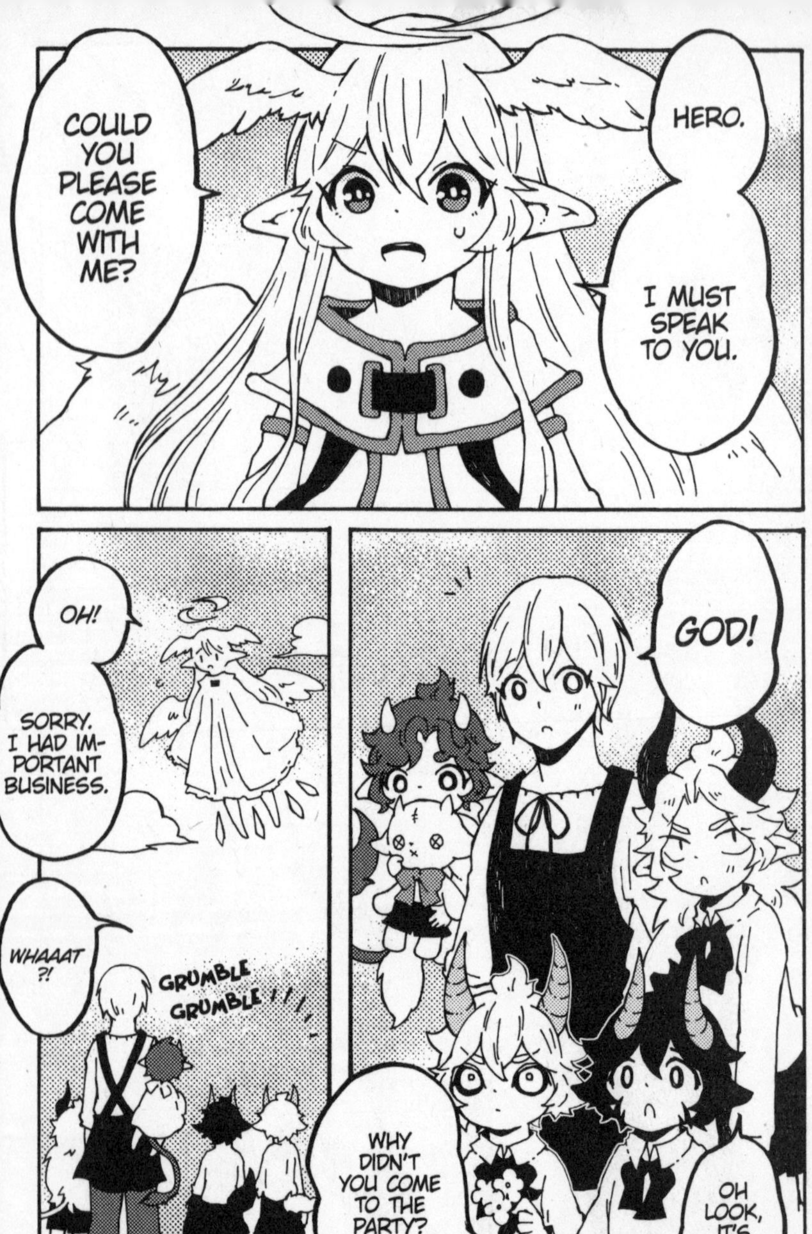
HERO.
I MUST SPEAK TO YOU.
COULD YOU PLEASE COME WITH ME?
GOD!
OH LOOK, IT'S GOD.
WHY DIDN'T YOU COME TO THE PARTY?
OH!
SORRY. I HAD IM-PORTANT BUSINESS.
WHAAAT?!
GRUMBLE GRUMBLE

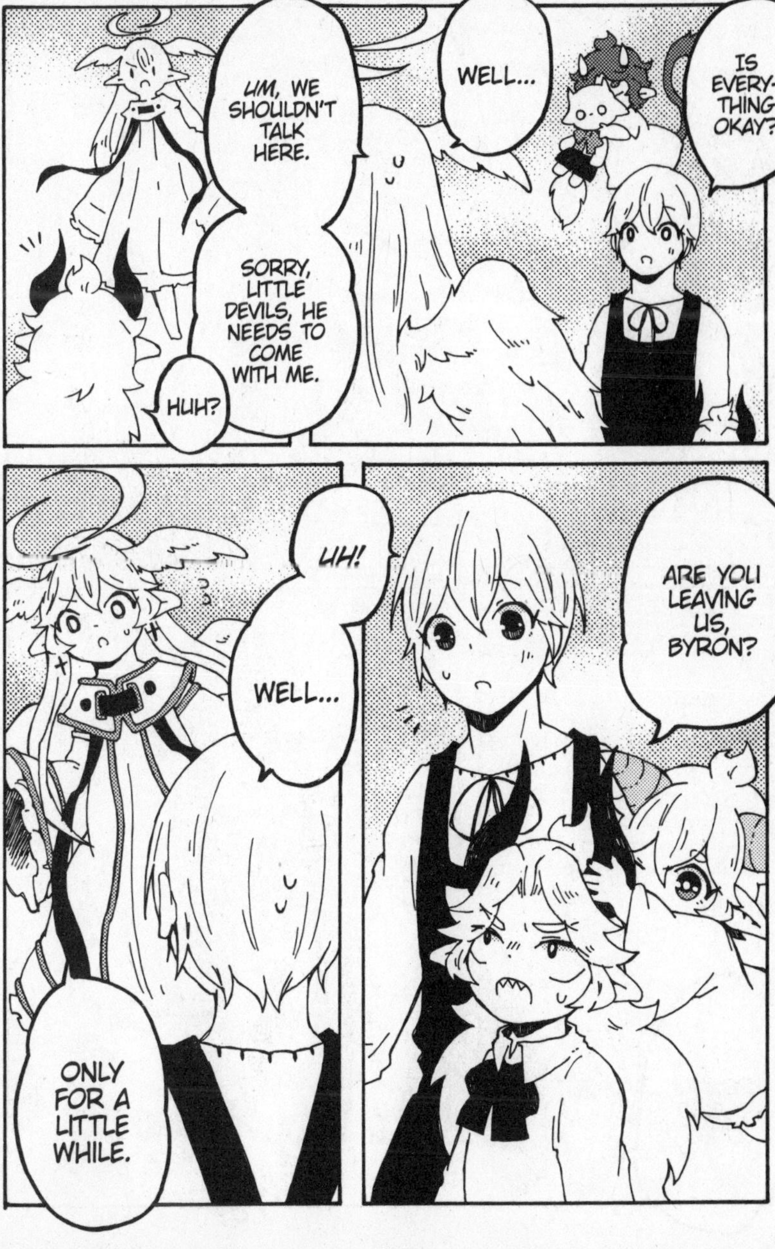
IS EVERY-THING OKAY?
WELL...
UM, WE SHOULDN'T TALK HERE.
SORRY, LITTLE DEVILS, HE NEEDS TO COME WITH ME.
HUH?
ARE YOU LEAVING US, BYRON?
UH!
WELL...
ONLY FOR A LITTLE WHILE.

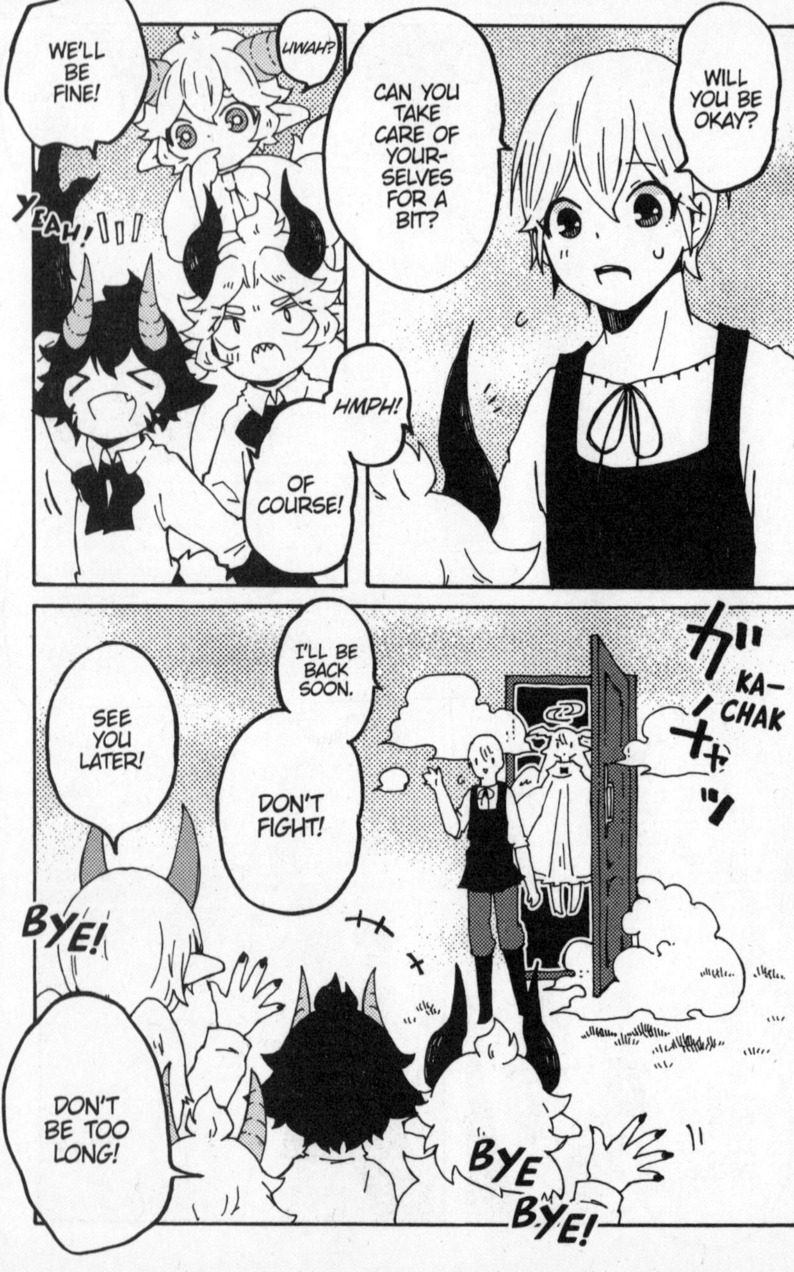
WILL YOU BE OKAY?
CAN YOU TAKE CARE OF YOUR-SELVES FOR A BIT?
UWAH?
WE'LL BE FINE!
YEAH!
HMPH!
OF COURSE!
ガチャッ
KA-CHAK
I'LL BE BACK SOON.
DON'T FIGHT!
SEE YOU LATER!
BYE!
DON'T BE TOO LONG!
BYE BYE!

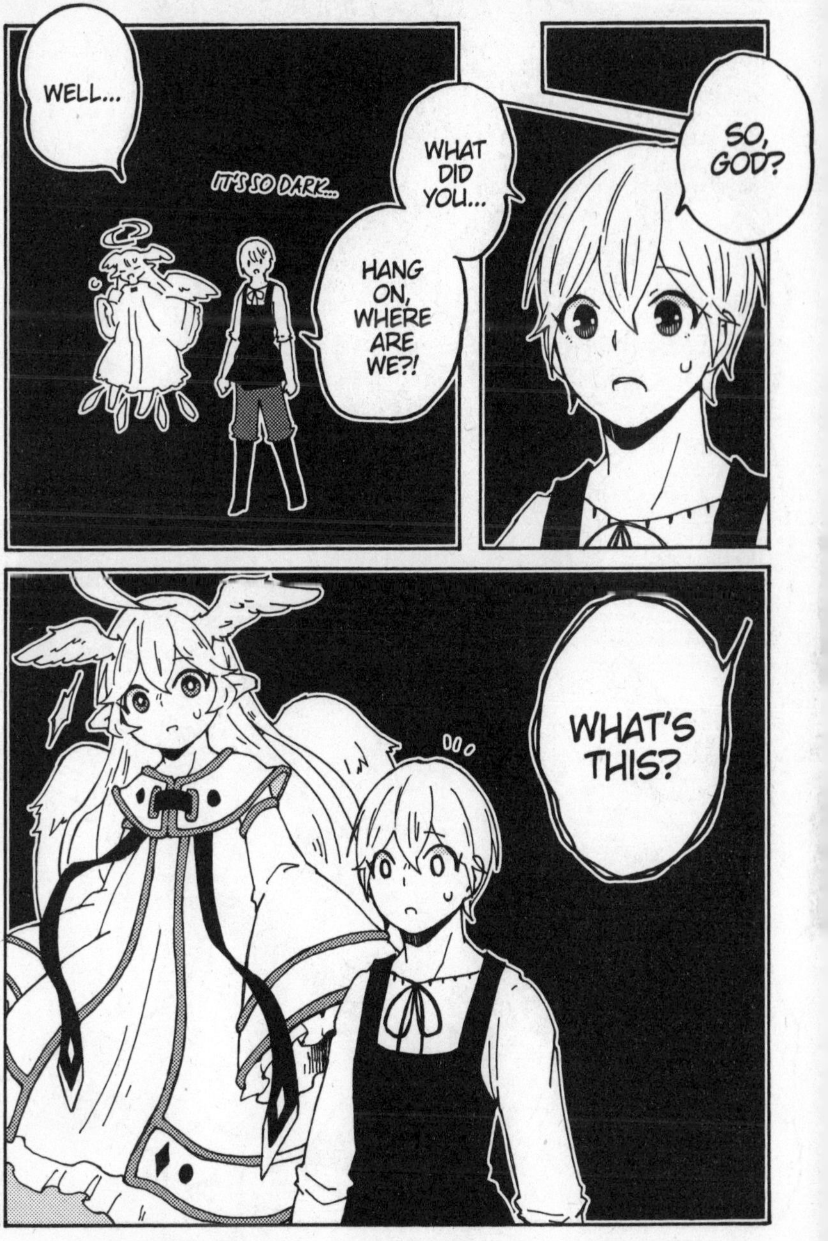
SO, GOD?
WHAT DID YOU...
HANG ON, WHERE ARE WE?!
IT'S SO DARK...
WELL...
WHAT'S THIS?

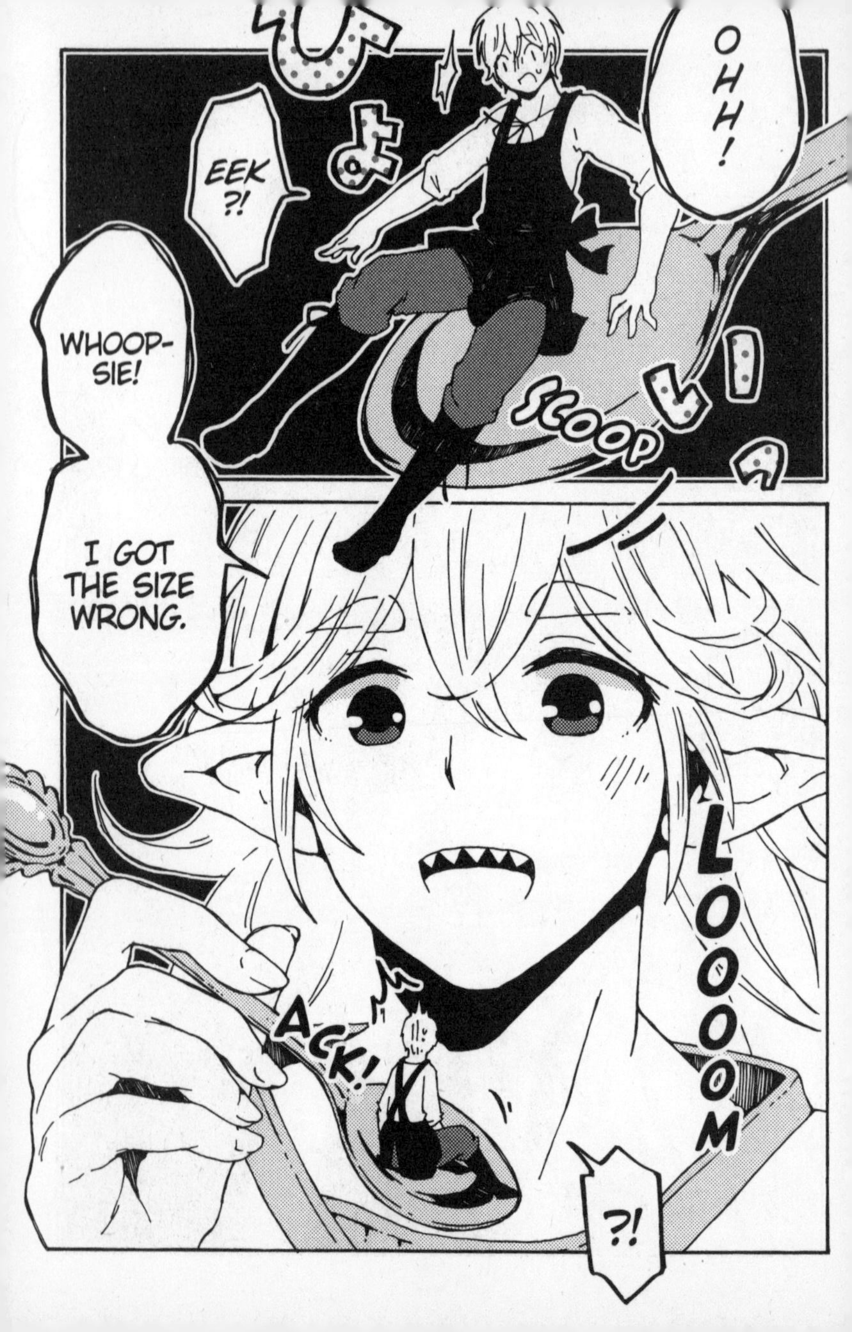
OHHH!
EEK ?!
SCOOP
WHOOP-SIE!
I GOT THE SIZE WRONG.
LOOOOOM
?!
ACK!

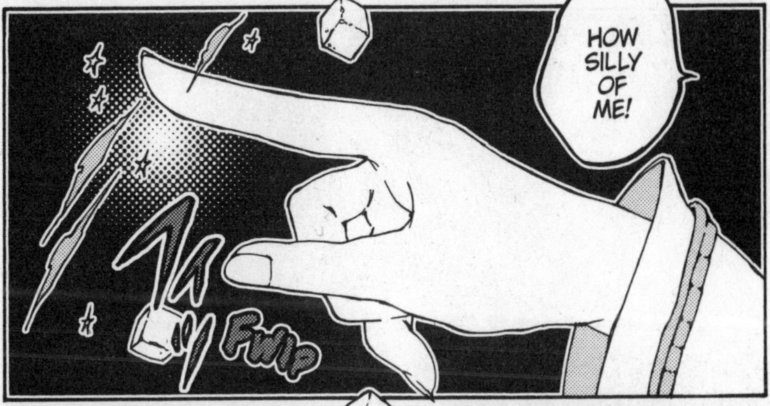
HOW SILLY OF ME!
FWIP

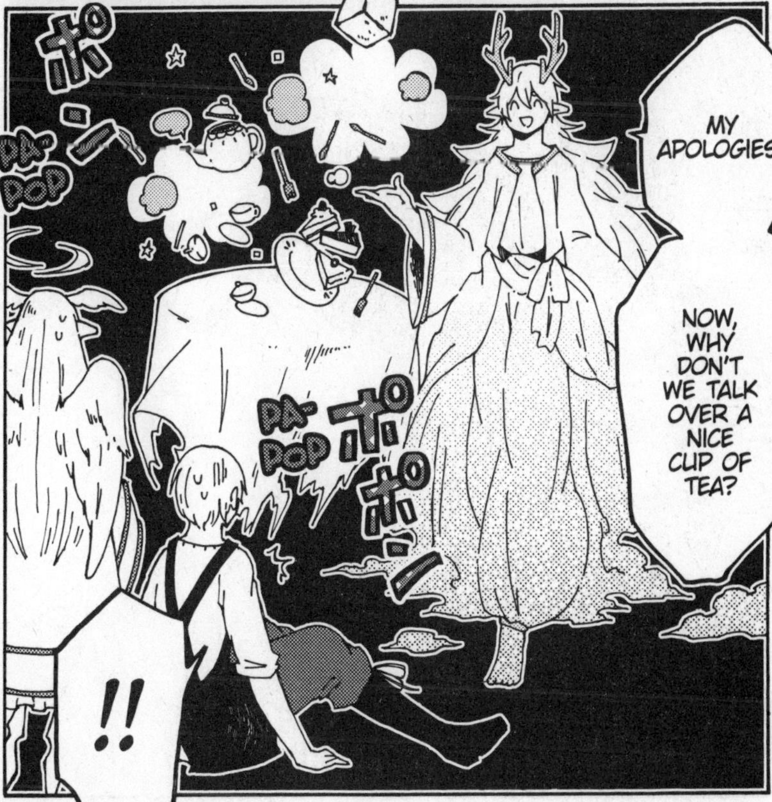
MY APOLOGIES!
NOW, WHY DON'T WE TALK OVER A NICE CUP OF TEA?
PA-POP
PA-POP
!!

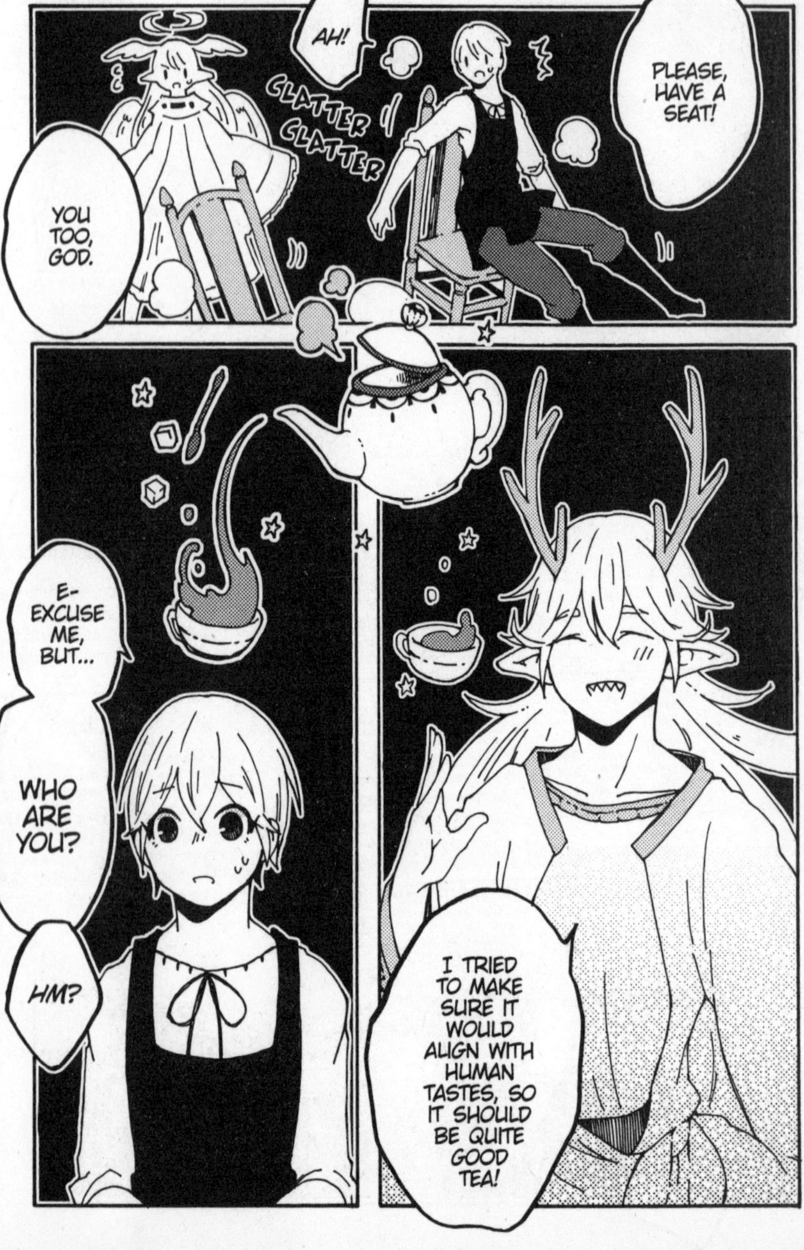
PLEASE, HAVE A SEAT!
AH!
CLATTER CLATTER
YOU TOO, GOD.
I TRIED TO MAKE SURE IT WOULD ALIGN WITH HUMAN TASTES, SO IT SHOULD BE QUITE GOOD TEA!
E-EXCUSE ME, BUT...
WHO ARE YOU?
HM?

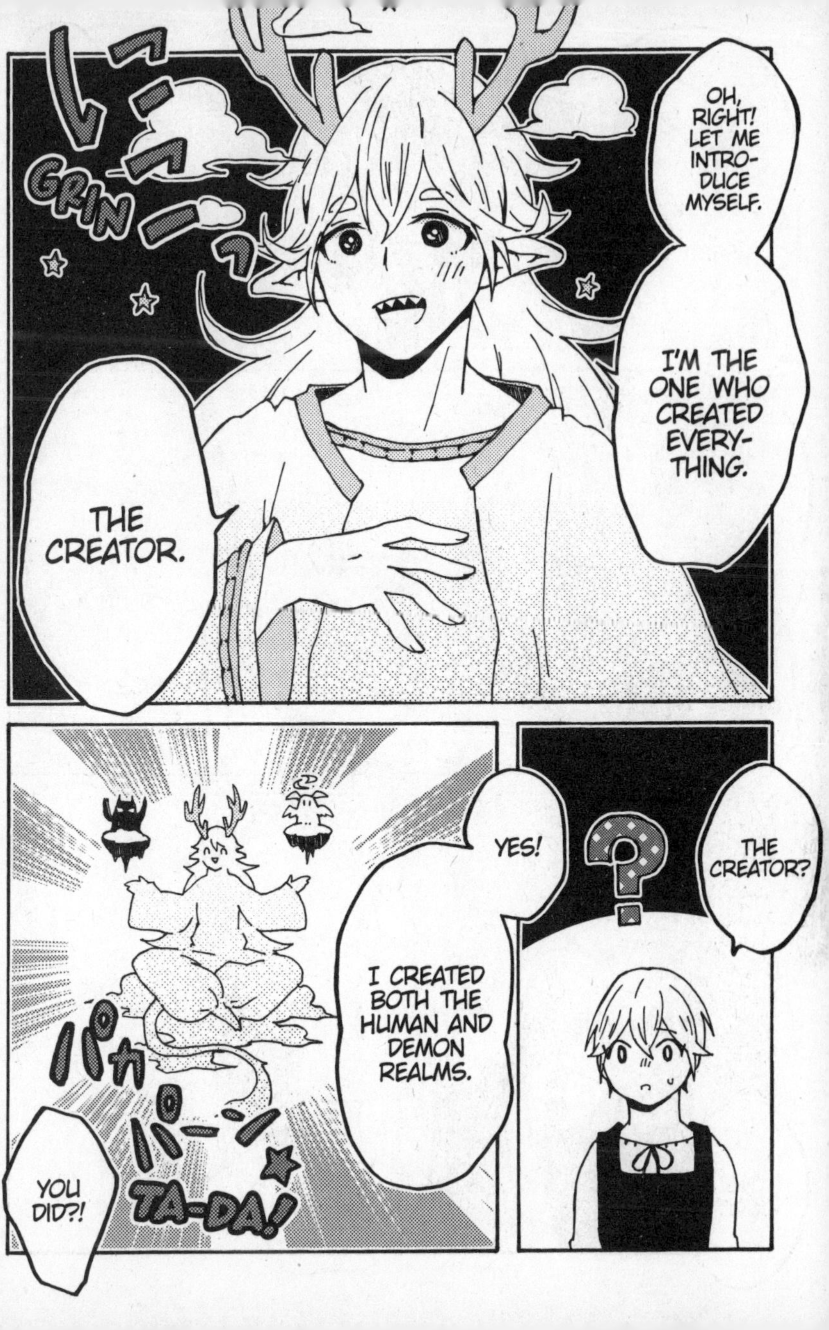
OH, RIGHT! LET ME INTRO-DUCE MYSELF.
I'M THE ONE WHO CREATED EVERY-THING.
THE CREATOR.
GRIN
THE CREATOR?
YES!
I CREATED BOTH THE HUMAN AND DEMON REALMS.
TA-DA!
YOU DID?!

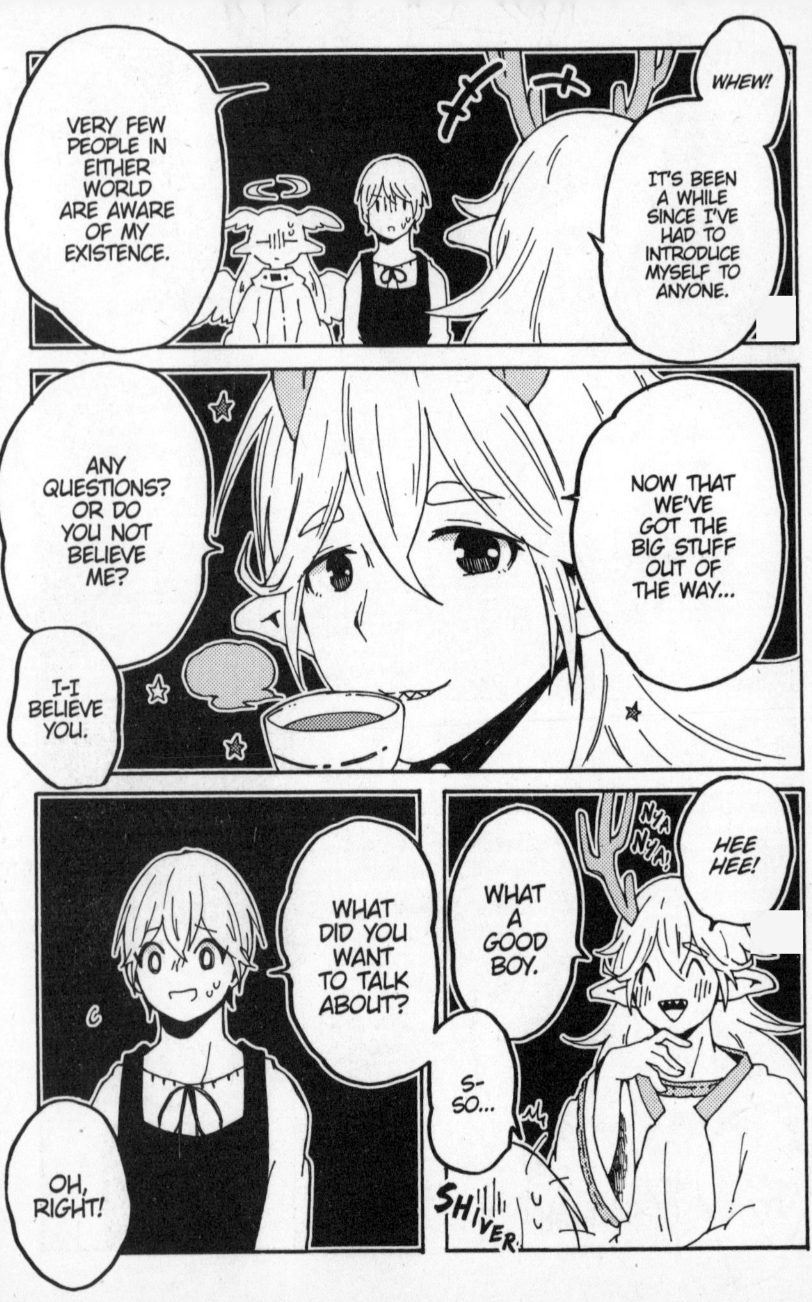
WHEW!
IT'S BEEN A WHILE SINCE I'VE HAD TO INTRODUCE MYSELF TO ANYONE.
VERY FEW PEOPLE IN EITHER WORLD ARE AWARE OF MY EXISTENCE.
NOW THAT WE'VE GOT THE BIG STUFF OUT OF THE WAY...
ANY QUESTIONS? OR DO YOU NOT BELIEVE ME?
I-I BELIEVE YOU.
HEE HEE!
NYA NYA!
WHAT A GOOD BOY.
S-SO...
SHIVER
WHAT DID YOU WANT TO TALK ABOUT?
OH, RIGHT!

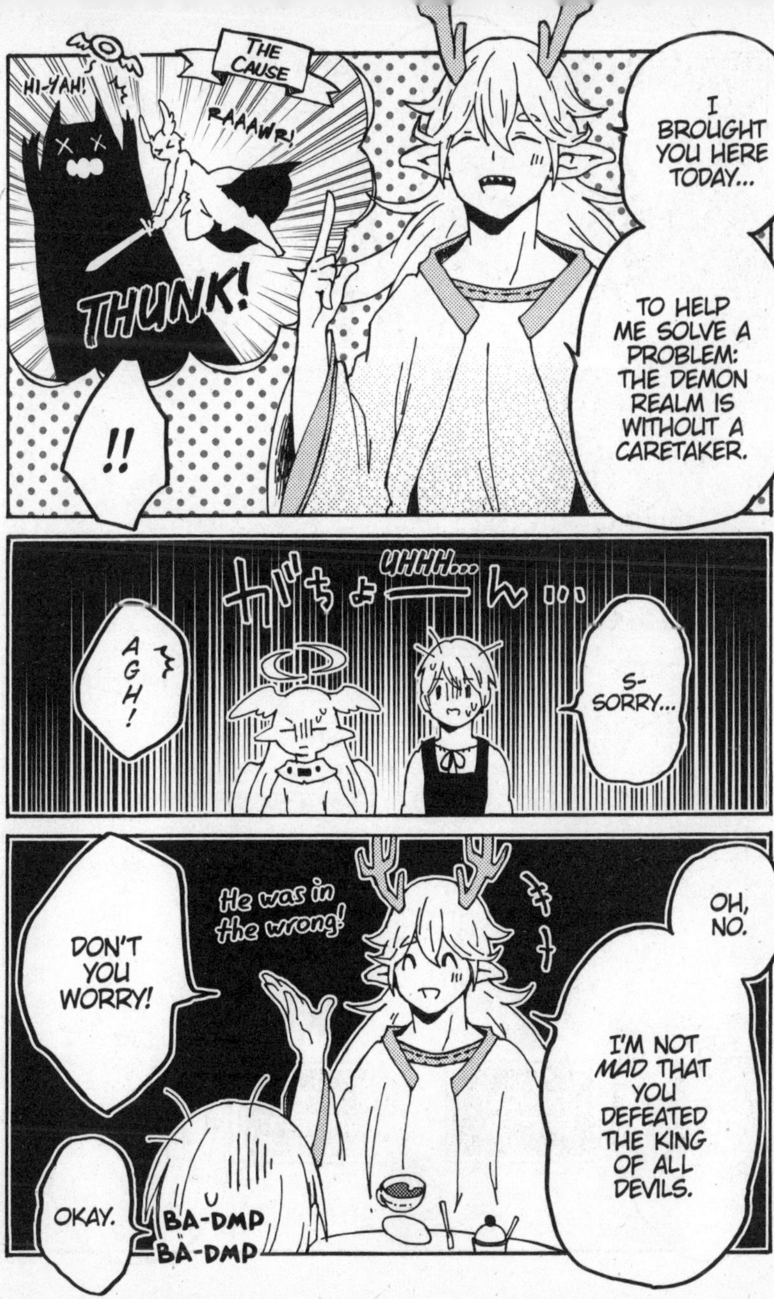
I BROUGHT YOU HERE TODAY...
TO HELP ME SOLVE A PROBLEM: THE DEMON REALM IS WITHOUT A CARETAKER.
THE CAUSE
RAAAWR!
HI-YAH!
THUNK!
!!
UHHH...
ガちょーん...
S-SORRY...
AGH!
OH, NO.
I'M NOT *MAD* THAT YOU DEFEATED THE KING OF ALL DEVILS.
キッ
He was in the wrong!
DON'T YOU WORRY!
BA-DMP BA-DMP
OKAY.

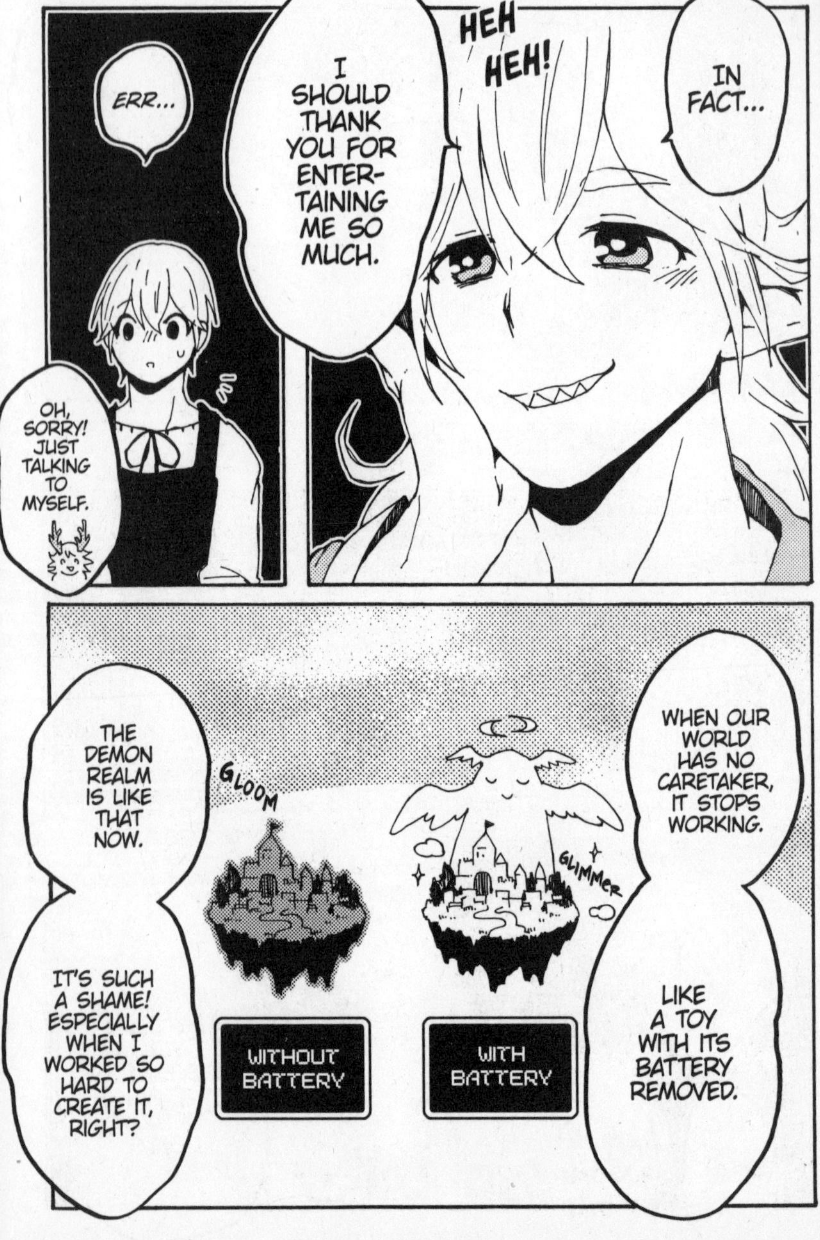
IN FACT...
HEH HEH!
I SHOULD THANK YOU FOR ENTER-TAINING ME SO MUCH.
ERR...
OH, SORRY! JUST TALKING TO MYSELF.
WHEN OUR WORLD HAS NO CARETAKER, IT STOPS WORKING.
LIKE A TOY WITH ITS BATTERY REMOVED.
GLIMMER
WITH BATTERY
GLOOM
WITHOUT BATTERY
THE DEMON REALM IS LIKE THAT NOW.
IT'S SUCH A SHAME! ESPECIALLY WHEN I WORKED SO HARD TO CREATE IT, RIGHT?

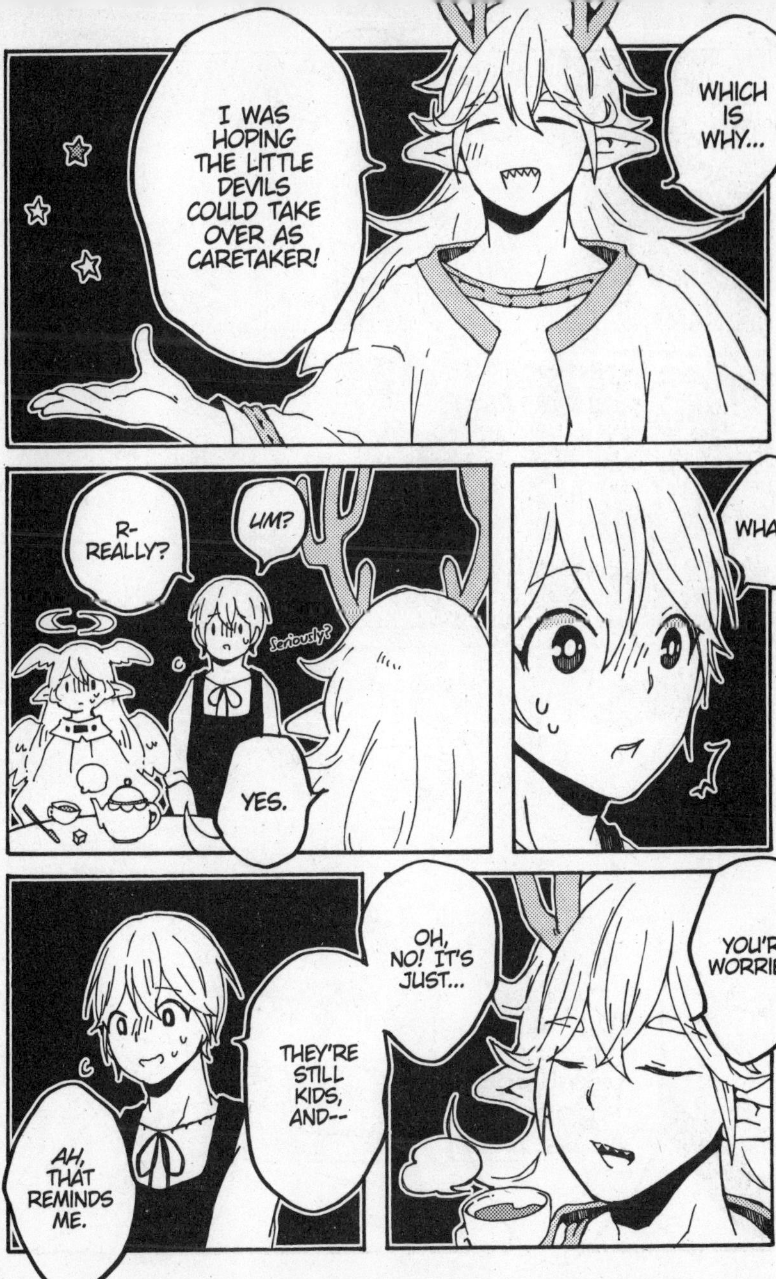
WHICH IS WHY...
I WAS HOPING THE LITTLE DEVILS COULD TAKE OVER AS CARETAKER!
WHAT?
UM?
R-REALLY?
Seriously?
YES.
YOU'RE WORRIED?
OH, NO! IT'S JUST...
THEY'RE STILL KIDS, AND--
AH, THAT REMINDS ME.

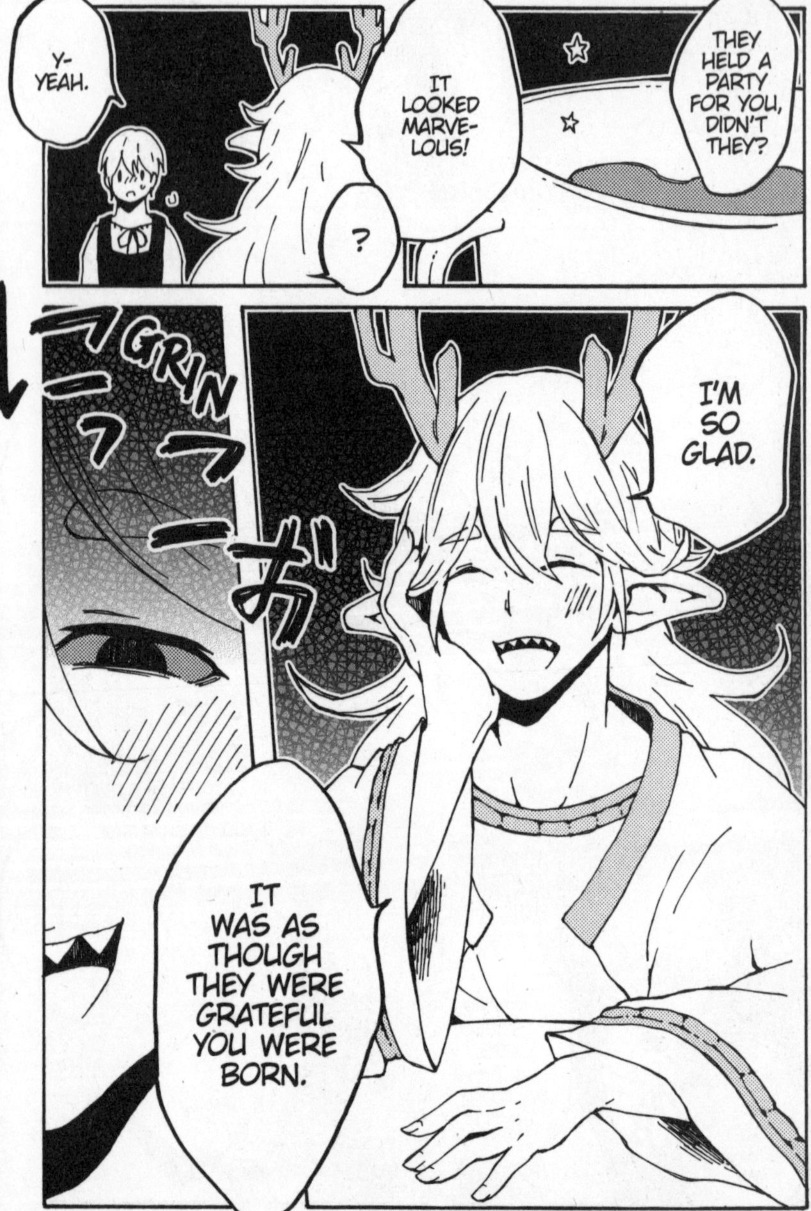
THEY HELD A PARTY FOR YOU, DIDN'T THEY?
IT LOOKED MARVE-LOUS!
?
Y-YEAH.
I'M SO GLAD.
GRIN
IT WAS AS THOUGH THEY WERE GRATEFUL YOU WERE BORN.

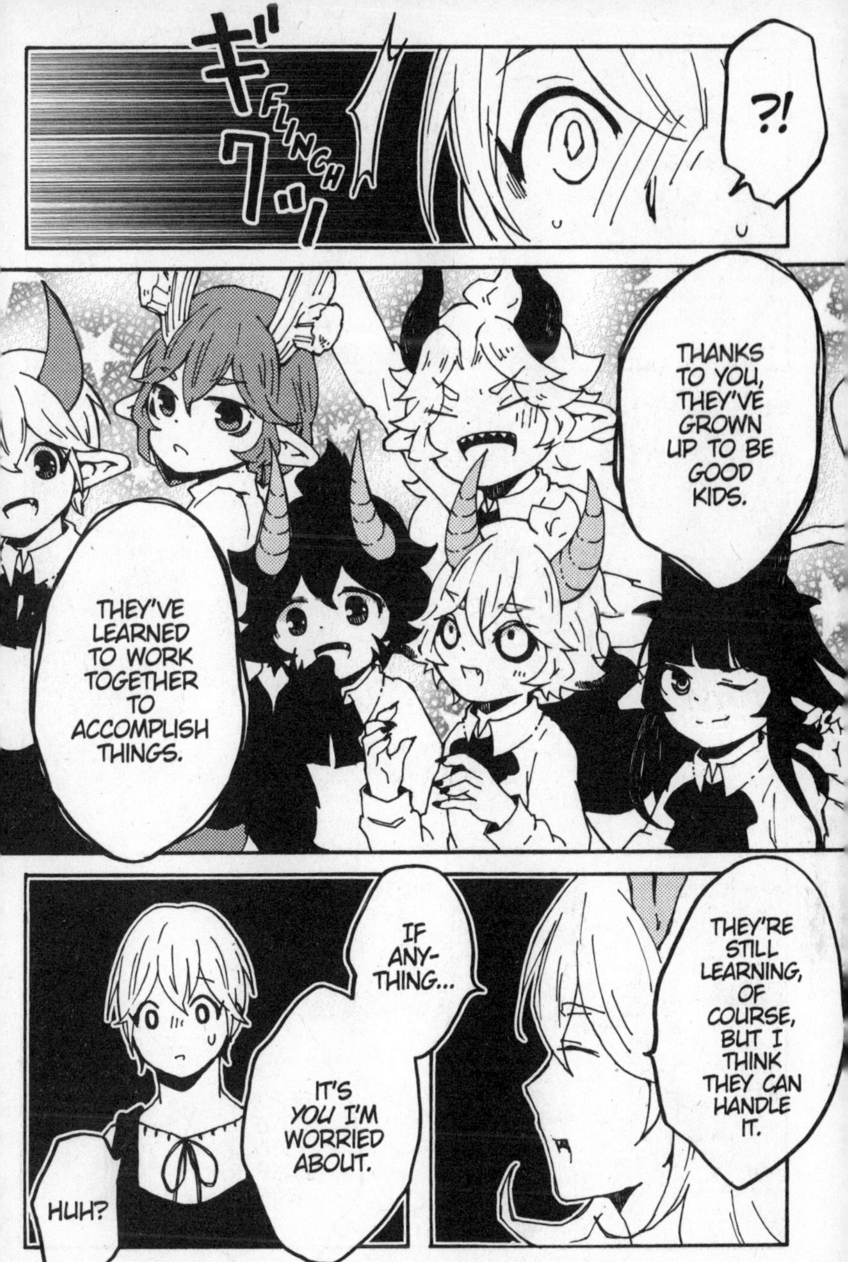
?!
ギクッ
FLINCH
THANKS TO YOU, THEY'VE GROWN UP TO BE GOOD KIDS.
THEY'VE LEARNED TO WORK TOGETHER TO ACCOMPLISH THINGS.
THEY'RE STILL LEARNING, OF COURSE, BUT I THINK THEY CAN HANDLE IT.
IF ANY-THING...
IT'S *YOU* I'M WORRIED ABOUT.
HUH?

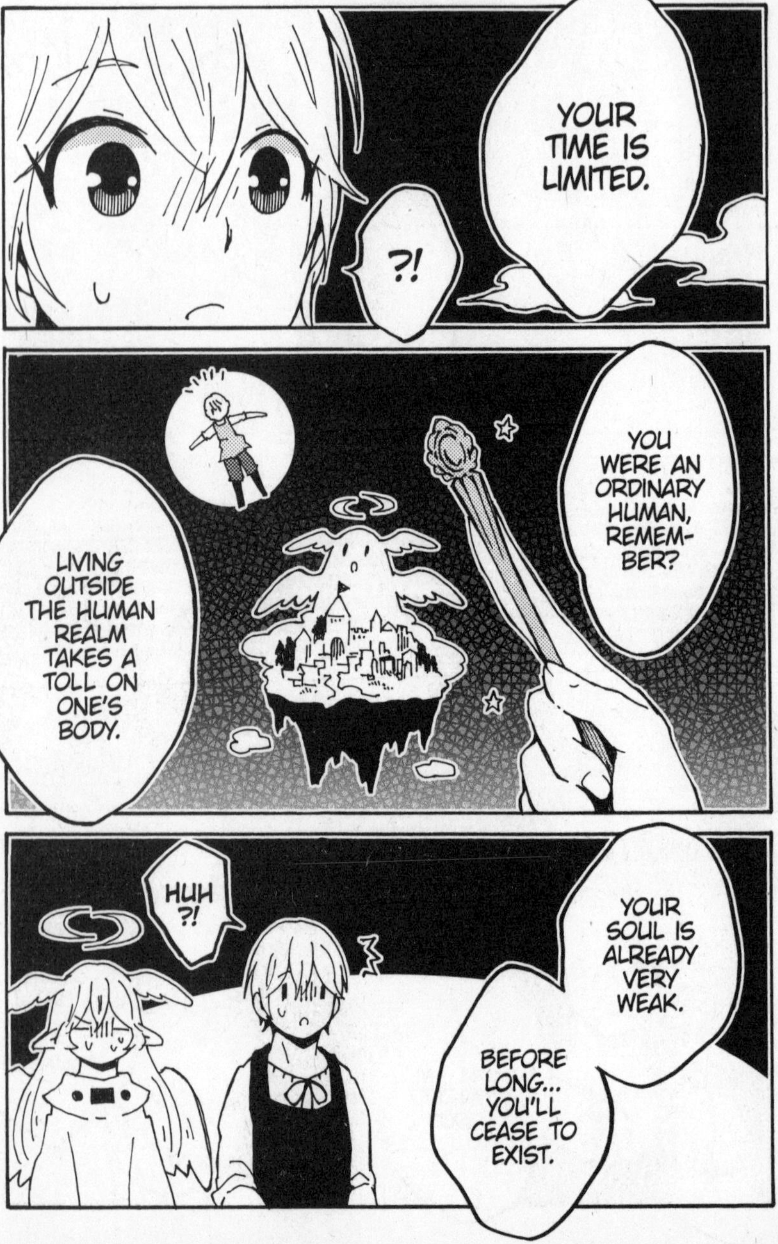
YOUR TIME IS LIMITED.
?!
YOU WERE AN ORDINARY HUMAN, REMEMBER?
LIVING OUTSIDE THE HUMAN REALM TAKES A TOLL ON ONE'S BODY.
YOUR SOUL IS ALREADY VERY WEAK.
BEFORE LONG... YOU'LL CEASE TO EXIST.
HUH ?!

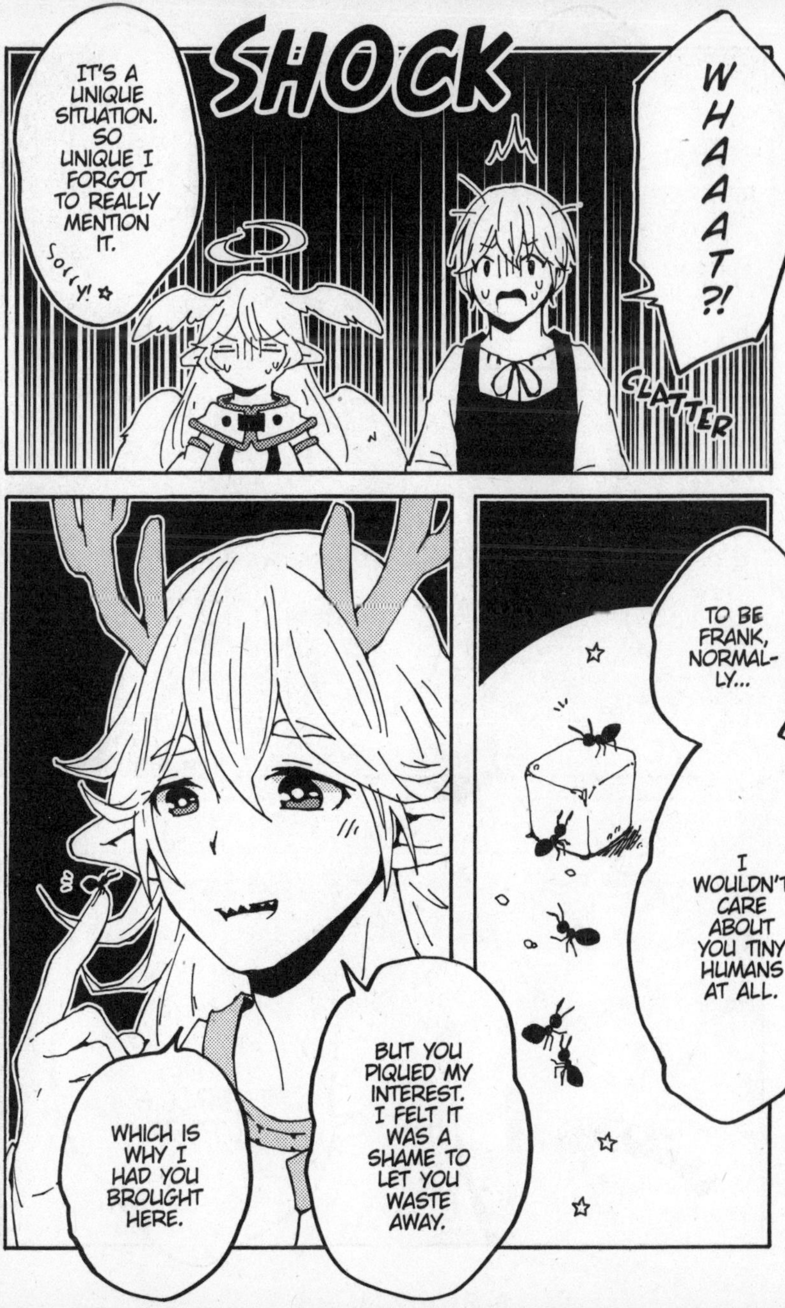
WHAAAAT?!
SHOCK
IT'S A UNIQUE SITUATION. SO UNIQUE I FORGOT TO REALLY MENTION IT.
CLATTER
Sorry! ☆
TO BE FRANK, NORMAL-LY...
I WOULDN'T CARE ABOUT YOU TINY HUMANS AT ALL.
BUT YOU PIQUED MY INTEREST. I FELT IT WAS A SHAME TO LET YOU WASTE AWAY.
WHICH IS WHY I HAD YOU BROUGHT HERE.

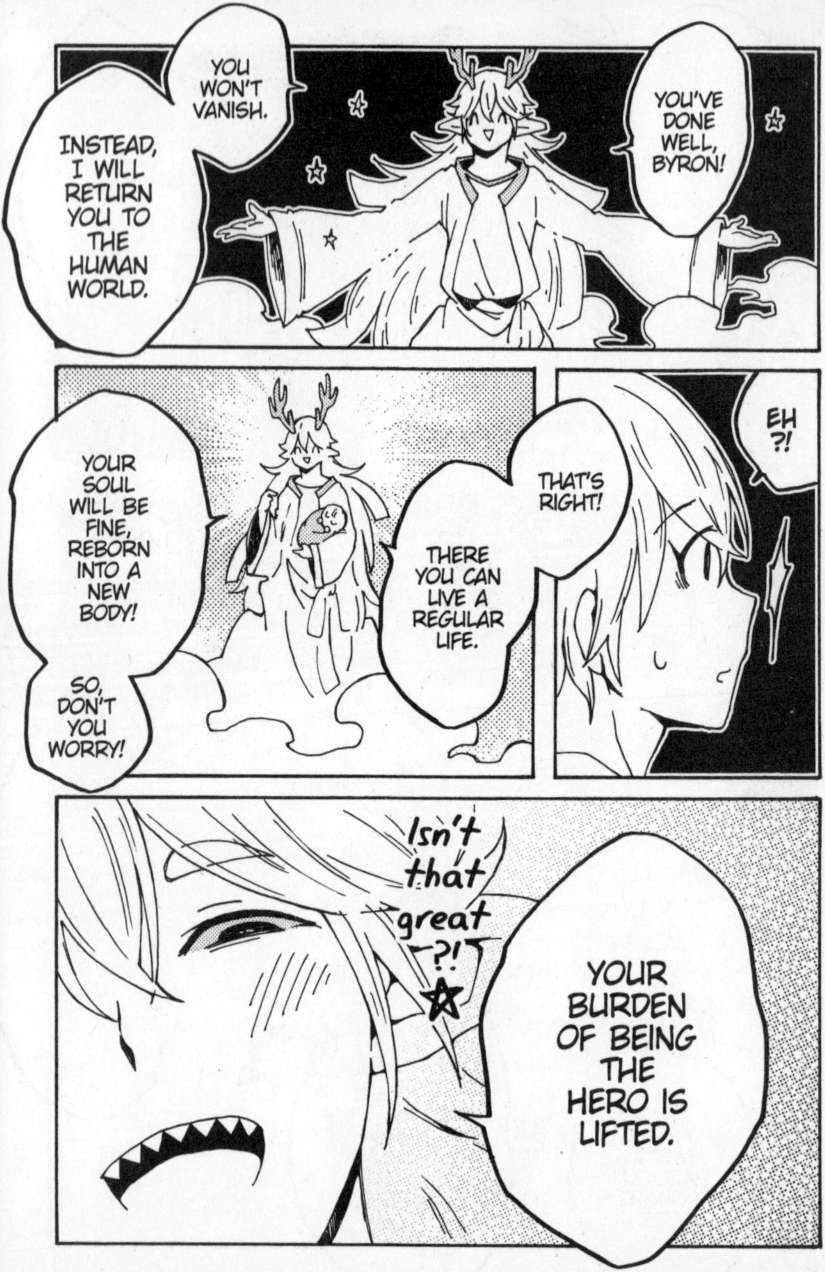
YOU'VE DONE WELL, BYRON!
YOU WON'T VANISH.
INSTEAD, I WILL RETURN YOU TO THE HUMAN WORLD.
EH ?!
THAT'S RIGHT!
THERE YOU CAN LIVE A REGULAR LIFE.
YOUR SOUL WILL BE FINE, REBORN INTO A NEW BODY!
SO, DON'T YOU WORRY!
YOUR BURDEN OF BEING THE HERO IS LIFTED.
Isn't that great?! ☆

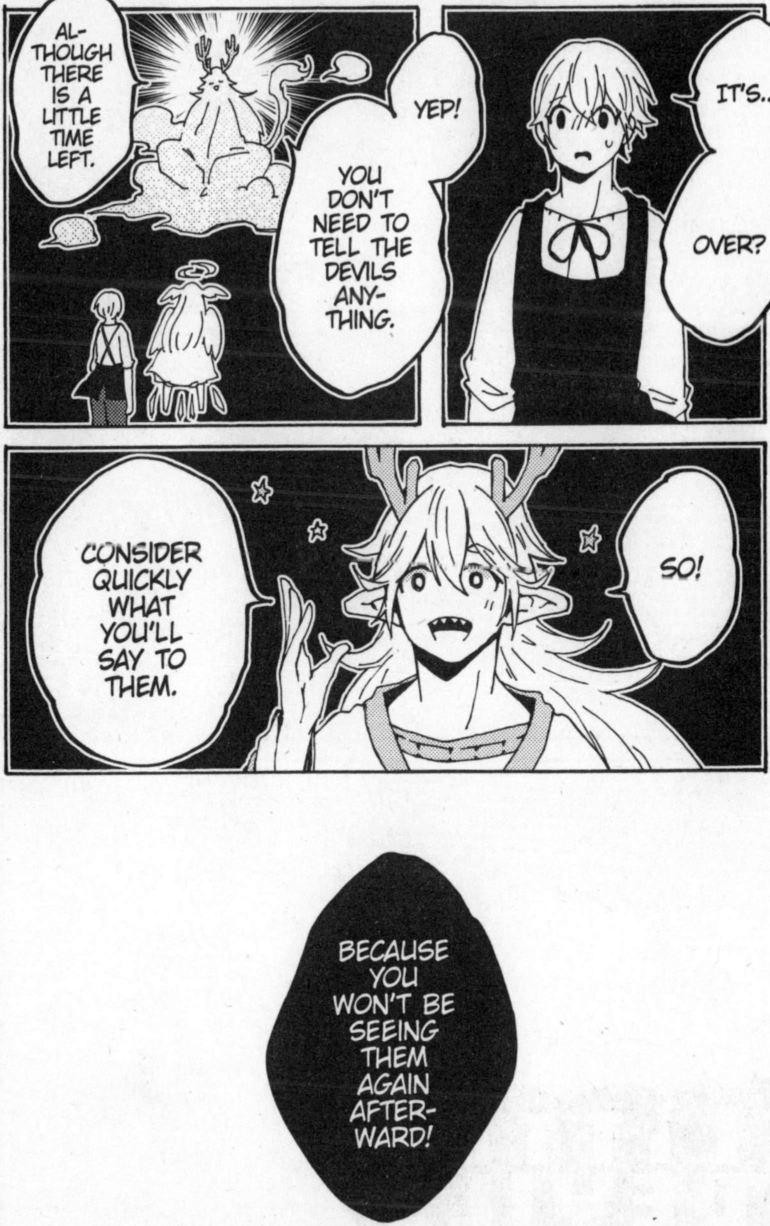
IT'S... OVER?
YEP!
YOU DON'T NEED TO TELL THE DEVILS ANY-THING.
AL-THOUGH THERE IS A LITTLE TIME LEFT.
SO!
CONSIDER QUICKLY WHAT YOU'LL SAY TO THEM.
BECAUSE YOU WON'T BE SEEING THEM AGAIN AFTER-WARD!

LITTLE DEVILS

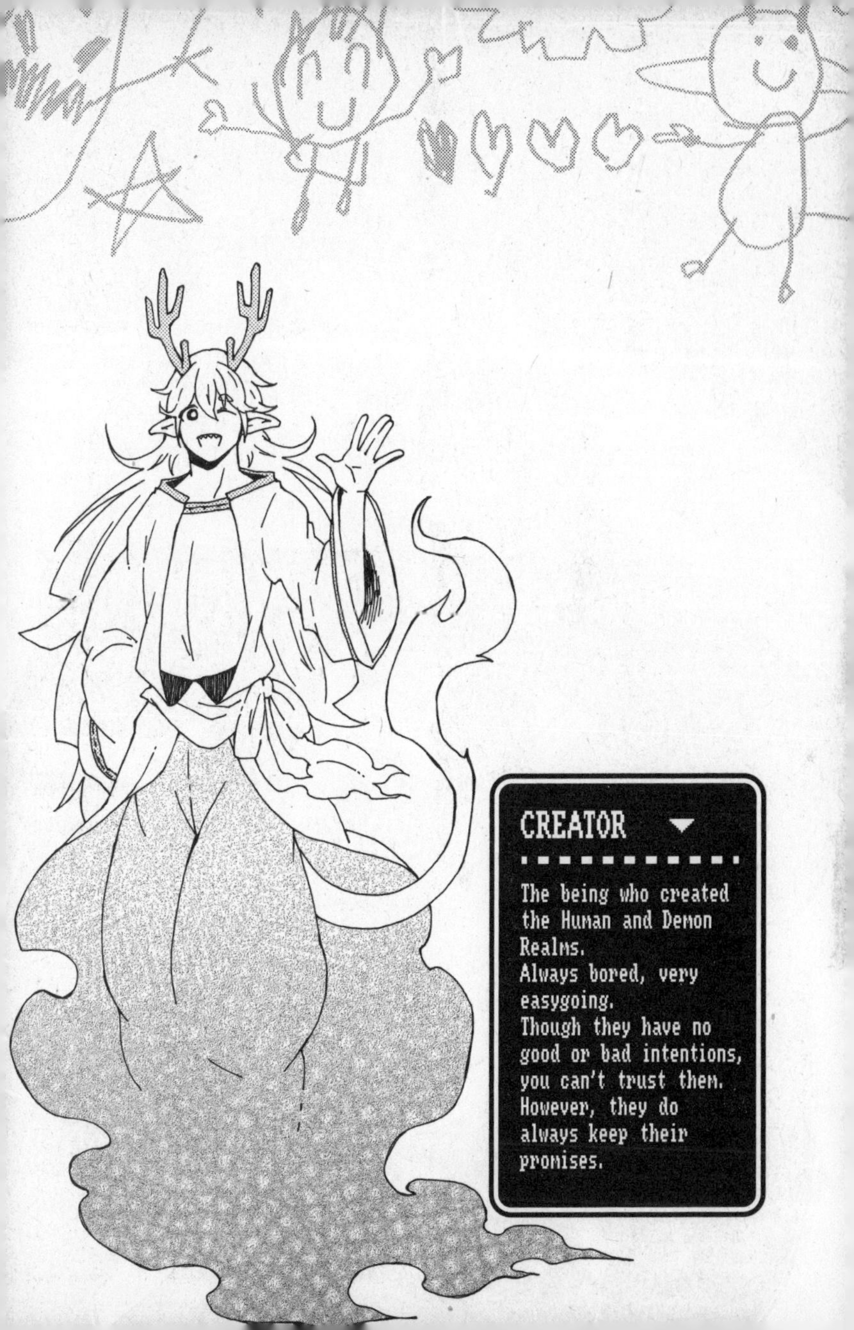
CREATOR
The being who created the Human and Demon Realms.
Always bored, very easygoing.
Though they have no good or bad intentions, you can't trust them.
However, they do always keep their promises.

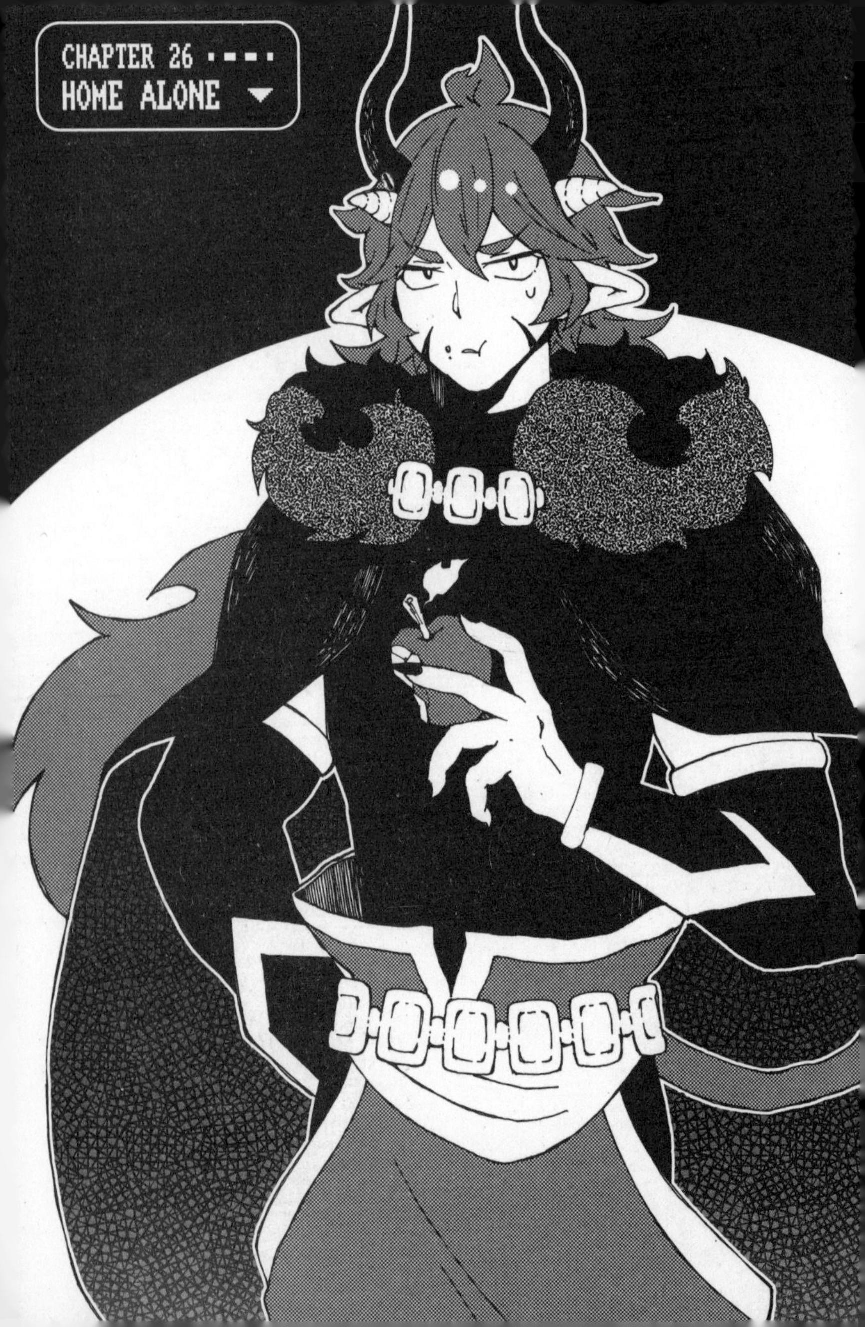
CHAPTER 26
HOME ALONE

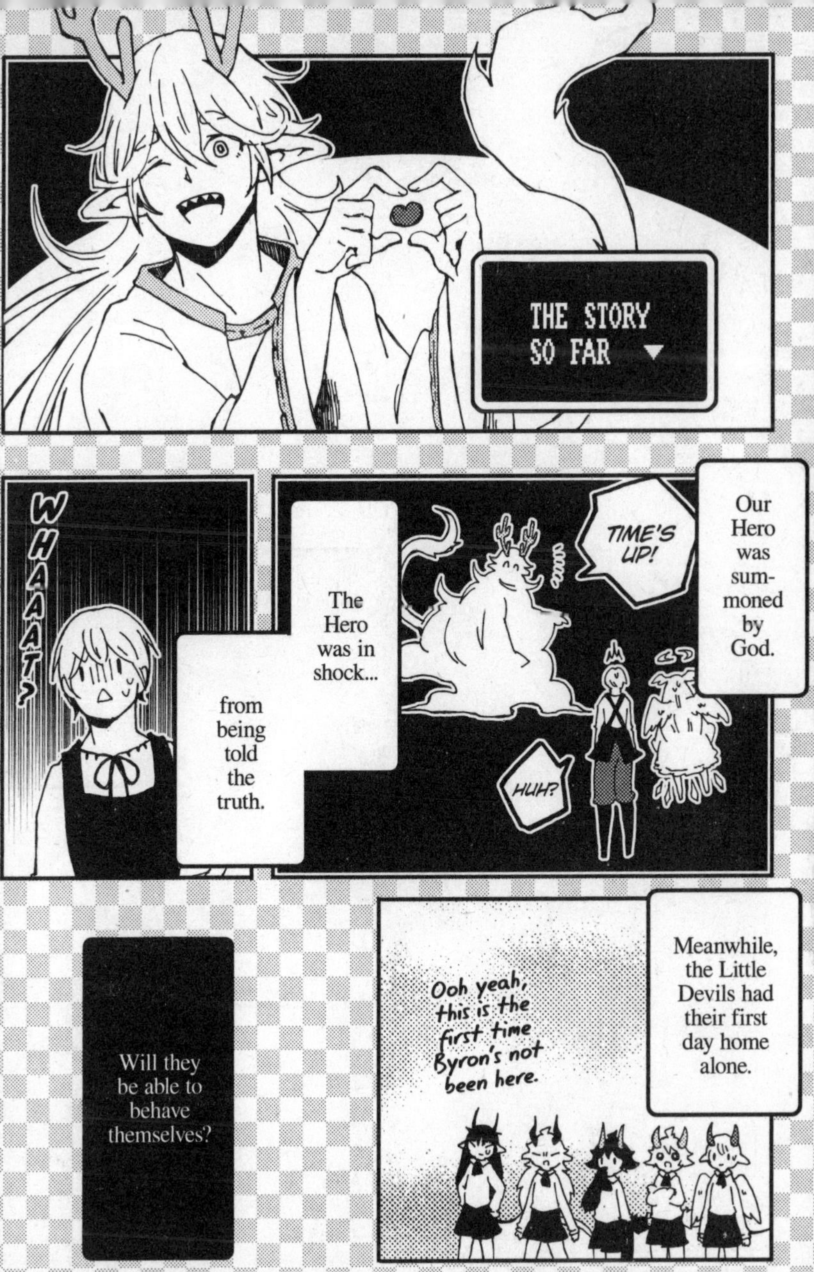
THE STORY SO FAR ▼
Our Hero was summoned by God.
TIME'S UP!
HUH?
The Hero was in shock...
from being told the truth.
WHAAAAT?
Meanwhile, the Little Devils had their first day home alone.
Ooh yeah, this is the first time Byron's not been here.
Will they be able to behave themselves?

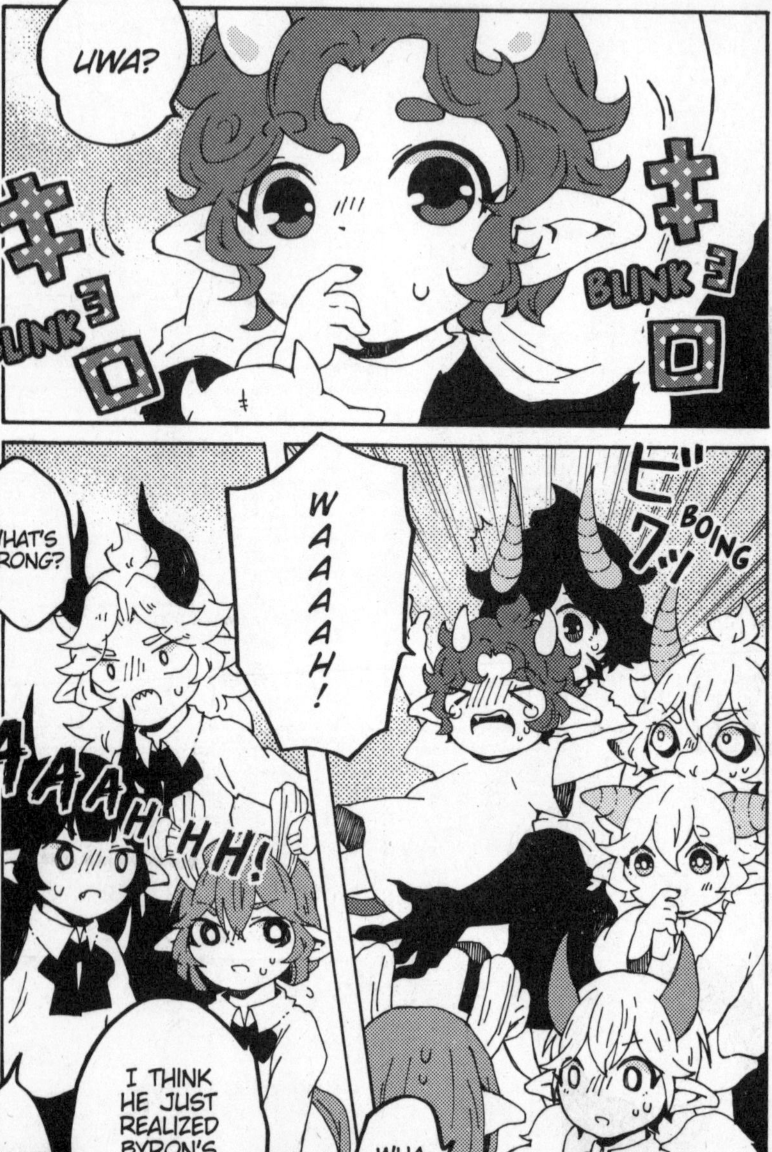

キョ
BLINK
ロ
UWA?
キョ
BLINK
ロ
ビクッ
BOING
WAAAAAH!
WHAT'S WRONG?
AAAHHH!
WHA?!
I THINK HE JUST REALIZED BYRON'S NOT HERE?
WHAT?

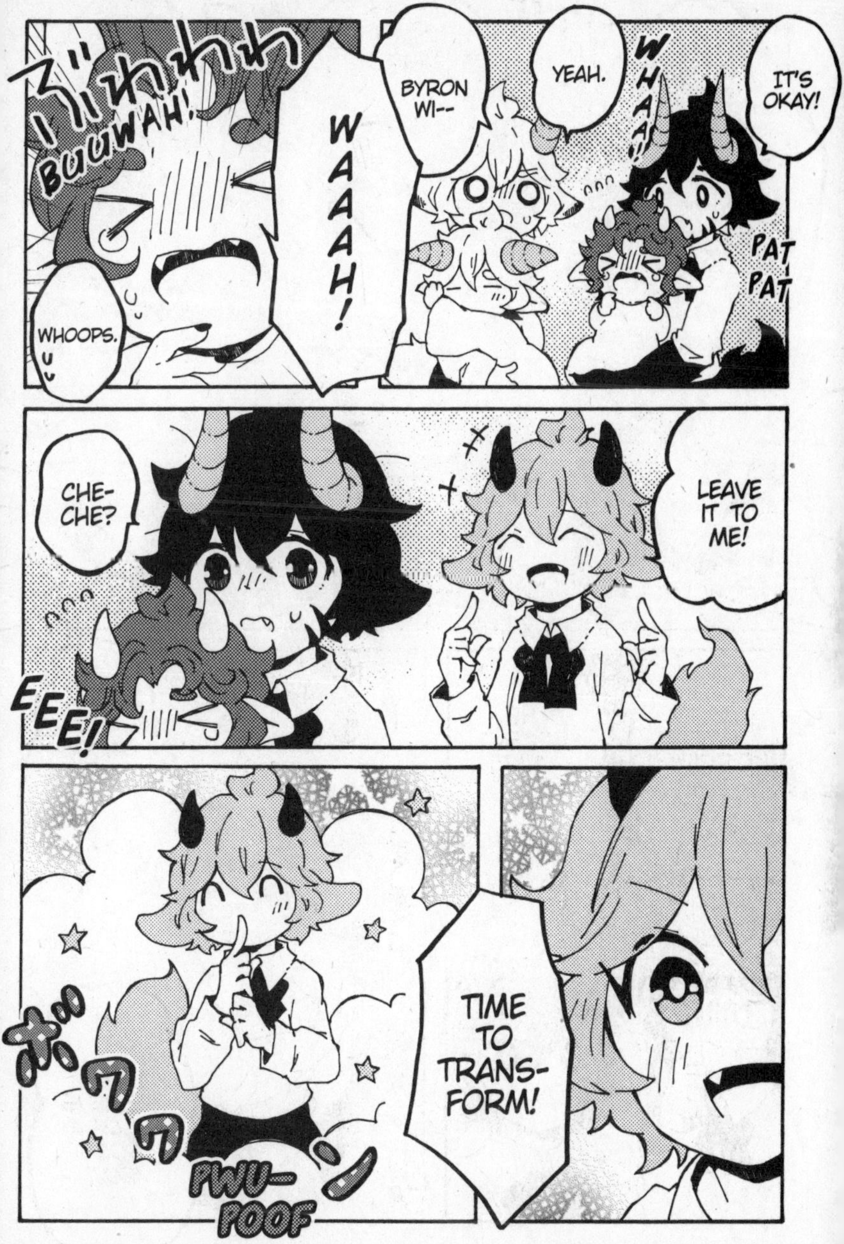
IT'S OKAY!
WHAAA!!
YEAH.
BYRON WI--
PAT PAT
WAAAAAH!
ぶわわわ
BUUWAH!
WHOOPS.
LEAVE IT TO ME!
CHE-CHE?
EEE!
TIME TO TRANS-FORM!
FWU-POOF

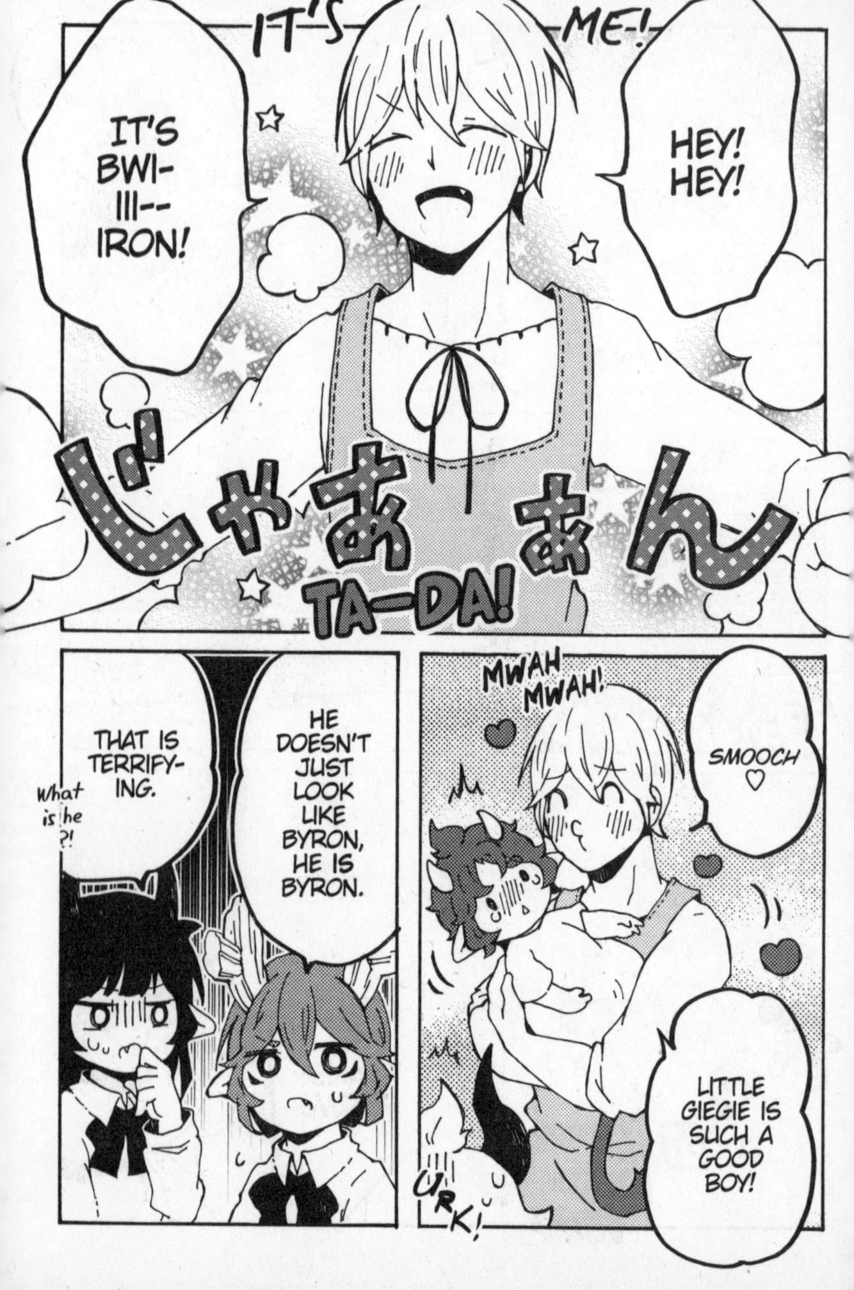
IT'S ME!
HEY! HEY!
IT'S BWI-IIII--IRON!
じゃあぁん
TA-DA!
MWAH MWAH!
SMOOCH ♡
LITTLE GIEGIE IS SUCH A GOOD BOY!
URK!
HE DOESN'T JUST LOOK LIKE BYRON, HE IS BYRON.
THAT IS TERRIFY-ING.
What is he ?!

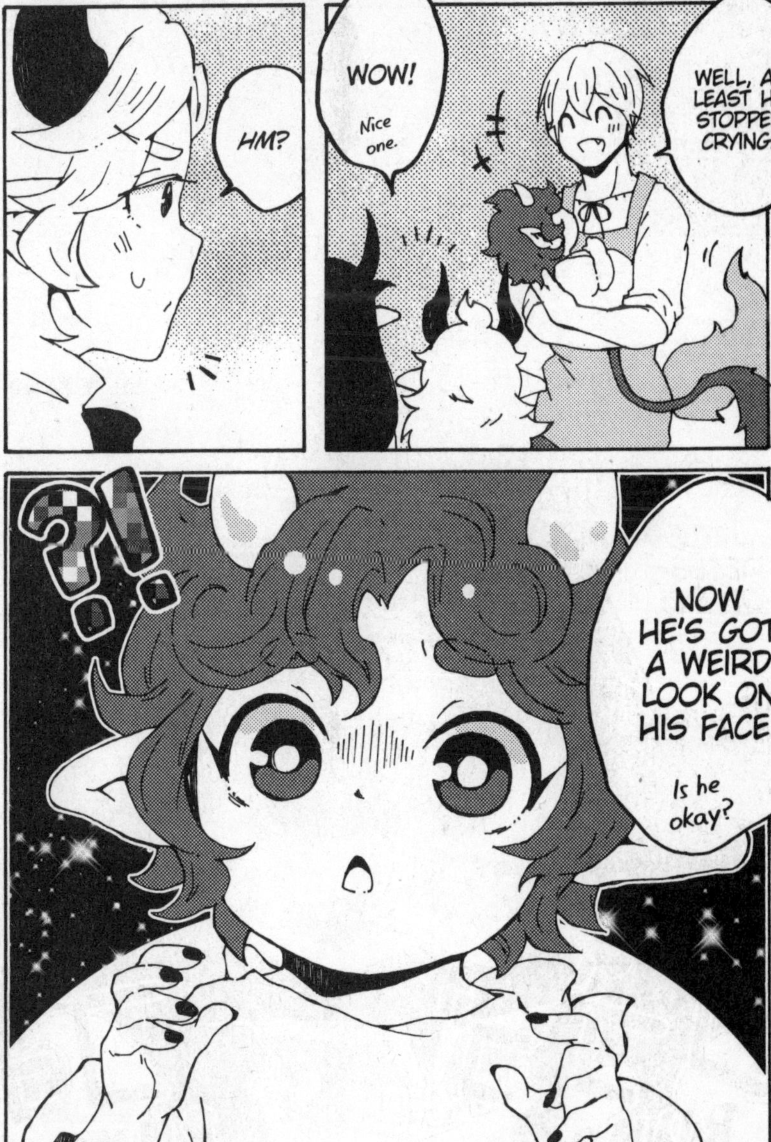
WELL, AT LEAST HE STOPPED CRYING!
WOW!
Nice one.
HM?
NOW HE'S GOT A WEIRD LOOK ON HIS FACE.
Is he okay?
?!

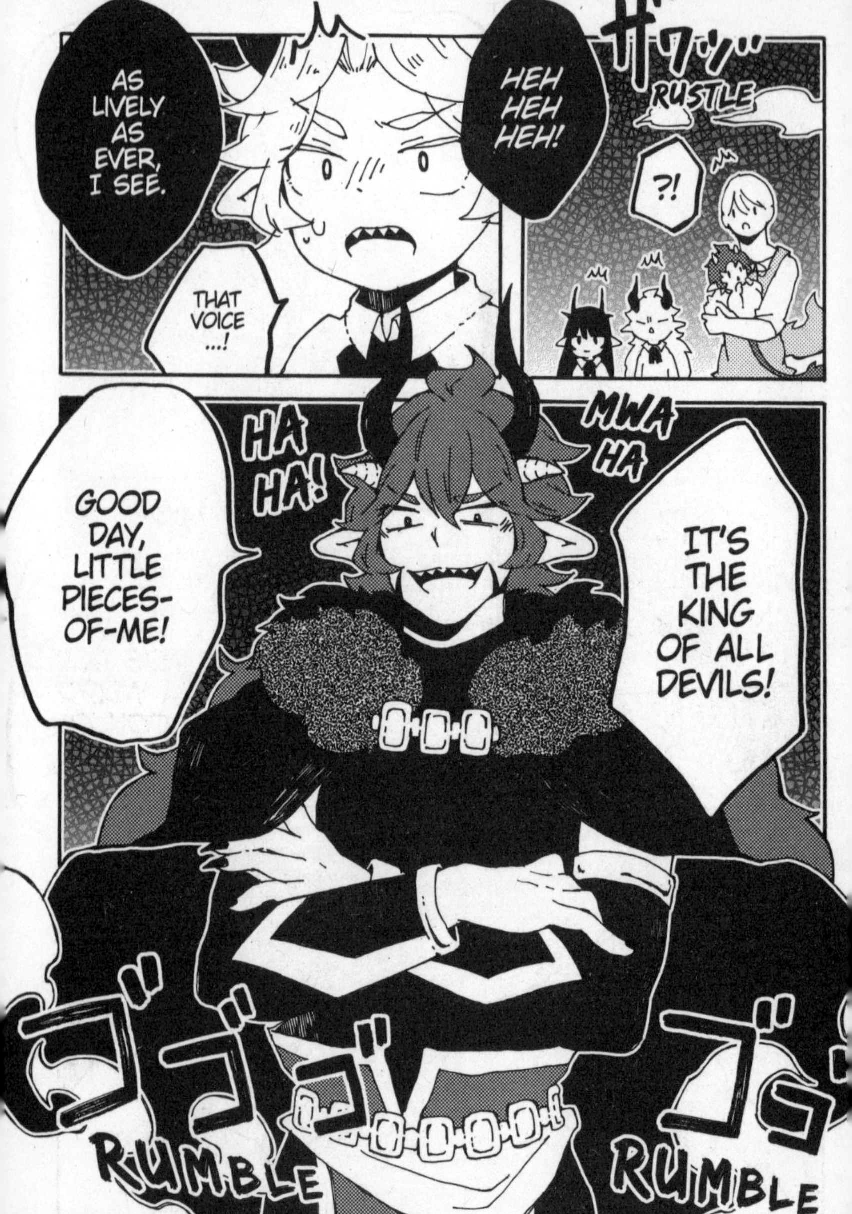
ザワッ
RUSTLE
?!
HEH HEH HEH!
AS LIVELY AS EVER, I SEE.
THAT VOICE ...!
MWA HA
IT'S THE KING OF ALL DEVILS!
HA HA!
GOOD DAY, LITTLE PIECES-OF-ME!
RUMBLE
RUMBLE

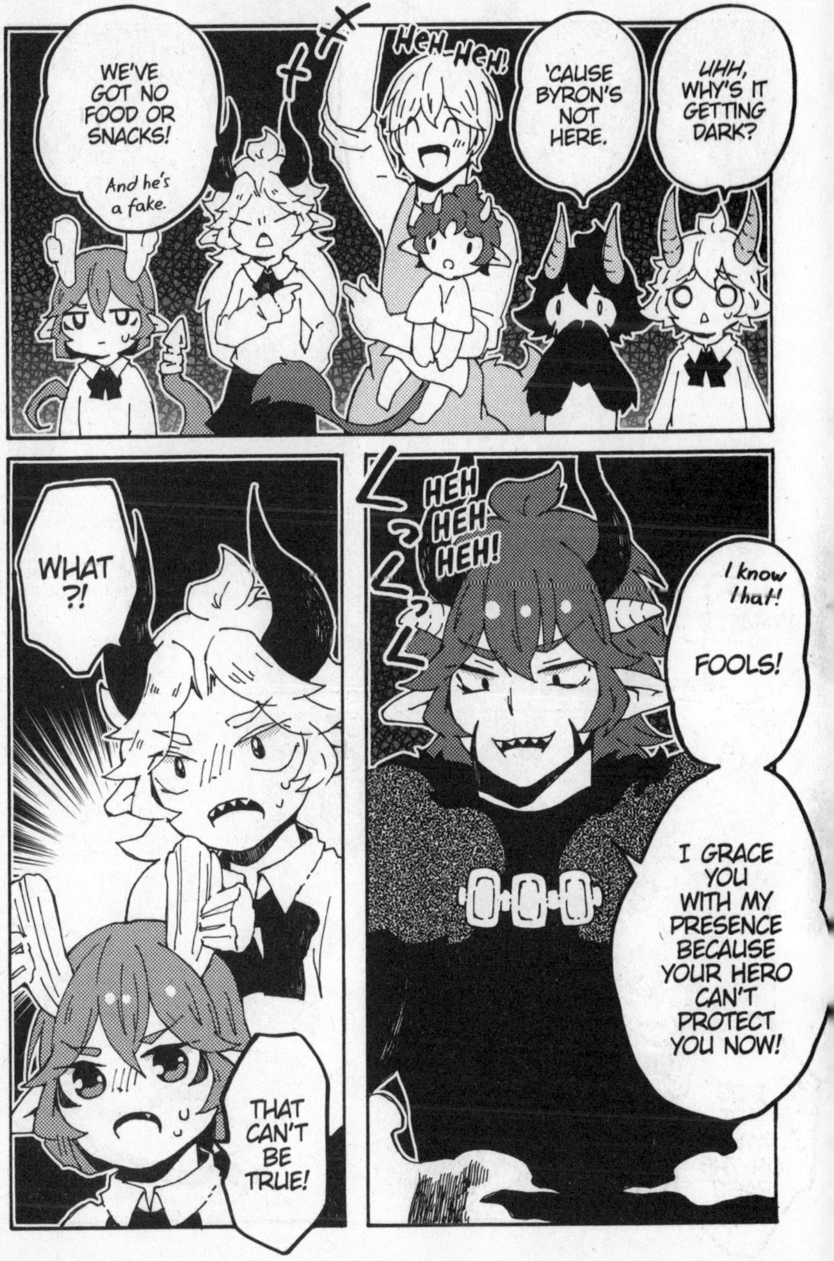
UHH, WHY'S IT GETTING DARK?
'CAUSE BYRON'S NOT HERE.
HEH-HEH!
WE'VE GOT NO FOOD OR SNACKS!
And he's a fake.
HEH HEH HEH!
I know that!
FOOLS!
I GRACE YOU WITH MY PRESENCE BECAUSE YOUR HERO CAN'T PROTECT YOU NOW!
WHAT ?!
THAT CAN'T BE TRUE!

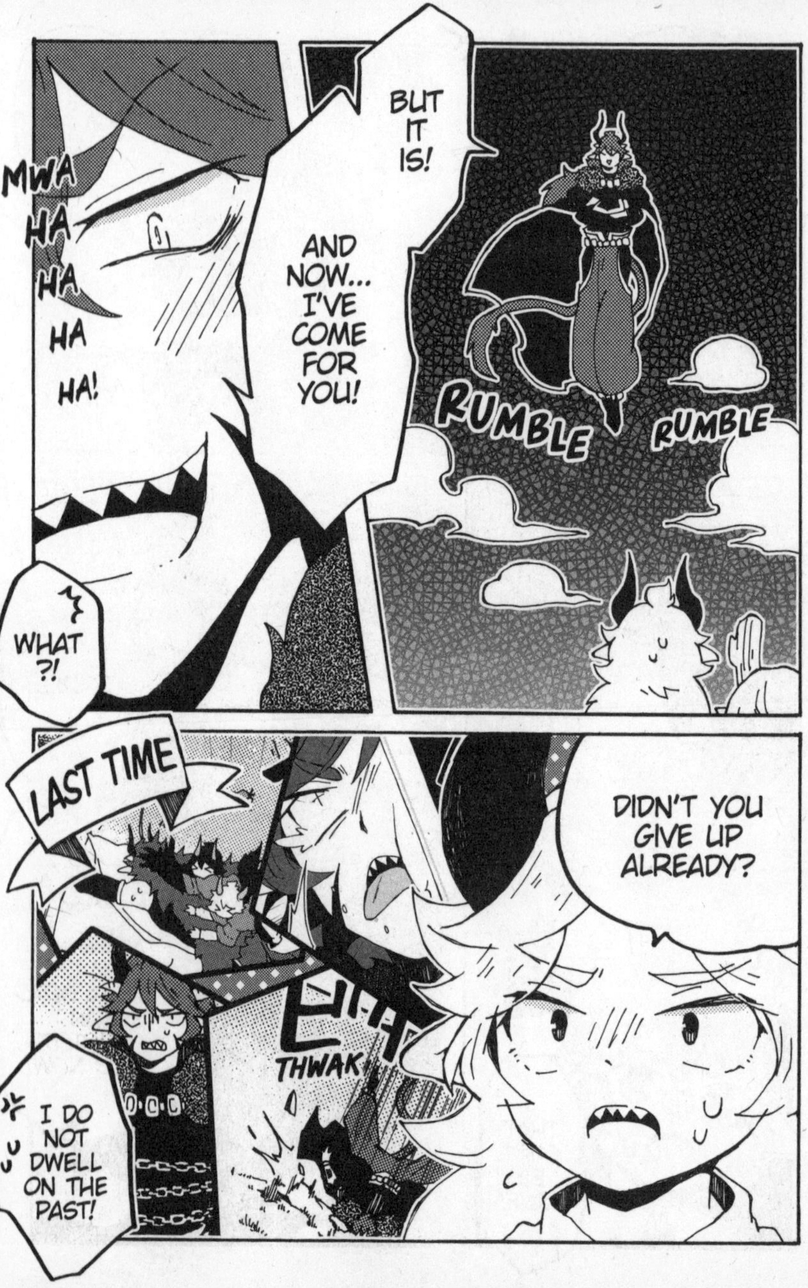

BUT IT IS!
AND NOW... I'VE COME FOR YOU!
RUMBLE
RUMBLE
MWA HA HA HA HA!
WHAT ?!
DIDN'T YOU GIVE UP ALREADY?
LAST TIME
THWAK
I DO NOT DWELL ON THE PAST!

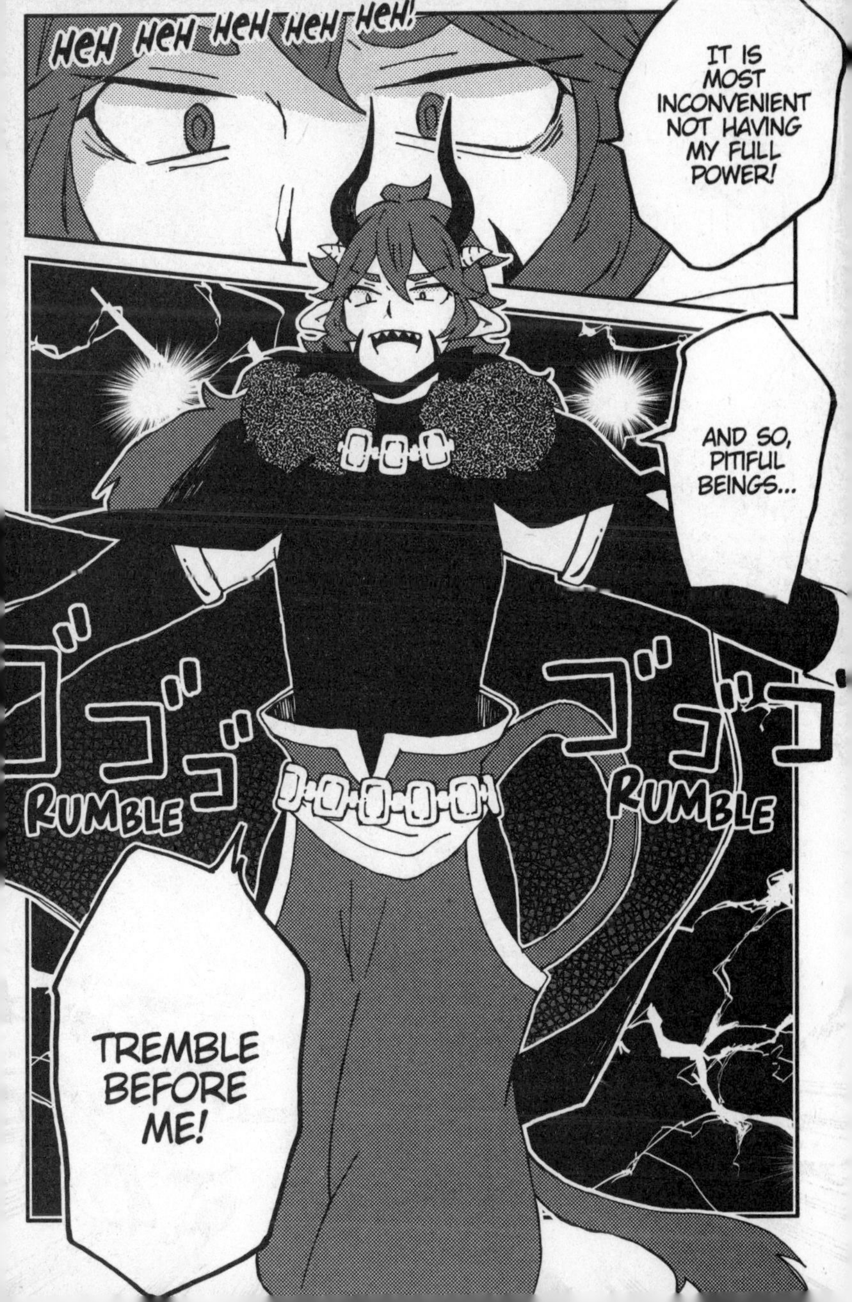
IT IS MOST INCONVENIENT NOT HAVING MY FULL POWER!
HEH HEH HEH HEH HEH!
AND SO, PITIFUL BEINGS...
ゴゴゴゴ
RUMBLE
ゴゴゴゴ
RUMBLE
TREMBLE BEFORE ME!

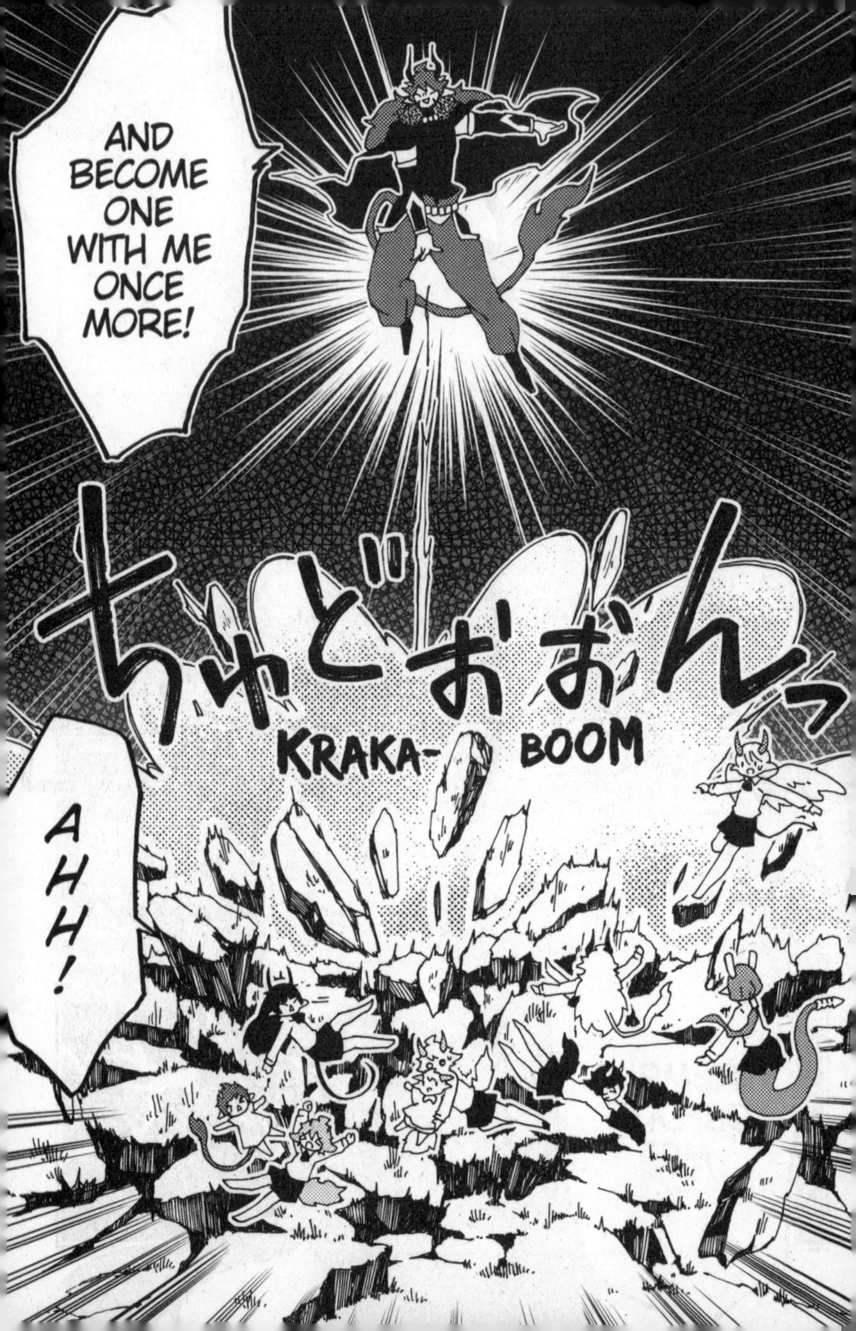
AND BECOME ONE WITH ME ONCE MORE!
ちゅどぉおんっ
KRAKA-BOOM
AHH!

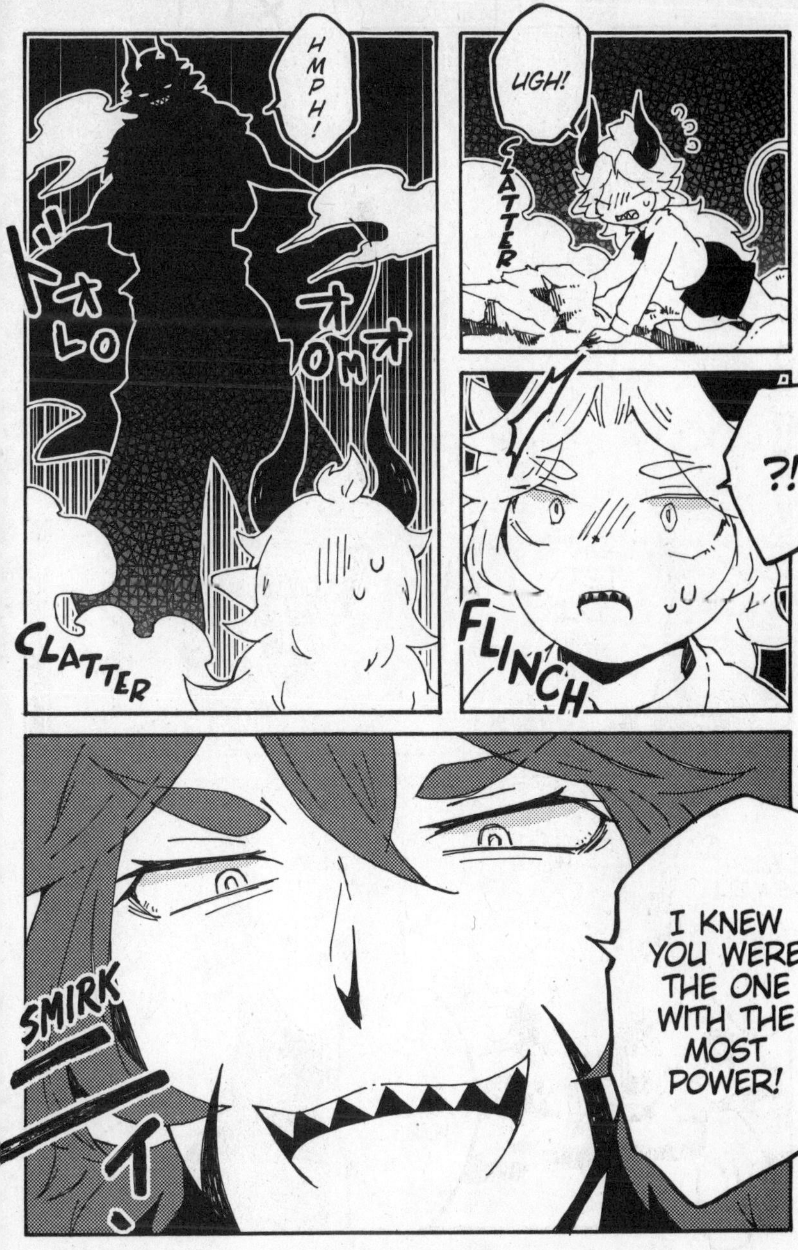
UGH!
CLATTER
?!
FLINCH
HMPH!
CLATTER
SMIRK
I KNEW YOU WERE THE ONE WITH THE MOST POWER!

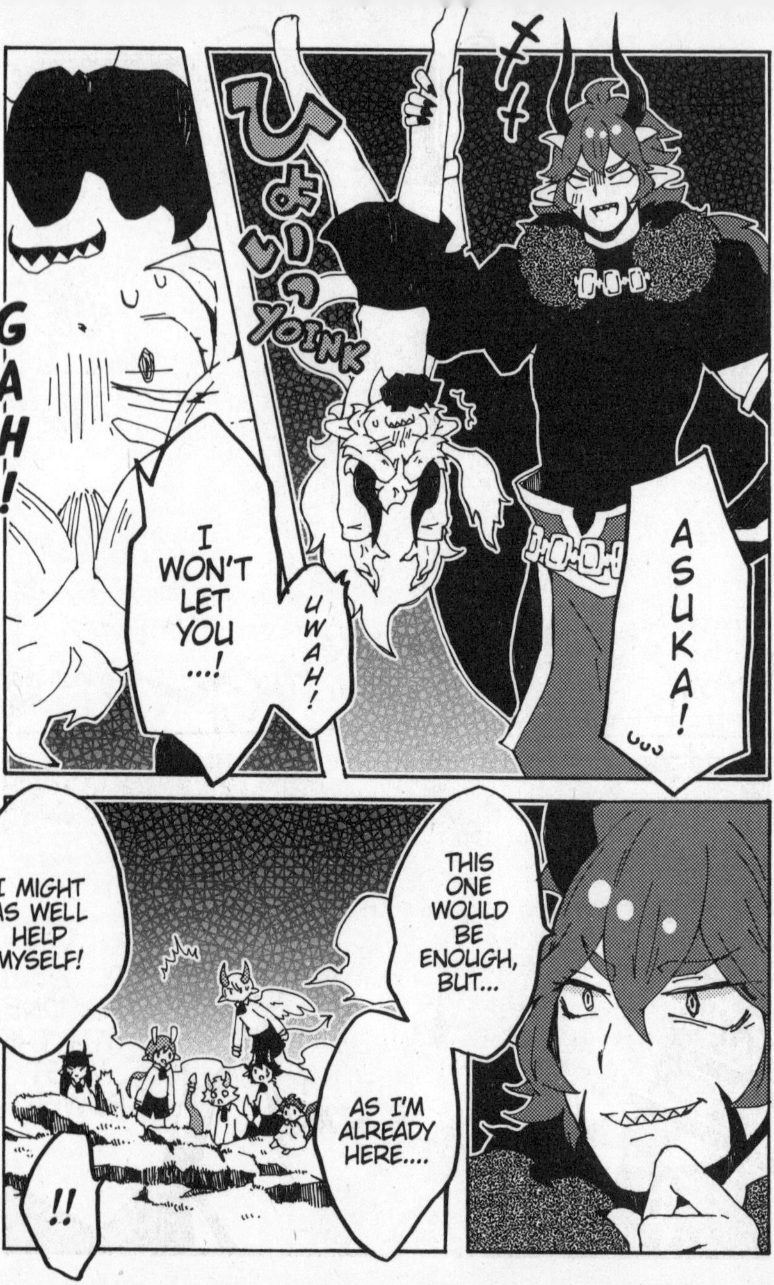
ひょいっ
YOINK
ASUKA!
UWAH!
GAH!
I WON'T LET YOU ...!
THIS ONE WOULD BE ENOUGH, BUT...
AS I'M ALREADY HERE....
I MIGHT AS WELL HELP MYSELF!
!!

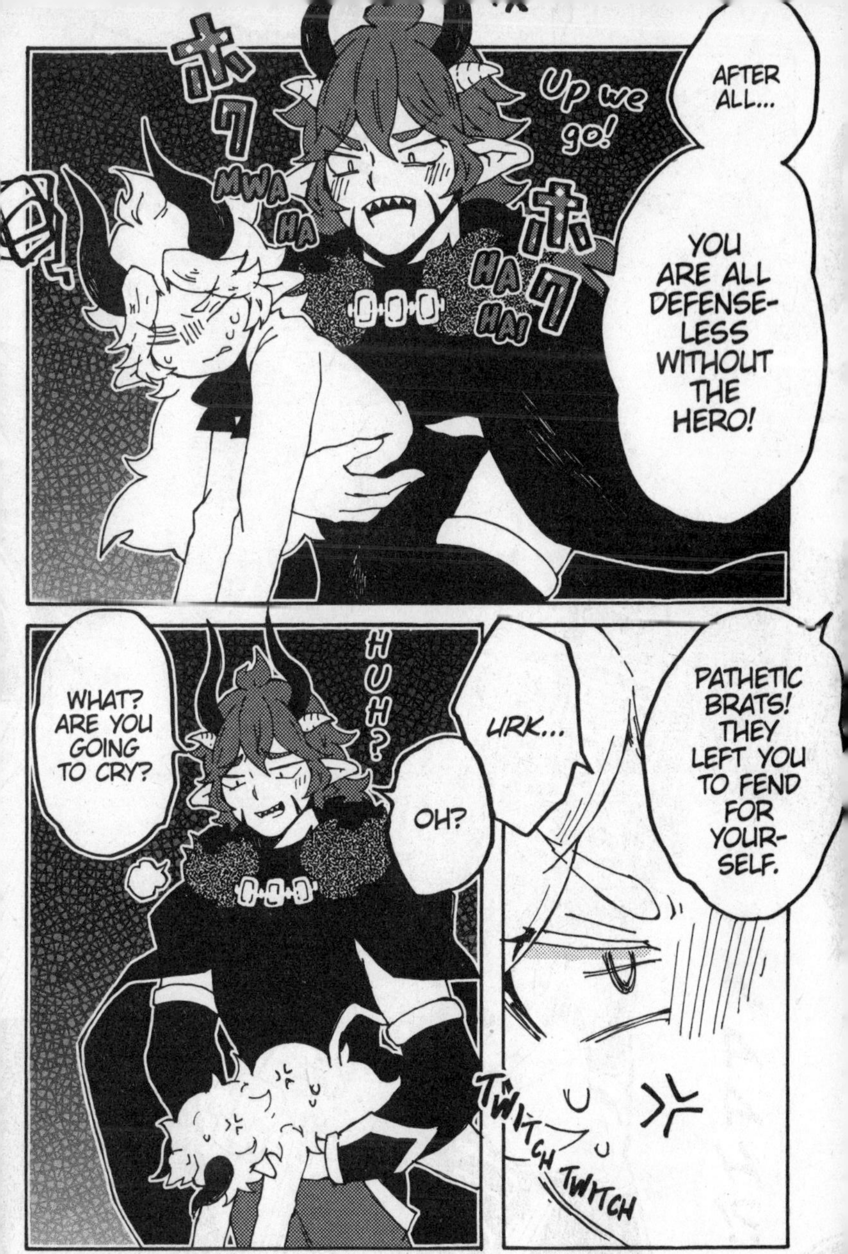

AFTER ALL...
YOU ARE ALL DEFENSE-LESS WITHOUT THE HERO!
Up we go!
HA HA HA
MWA HA HA
PATHETIC BRATS! THEY LEFT YOU TO FEND FOR YOURSELF.
URK...
TWITCH TWITCH
OH?
HUH?
WHAT? ARE YOU GOING TO CRY?

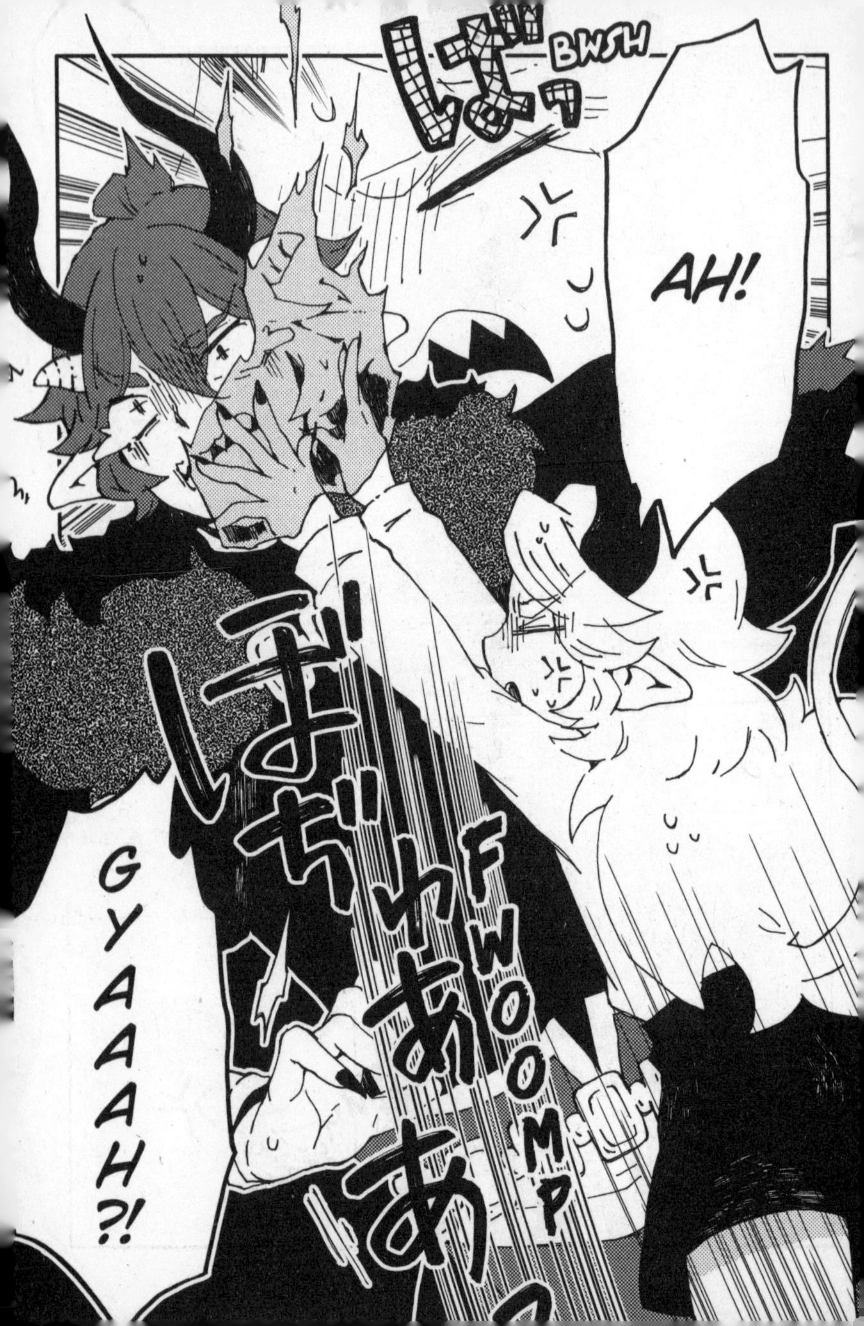
BWSH
AH!
FWOOMP
GYAAAAH?!

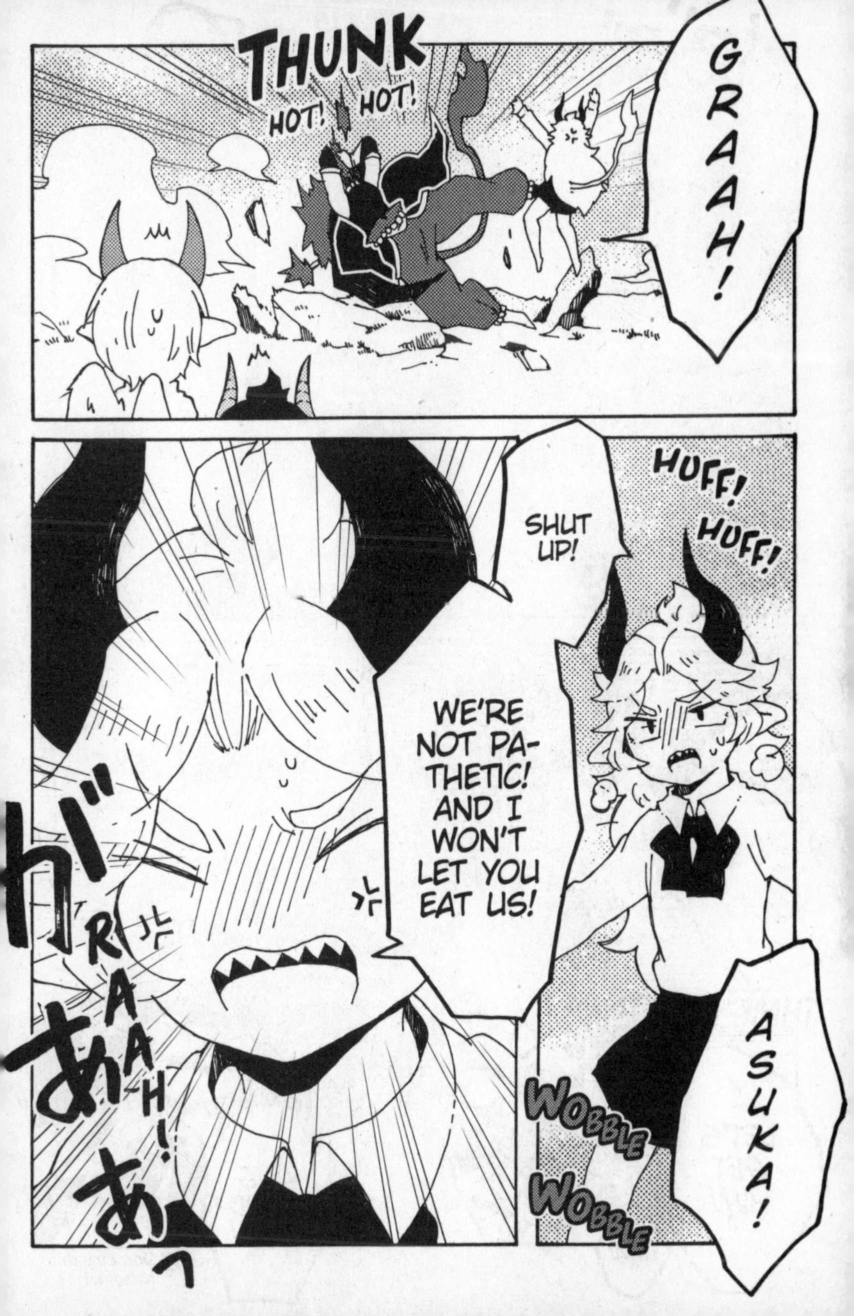
GRAAH!
THUNK
HOT! HOT!
HUFF! HUFF!
SHUT UP!
WE'RE NOT PATHETIC! AND I WON'T LET YOU EAT US!
ASUKA!
WOBBLE WOBBLE
がああ
RAAH!

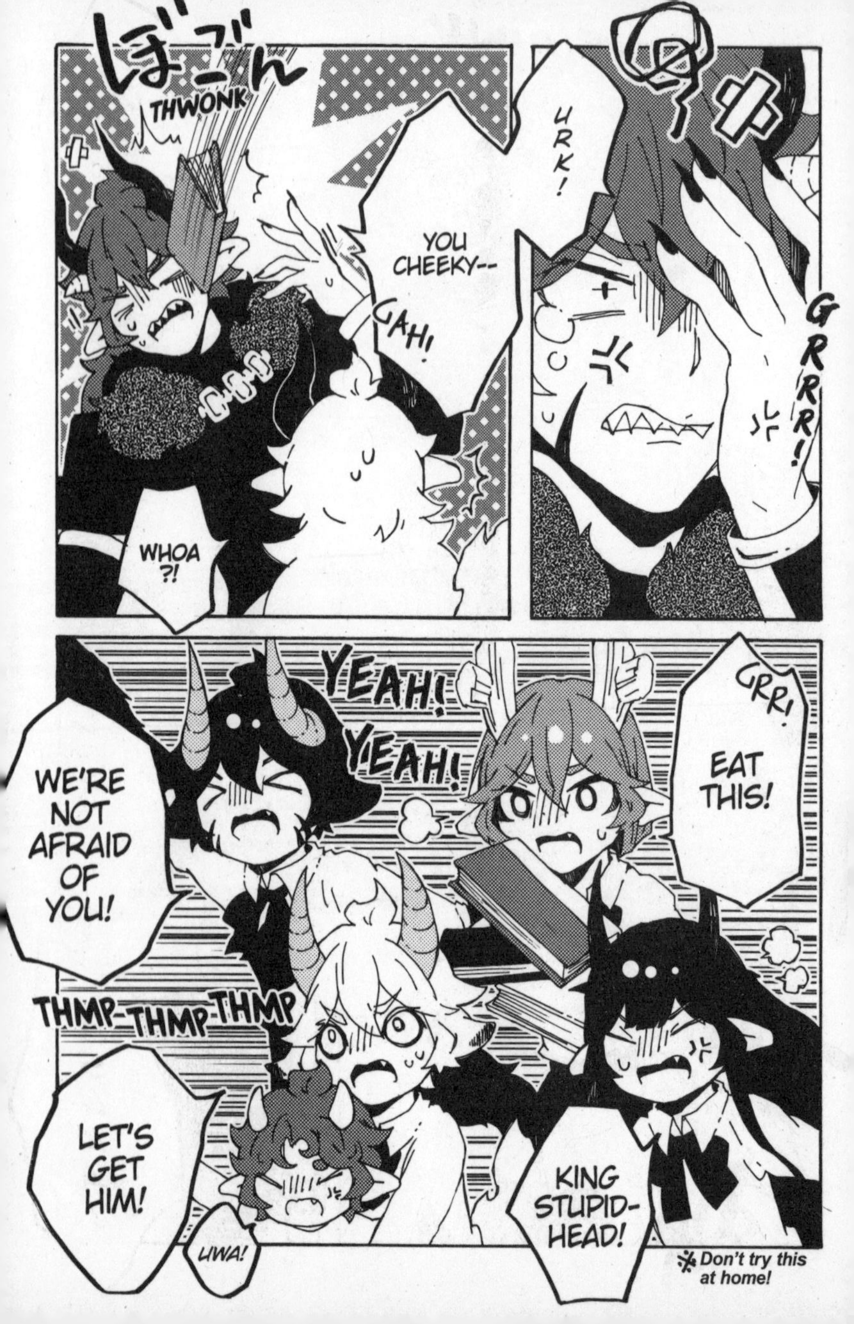
URK!
YOU CHEEKY--
GRRR!
ぼごーん
THWONK
GAH!
WHOA ?!
GRR!
EAT THIS!
YEAH!
YEAH!
WE'RE NOT AFRAID OF YOU!
THMP-THMP-THMP
KING STUPID-HEAD!
LET'S GET HIM!
UWA!

※ Don't try this at home!

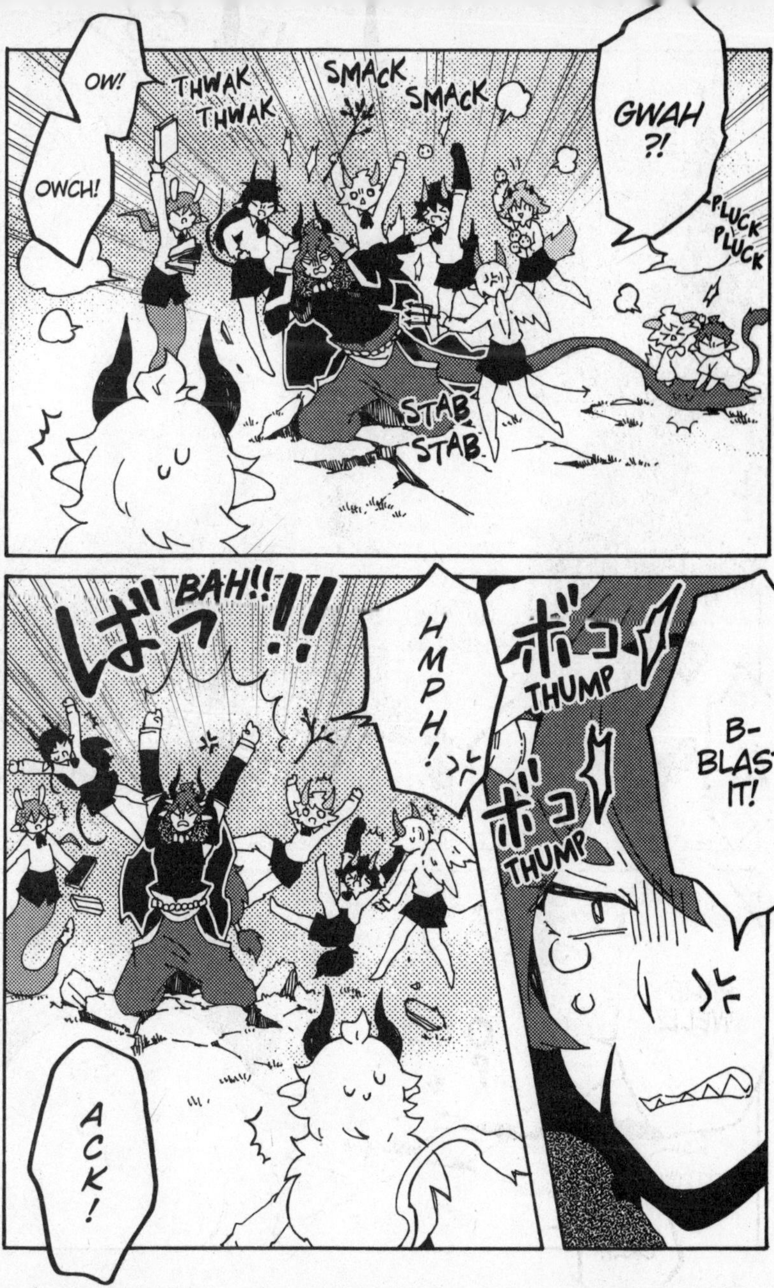
GWAH ?!
PLUCK PLUCK
SMACK SMACK
THWAK THWAK
OW!
OWCH!
STAB STAB
B-BLAST IT!
ボコ THUMP
ボコ THUMP
HMPH!
ばっ!! BAH!!
ACK!

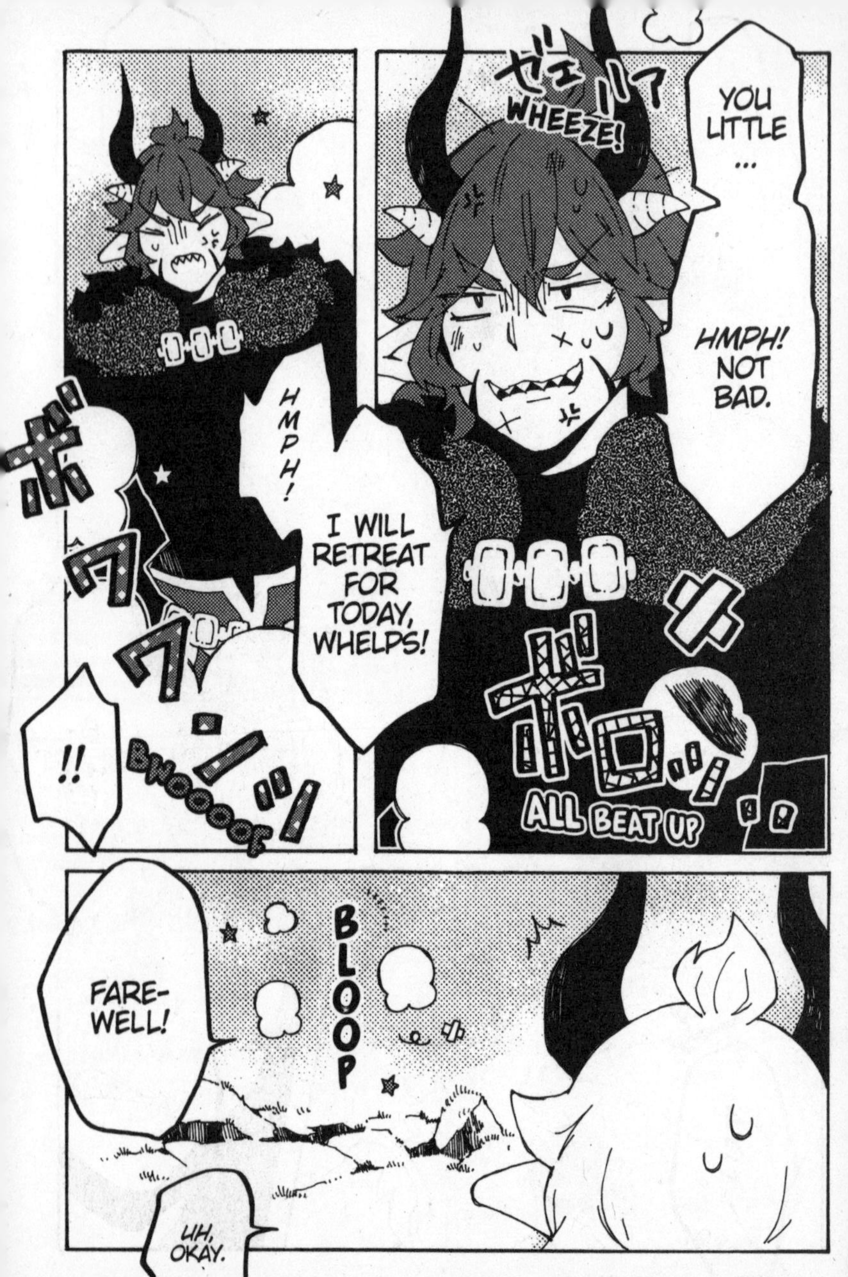
WHEEZE!
YOU LITTLE ...
HMPH! NOT BAD.
ALL BEAT UP
HMPH!
I WILL RETREAT FOR TODAY, WHELPS!
BWOOOOF
!!
FARE-WELL!
BLOOP
UH, OKAY.

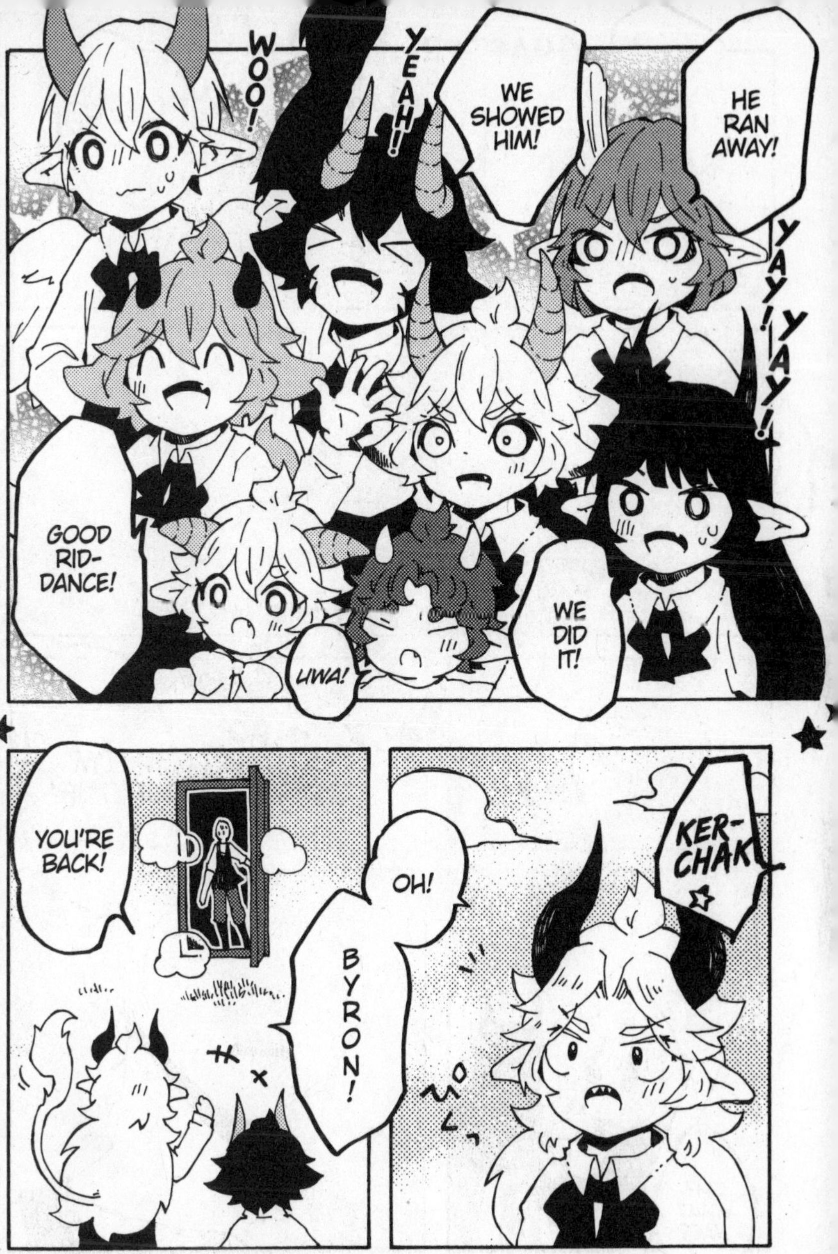
HE RAN AWAY!
WE SHOWED HIM!
YEAH!!
WOO!
YAY! YAY!
WE DID IT!
UWA!
GOOD RID-DANCE!
KER-CHAK
OH!
BYRON!
YOU'RE BACK!

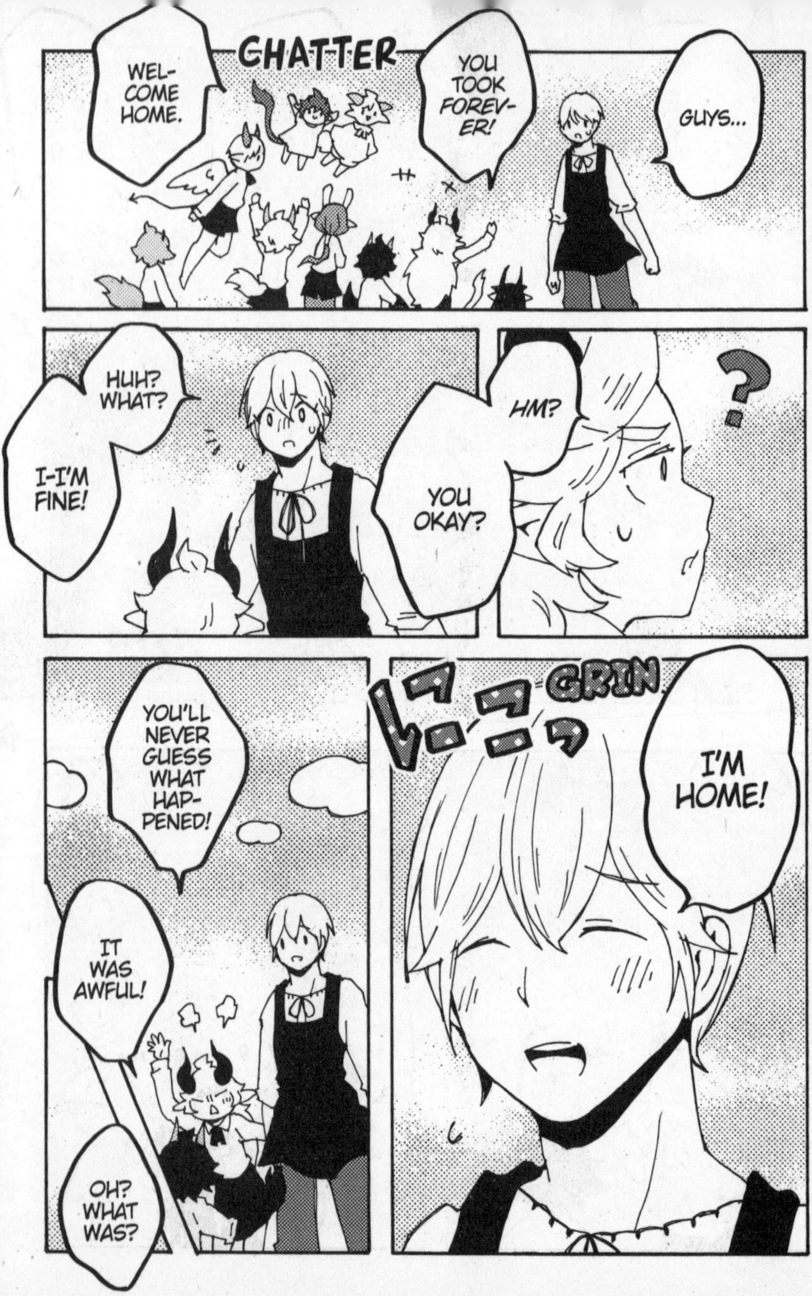
GUYS...
YOU TOOK FOREVER!
CHATTER
WELCOME HOME.
HM?
YOU OKAY?
HUH? WHAT?
I-I'M FINE!
GRIN
I'M HOME!
YOU'LL NEVER GUESS WHAT HAPPENED!
IT WAS AWFUL!
OH? WHAT WAS?

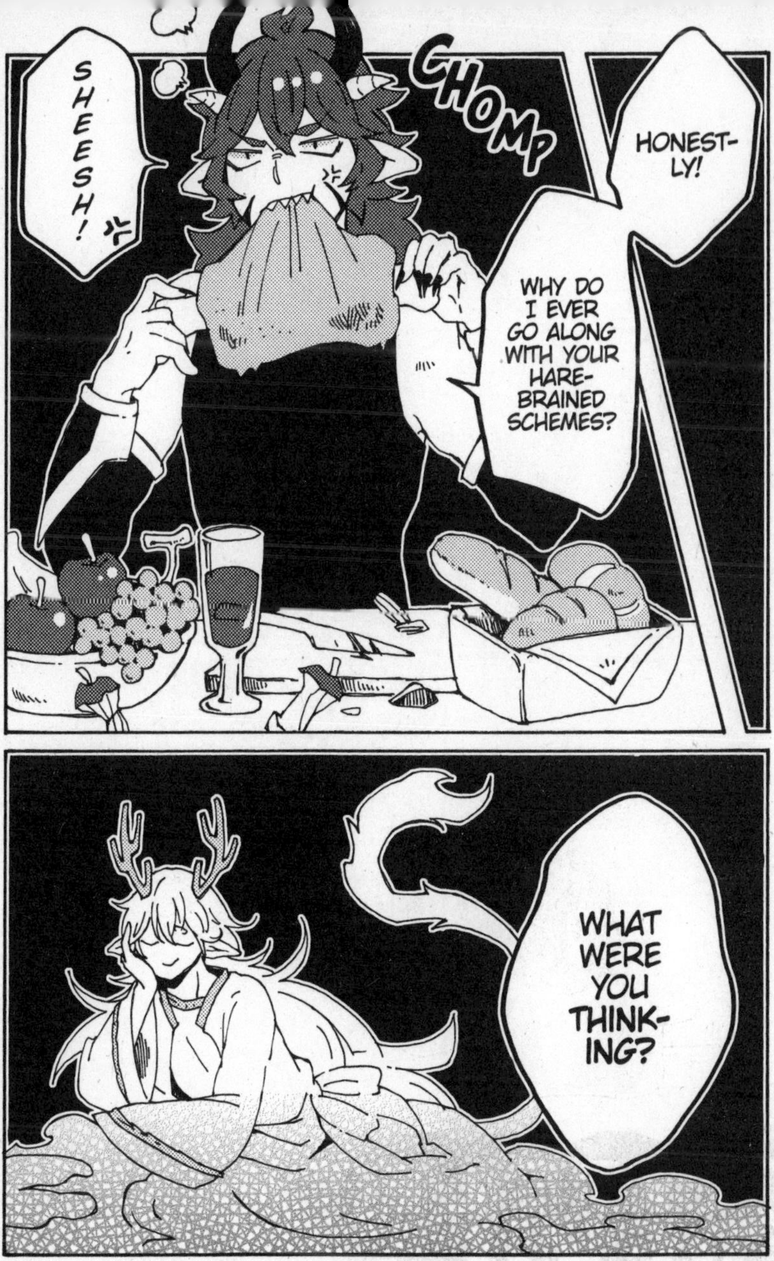
HONEST-LY!
CHOMP
SHEESH!
WHY DO I EVER GO ALONG WITH YOUR HARE-BRAINED SCHEMES?
WHAT WERE YOU THINK-ING?

LITTLE DEVILS

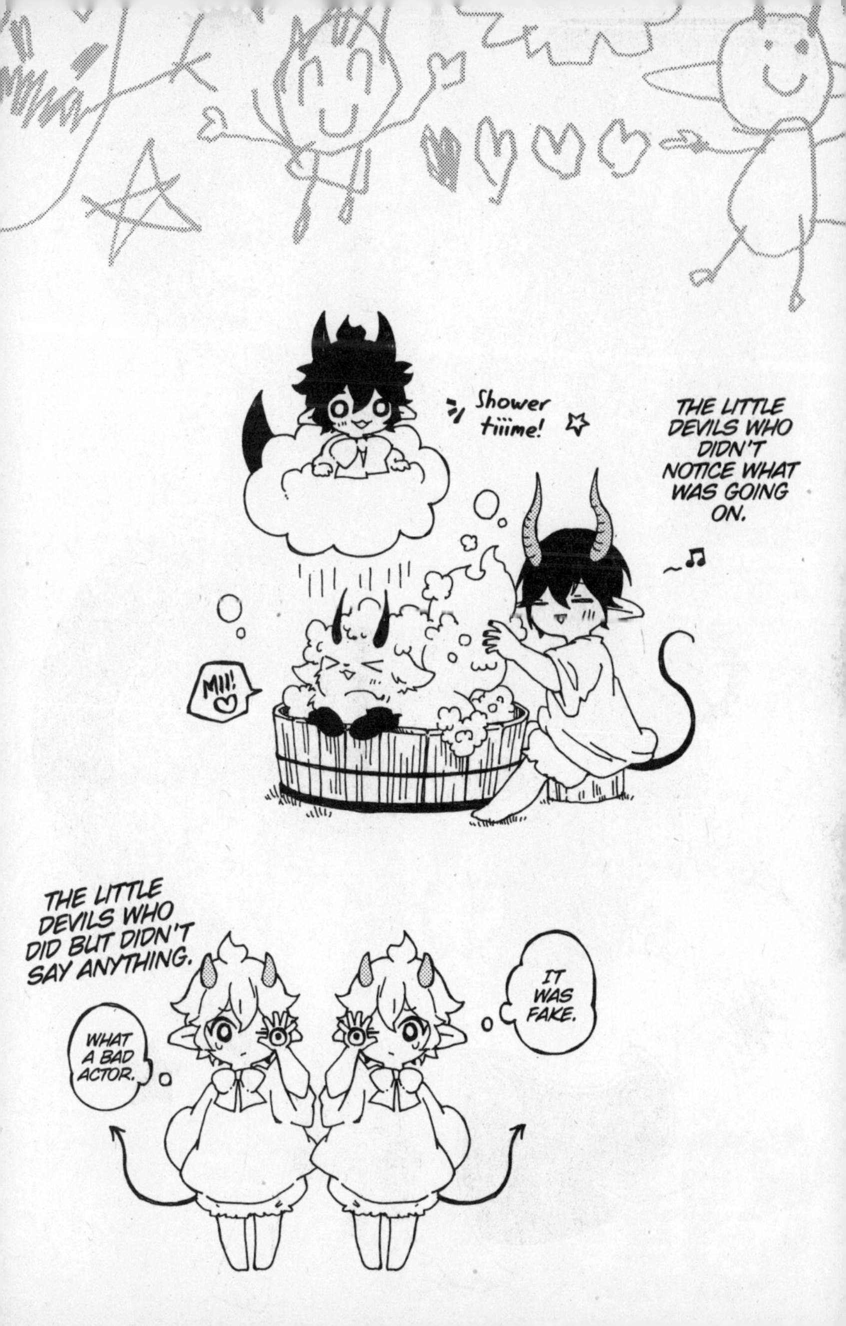
THE LITTLE DEVILS WHO DIDN'T NOTICE WHAT WAS GOING ON.
Shower tiiime!
MI!
THE LITTLE DEVILS WHO DID BUT DIDN'T SAY ANYTHING.
IT WAS FAKE.
WHAT A BAD ACTOR.

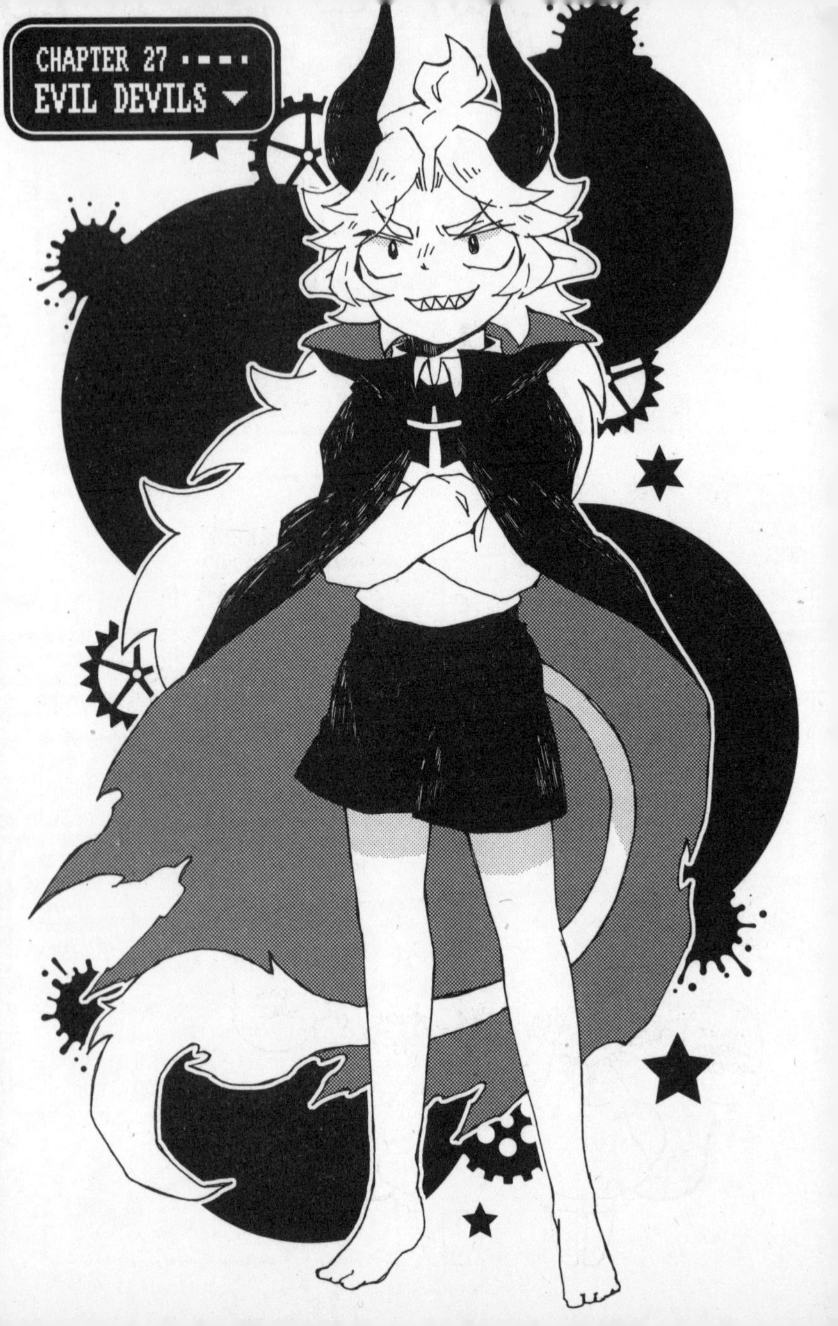
CHAPTER 27
EVIL DEVILS

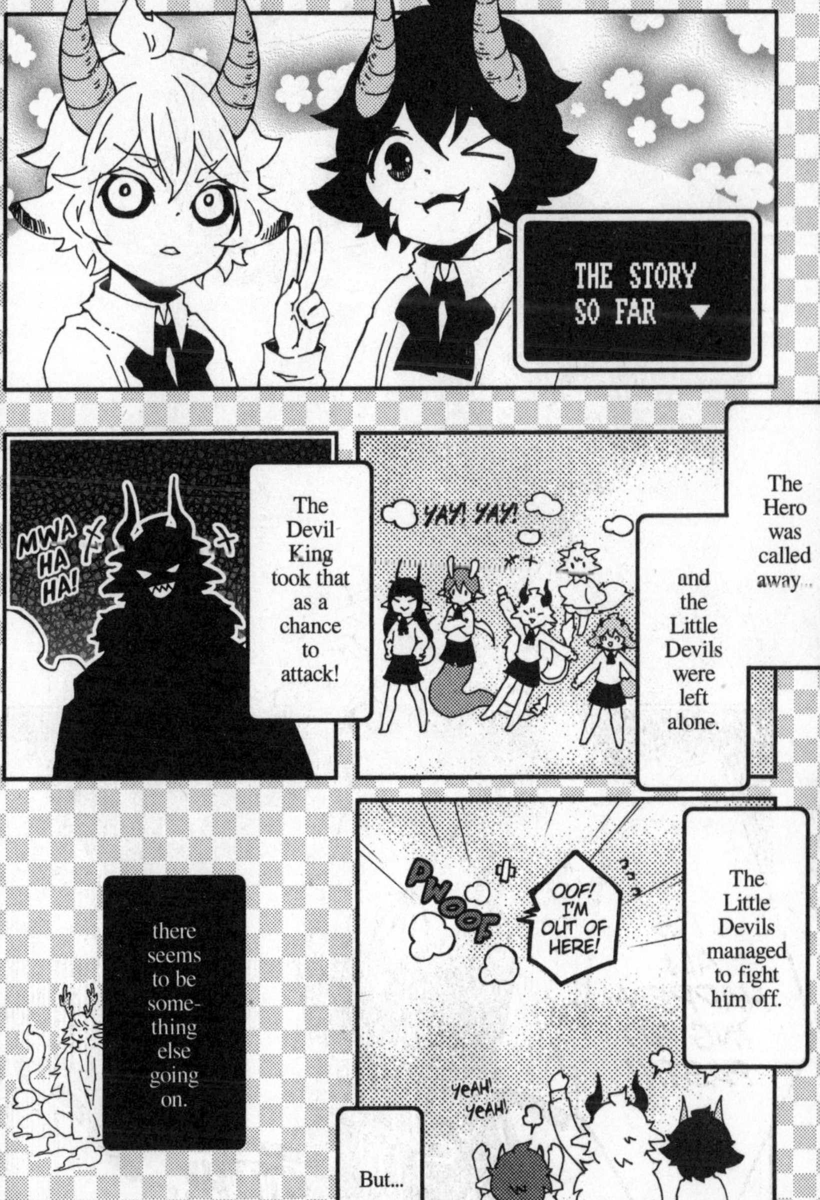
THE STORY SO FAR ▼
The Hero was called away...
and the Little Devils were left alone.
YAY! YAY!
The Devil King took that as a chance to attack!
MWA HA HA!
The Little Devils managed to fight him off.
PWOOF
OOF! I'M OUT OF HERE!
YEAH! YEAH!
But...
there seems to be some-thing else going on.

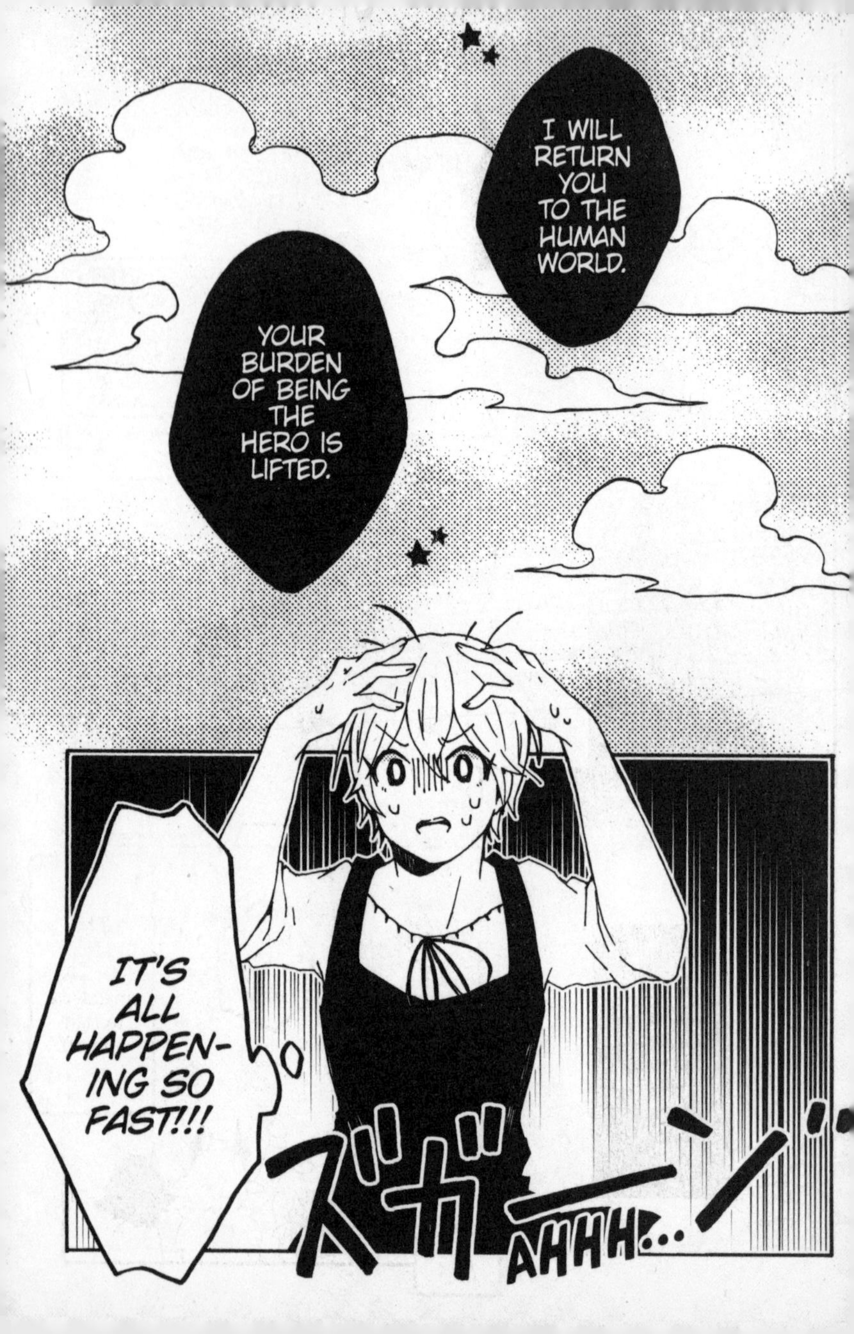
I WILL RETURN YOU TO THE HUMAN WORLD.
YOUR BURDEN OF BEING THE HERO IS LIFTED.
ズガーン
AHHH...
IT'S ALL HAPPEN-ING SO FAST!!!

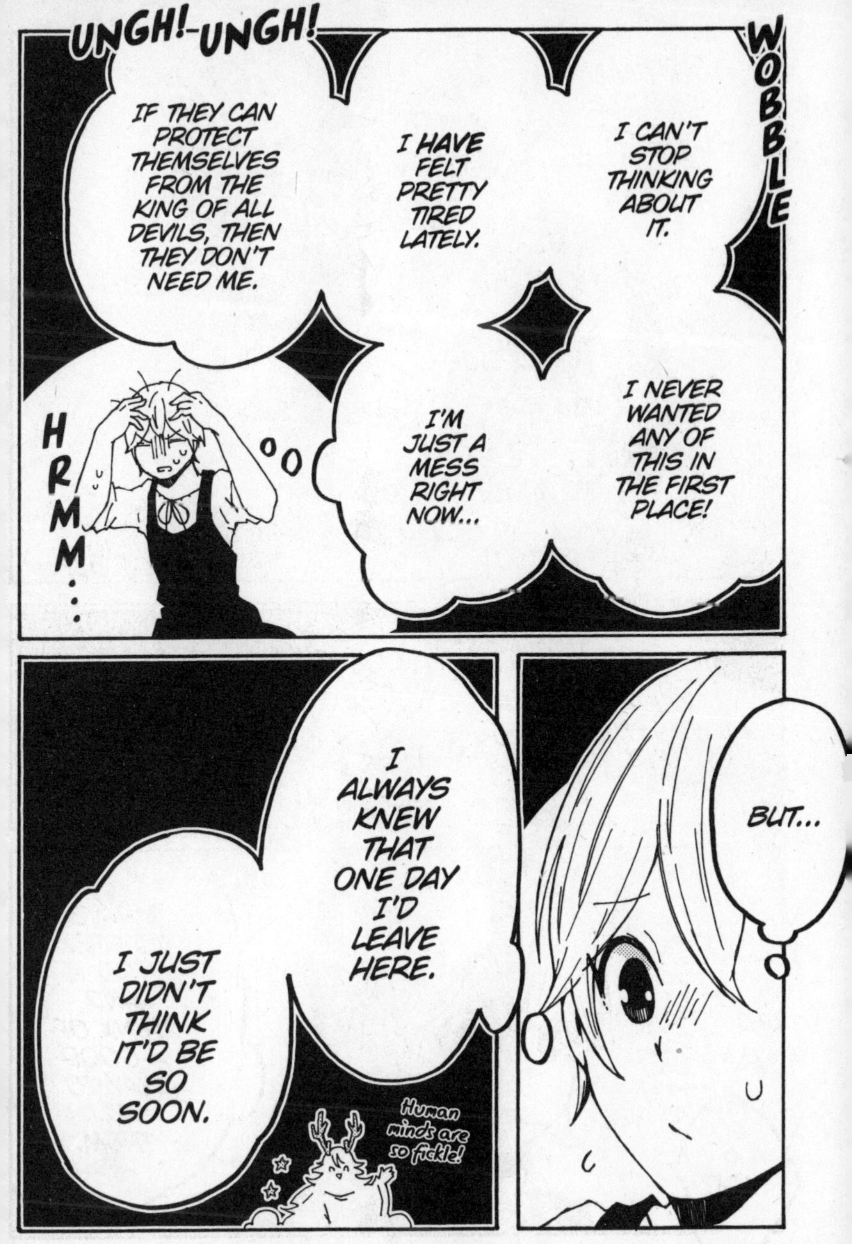
WOBBLE
I CAN'T STOP THINKING ABOUT IT.
I HAVE FELT PRETTY TIRED LATELY.
UNGH!-UNGH!
IF THEY CAN PROTECT THEMSELVES FROM THE KING OF ALL DEVILS, THEN THEY DON'T NEED ME.
I NEVER WANTED ANY OF THIS IN THE FIRST PLACE!
I'M JUST A MESS RIGHT NOW...
HRMM...
BUT...
I ALWAYS KNEW THAT ONE DAY I'D LEAVE HERE.
I JUST DIDN'T THINK IT'D BE SO SOON.
Human minds are so fickle!

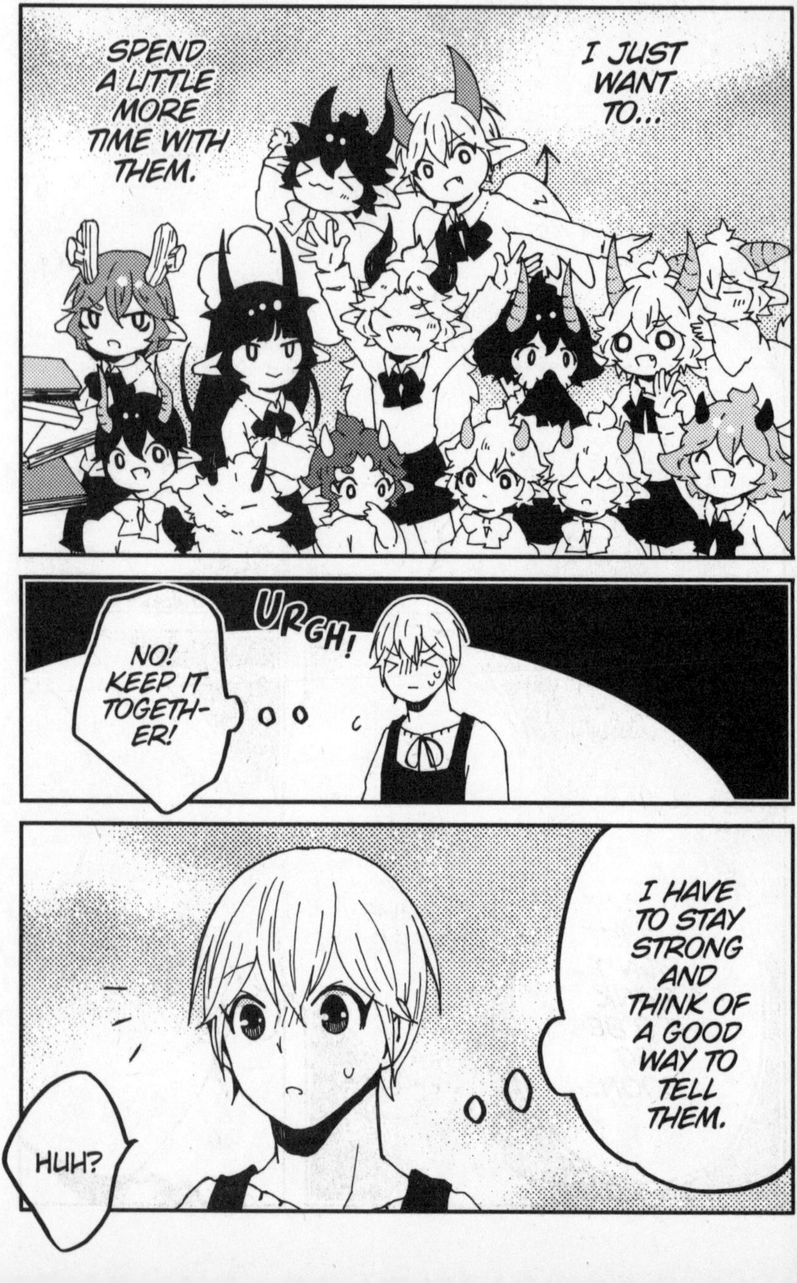
I JUST WANT TO...
SPEND A LITTLE MORE TIME WITH THEM.
URGH!
NO! KEEP IT TOGETH-ER!
I HAVE TO STAY STRONG AND THINK OF A GOOD WAY TO TELL THEM.
HUH?

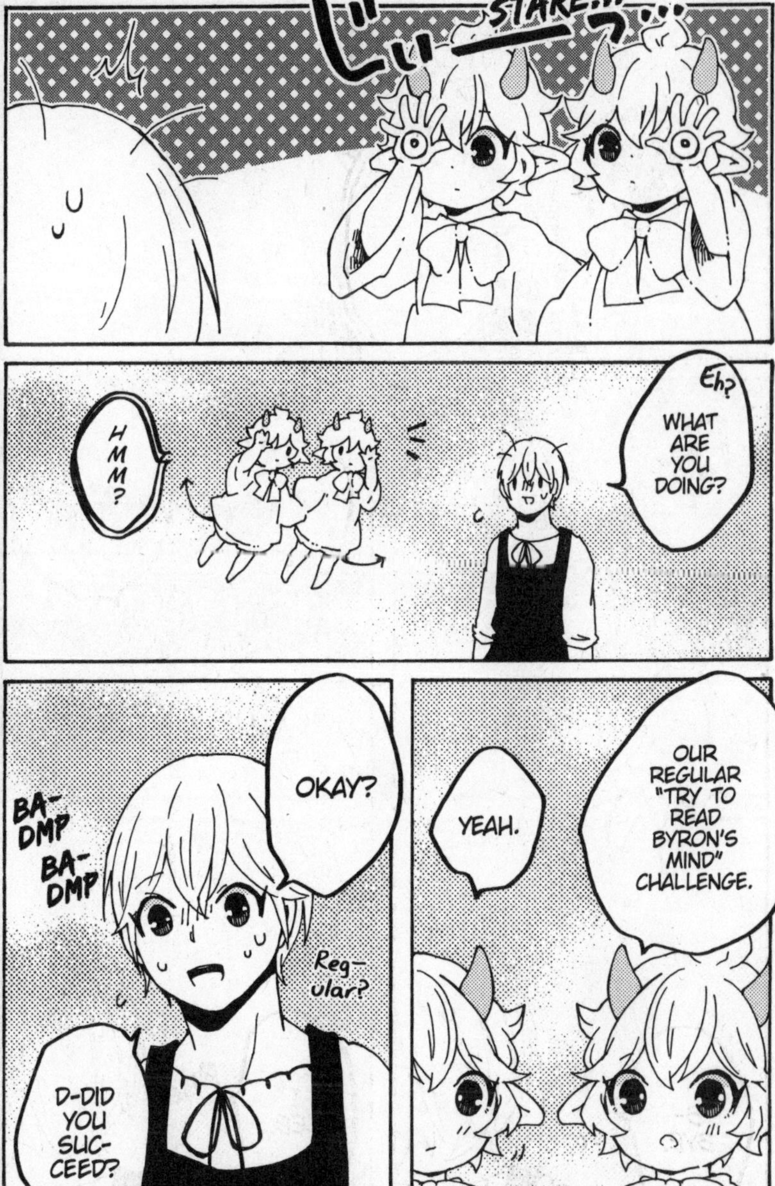
じぃーーっ
STARE...
Eh?
WHAT ARE YOU DOING?
HMM?
OUR REGULAR "TRY TO READ BYRON'S MIND" CHALLENGE.
YEAH.
OKAY?
Reg-ular?
BA-DMP BA-DMP
D-DID YOU SUC-CEED?

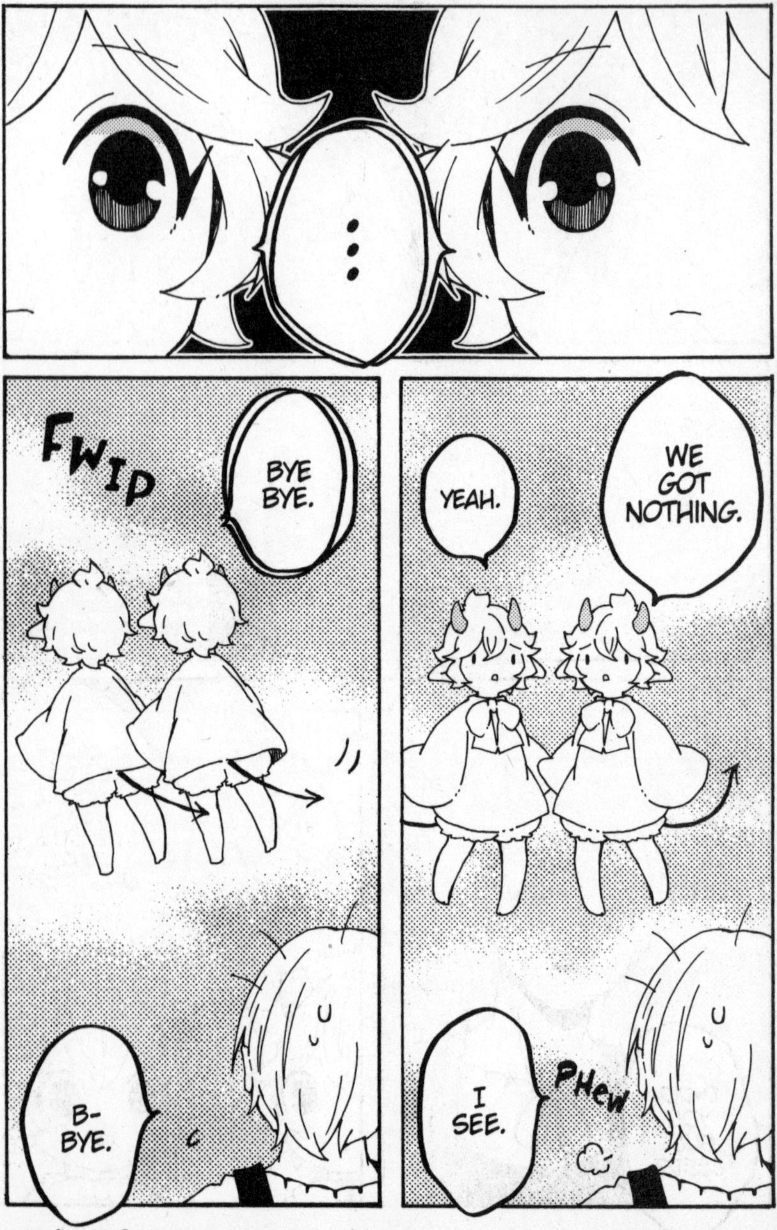
…
WE GOT NOTHING.
YEAH.
I SEE.
PHEW
BYE BYE.
FWIP
B-BYE.

You're going?

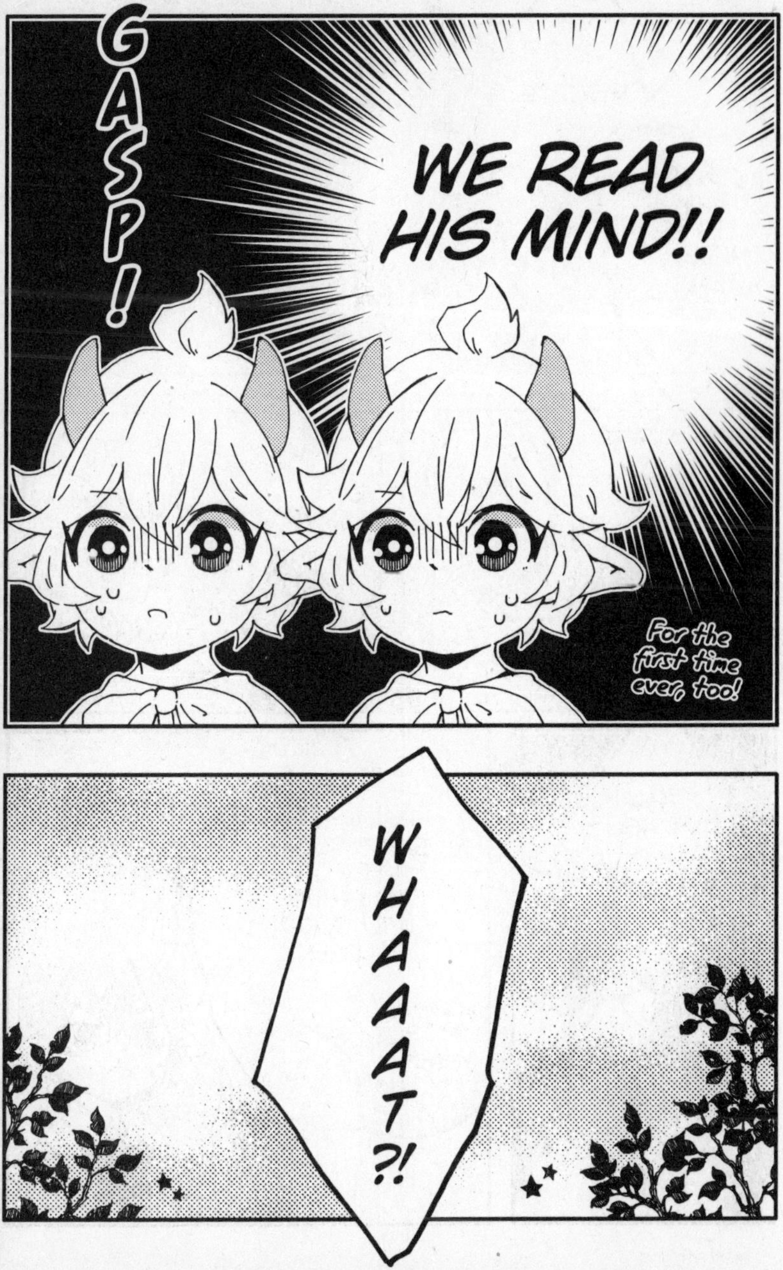
WE READ HIS MIND!!
For the first time ever, too!
GASP!
WHAAAAT?!

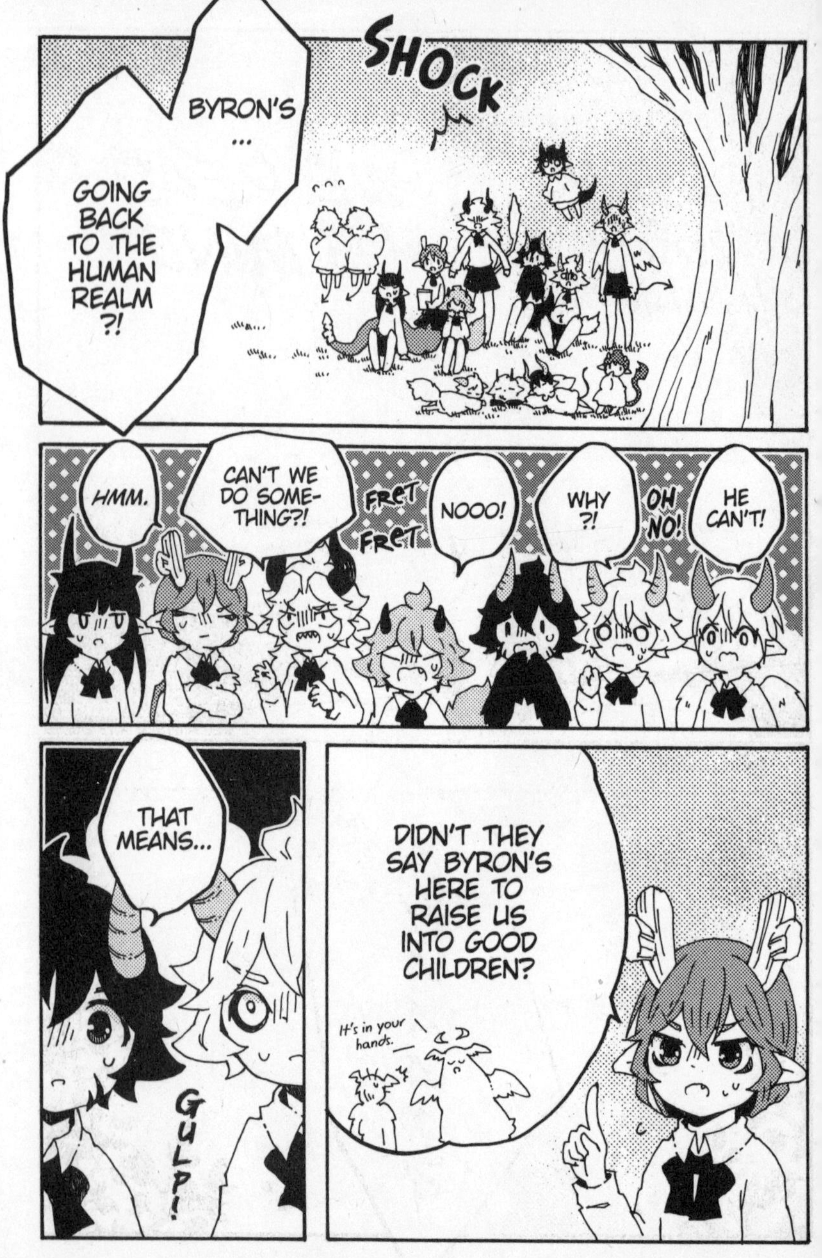
SHOCK
BYRON'S ... GOING BACK TO THE HUMAN REALM?!
HE CAN'T!
OH NO!
WHY?!
NOOO!
FRET FRET
CAN'T WE DO SOME-THING?!
HMM.
DIDN'T THEY SAY BYRON'S HERE TO RAISE US INTO GOOD CHILDREN?
It's in your hands.
THAT MEANS...
GULP!

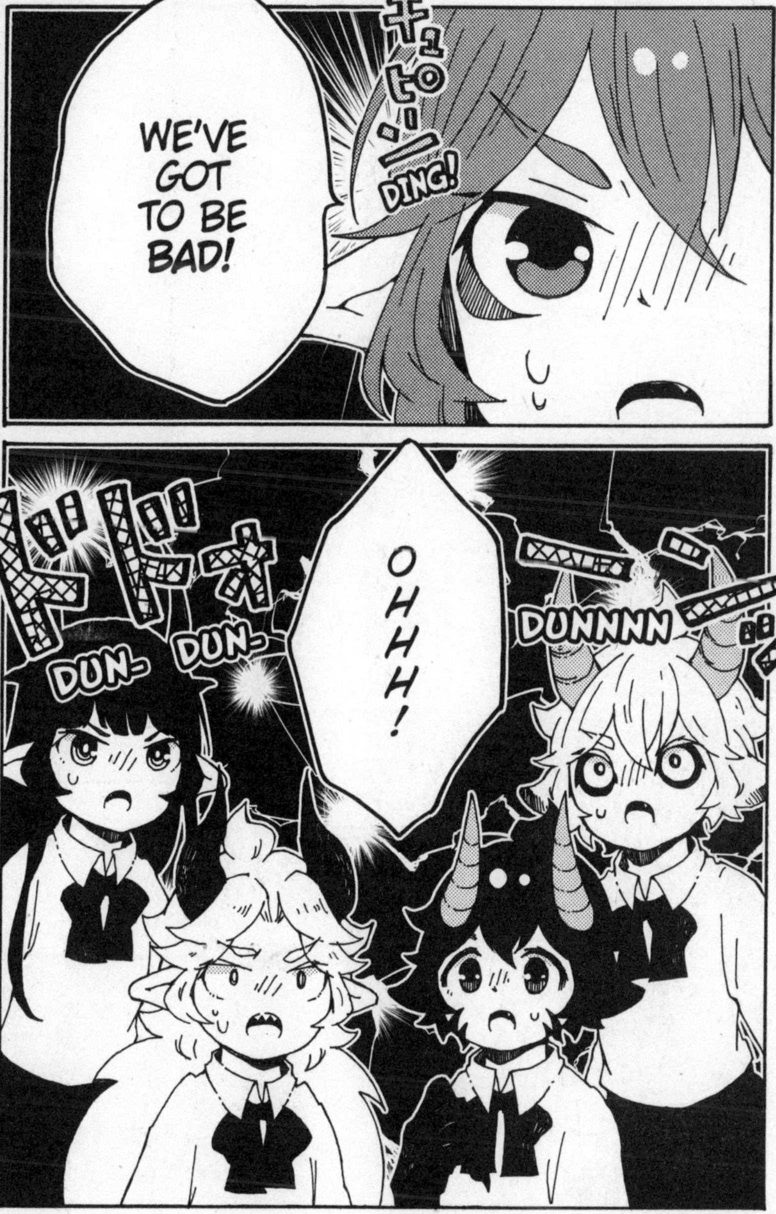
キュピーン
DING!
WE'VE GOT TO BE BAD!
ドドオーーン!!
DUN- DUN- DUNNNN
OHHHH!

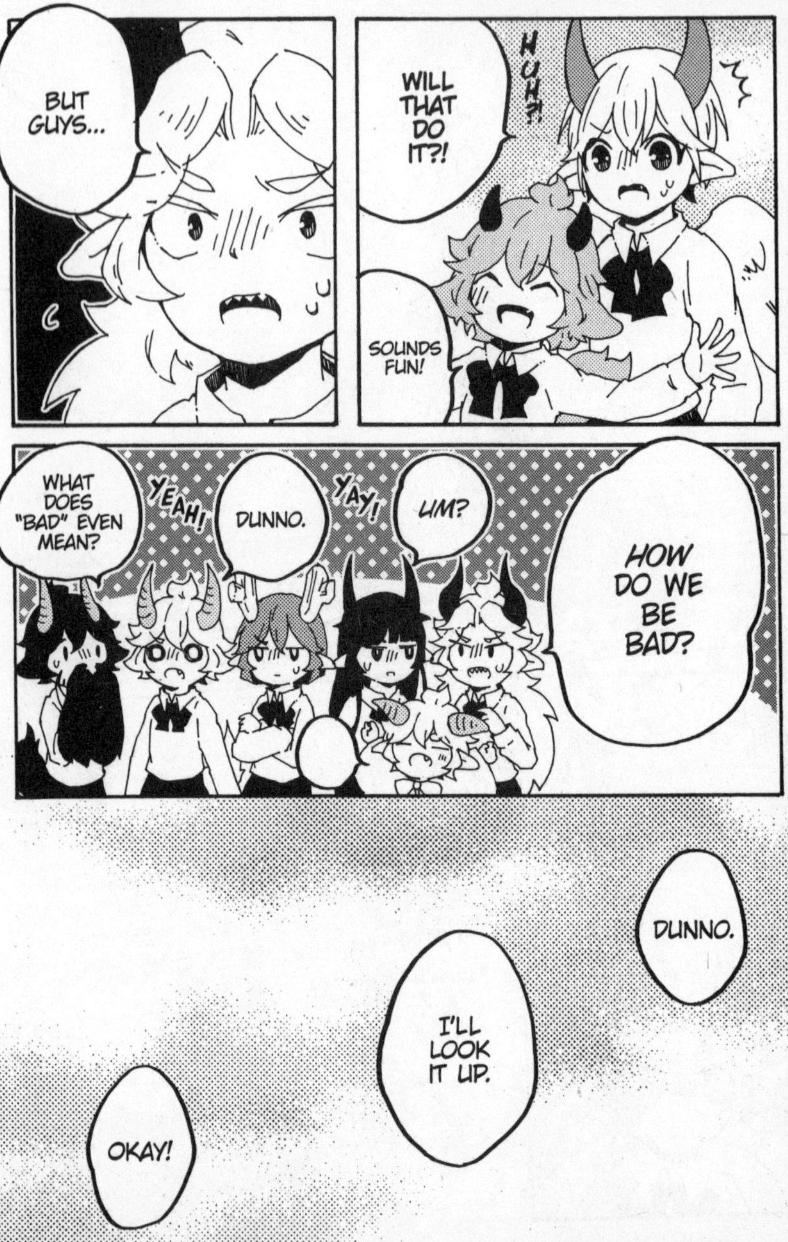
HUH?!
WILL THAT DO IT?!
SOUNDS FUN!
BUT GUYS...
HOW DO WE BE BAD?
UM?
YAY!
DUNNO.
YEAH!
WHAT DOES "BAD" EVEN MEAN?
DUNNO.
I'LL LOOK IT UP.
OKAY!

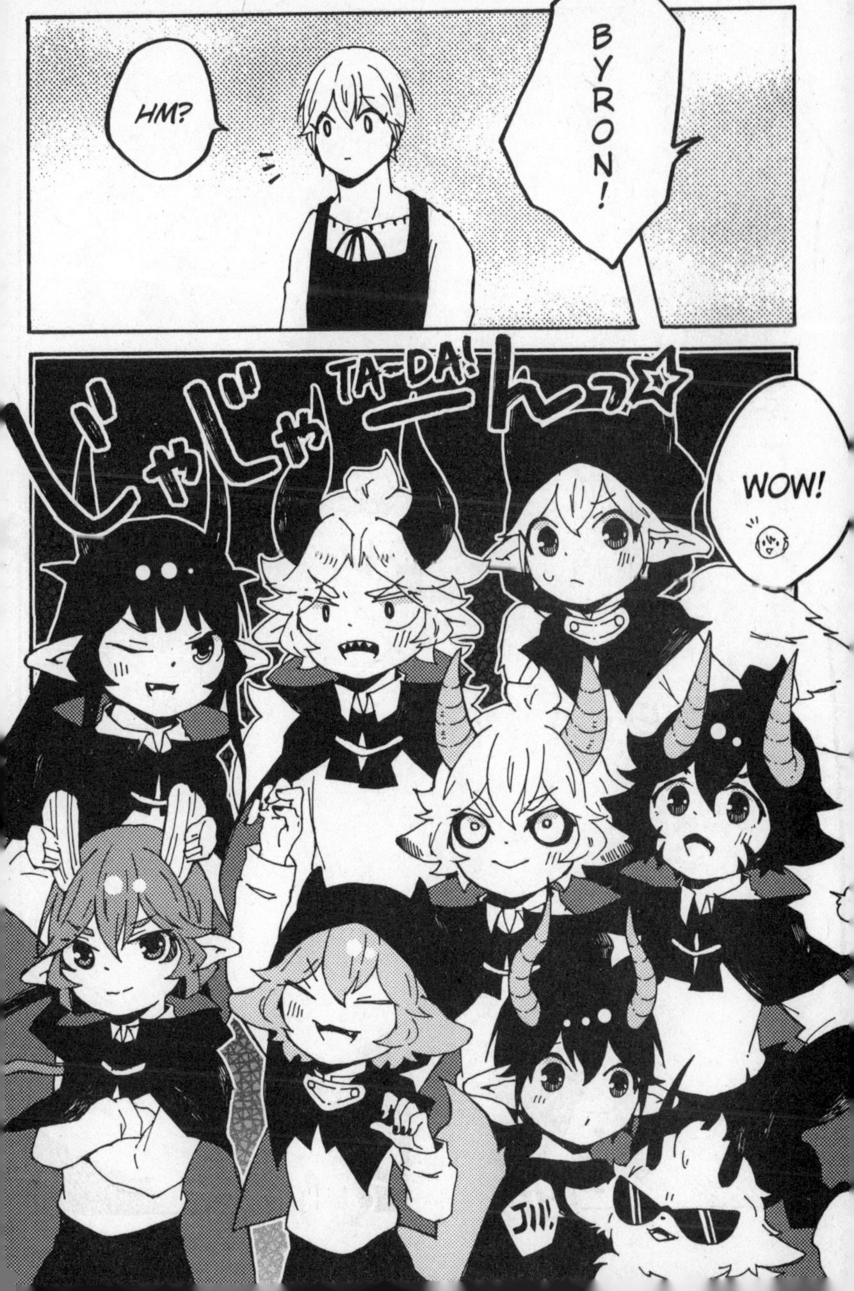
BYRON!
HM?
じゃじゃーんっ
TA-DA!
WOW!
JII!

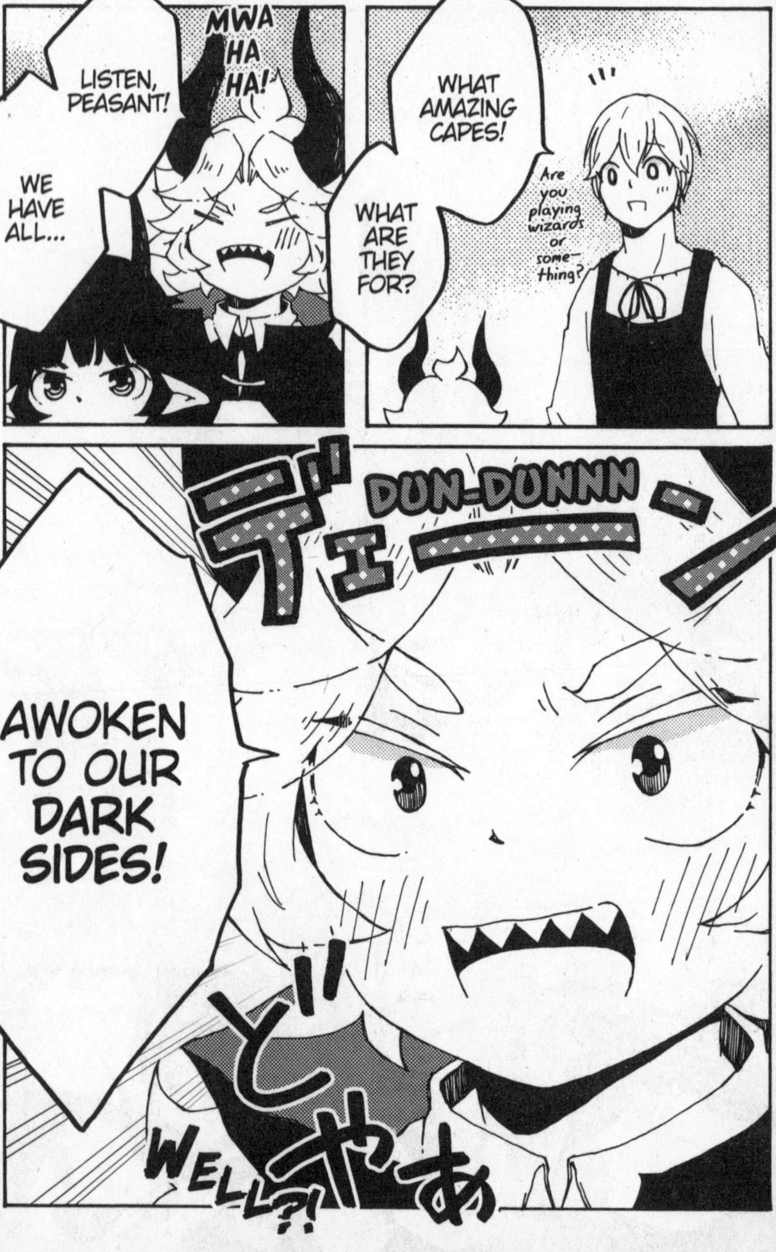
WHAT AMAZING CAPES!
WHAT ARE THEY FOR?
Are you playing wizards or some-thing?
MWA HA HA!
LISTEN, PEASANT!
WE HAVE ALL...
DUN-DUNNN
AWOKEN TO OUR DARK SIDES!
どやあ
WELL?!

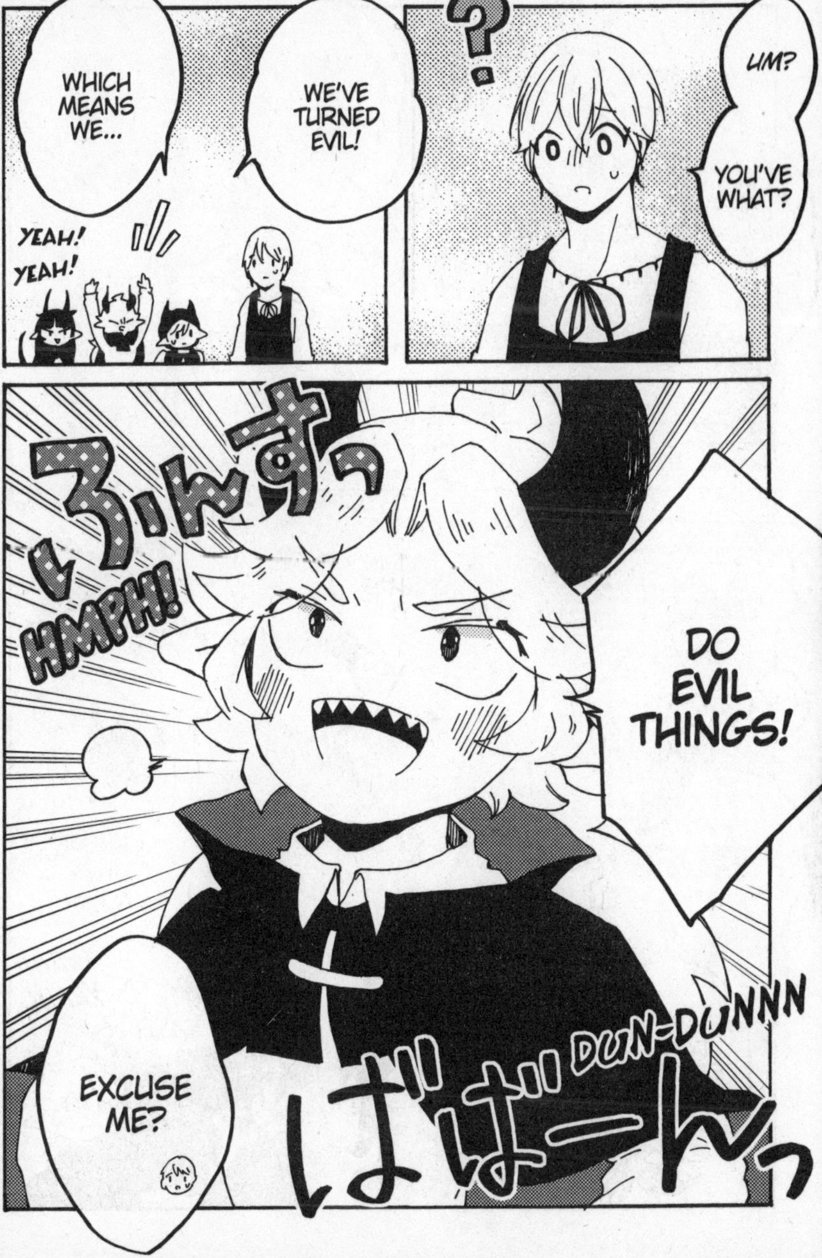
UM?
YOU'VE WHAT?
WE'VE TURNED EVIL!
WHICH MEANS WE...
YEAH!
YEAH!
ふんすっ
HMPH!
DO EVIL THINGS!
ばばーんっ
DUN-DUNNN
EXCUSE ME?

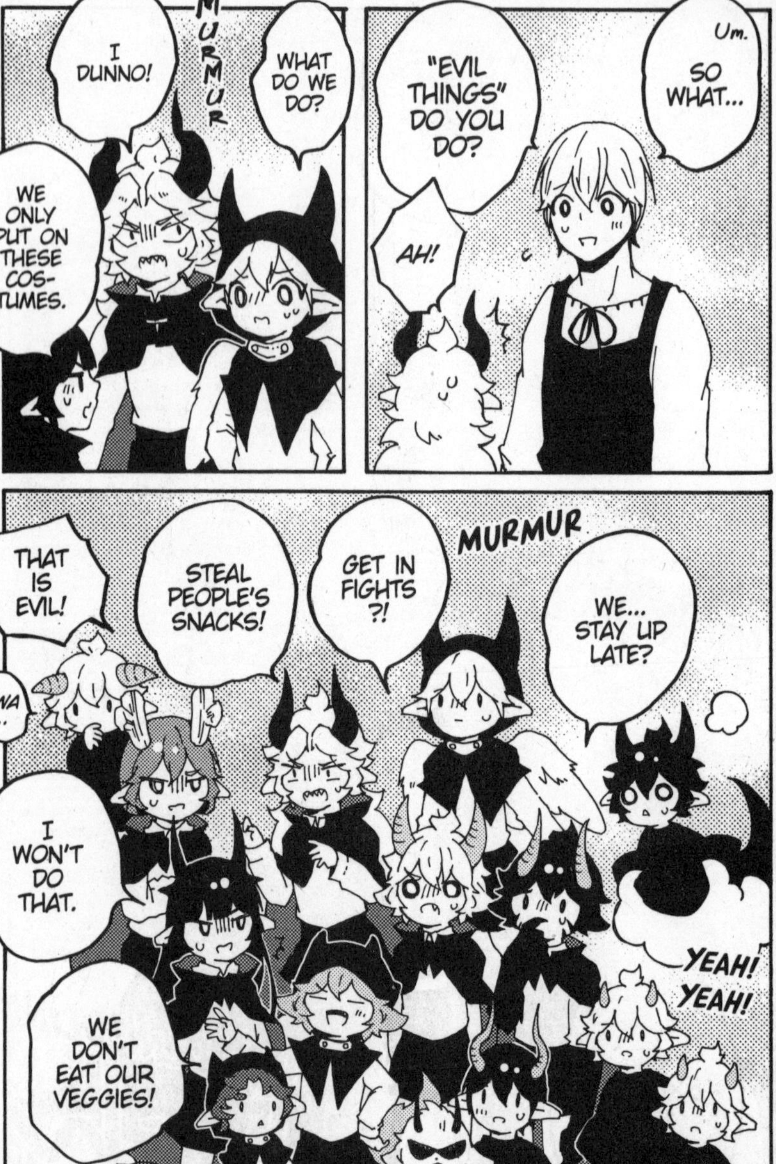
Um.
SO WHAT...
"EVIL THINGS" DO YOU DO?
AH!
WHAT DO WE DO?
MURMUR
I DUNNO!
WE ONLY PUT ON THESE COS-TUMES.
MURMUR
WE... STAY UP LATE?
GET IN FIGHTS?!
STEAL PEOPLE'S SNACKS!
THAT IS EVIL!
UWA...
YEAH! YEAH!
I WON'T DO THAT.
WE DON'T EAT OUR VEGGIES!

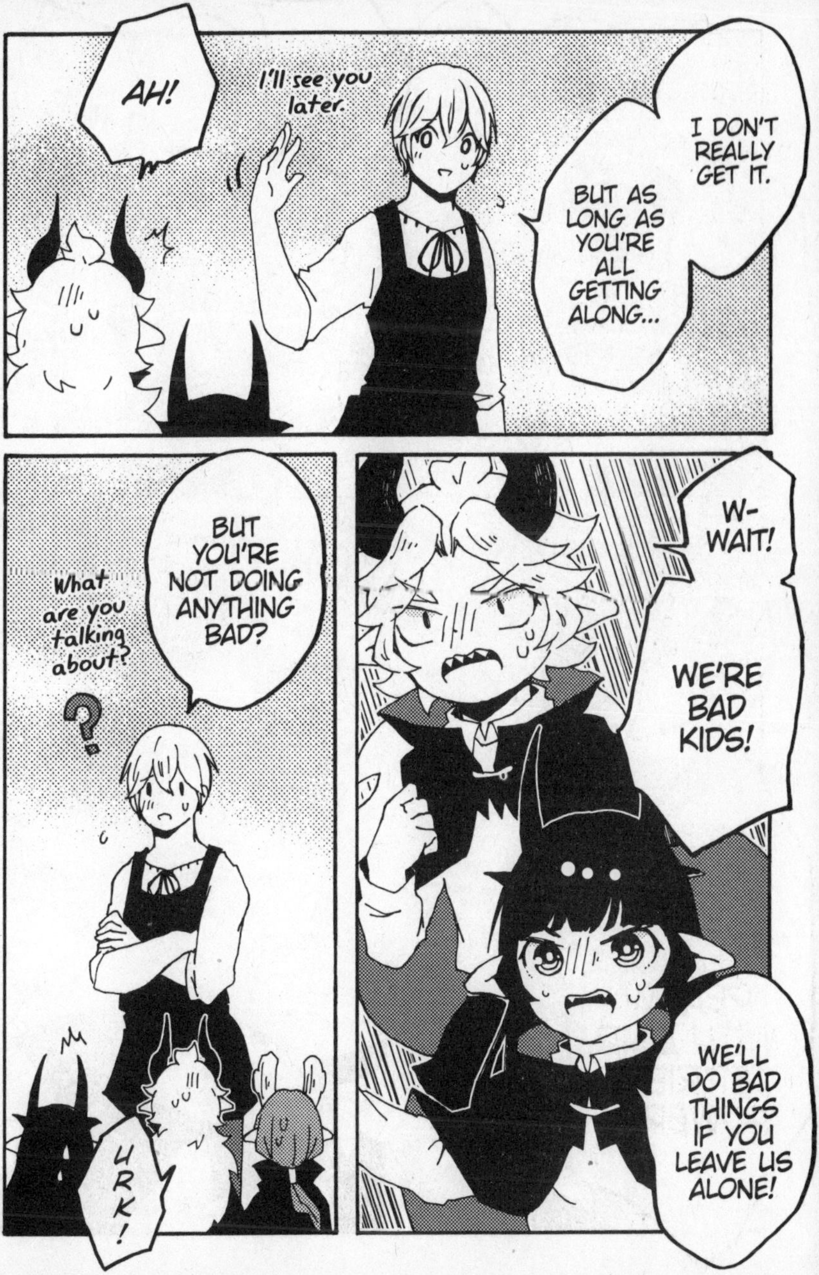
I DON'T REALLY GET IT.
BUT AS LONG AS YOU'RE ALL GETTING ALONG...
I'll see you later.
AH!
W-WAIT!
WE'RE BAD KIDS!
WE'LL DO BAD THINGS IF YOU LEAVE US ALONE!
BUT YOU'RE NOT DOING ANYTHING BAD?
What are you talking about?
URK!

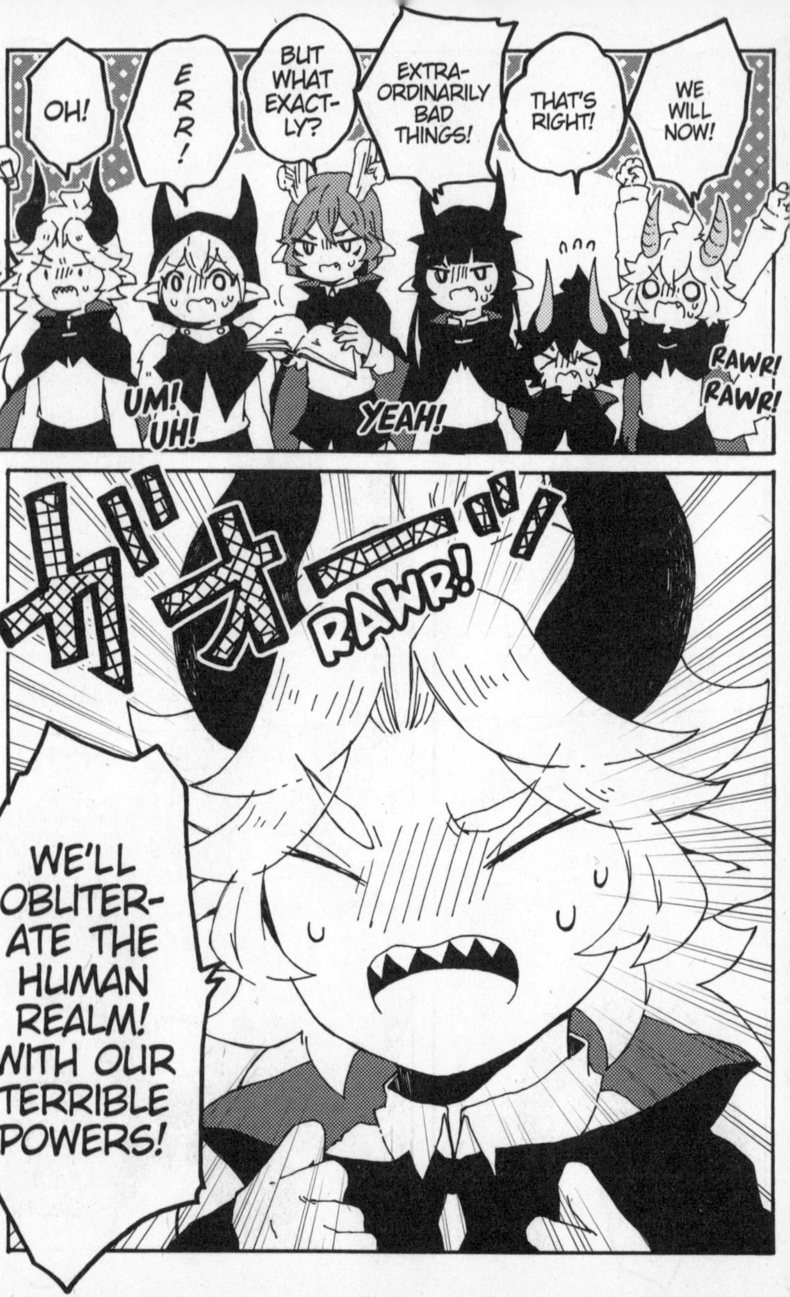
WE WILL NOW!
RAWR! RAWR!
THAT'S RIGHT!
EXTRA-ORDINARILY BAD THINGS!
YEAH!
BUT WHAT EXACTLY?
ERR!
UM! UH!
OH!
ガオーッ
RAWR!
WE'LL OBLITERATE THE HUMAN REALM! WITH OUR TERRIBLE POWERS!

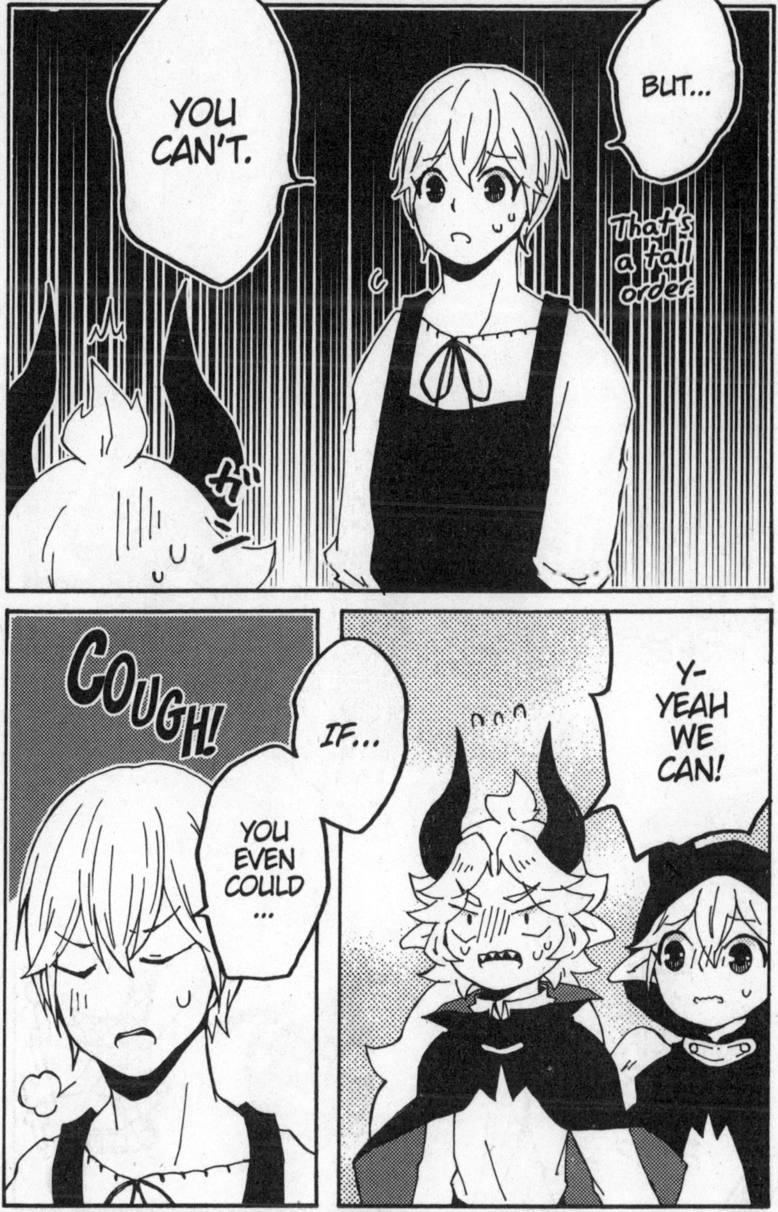
BUT...
That's a tall order.
YOU CAN'T.
ガ
Y- YEAH WE CAN!
IF... YOU EVEN COULD ...
COUGH!

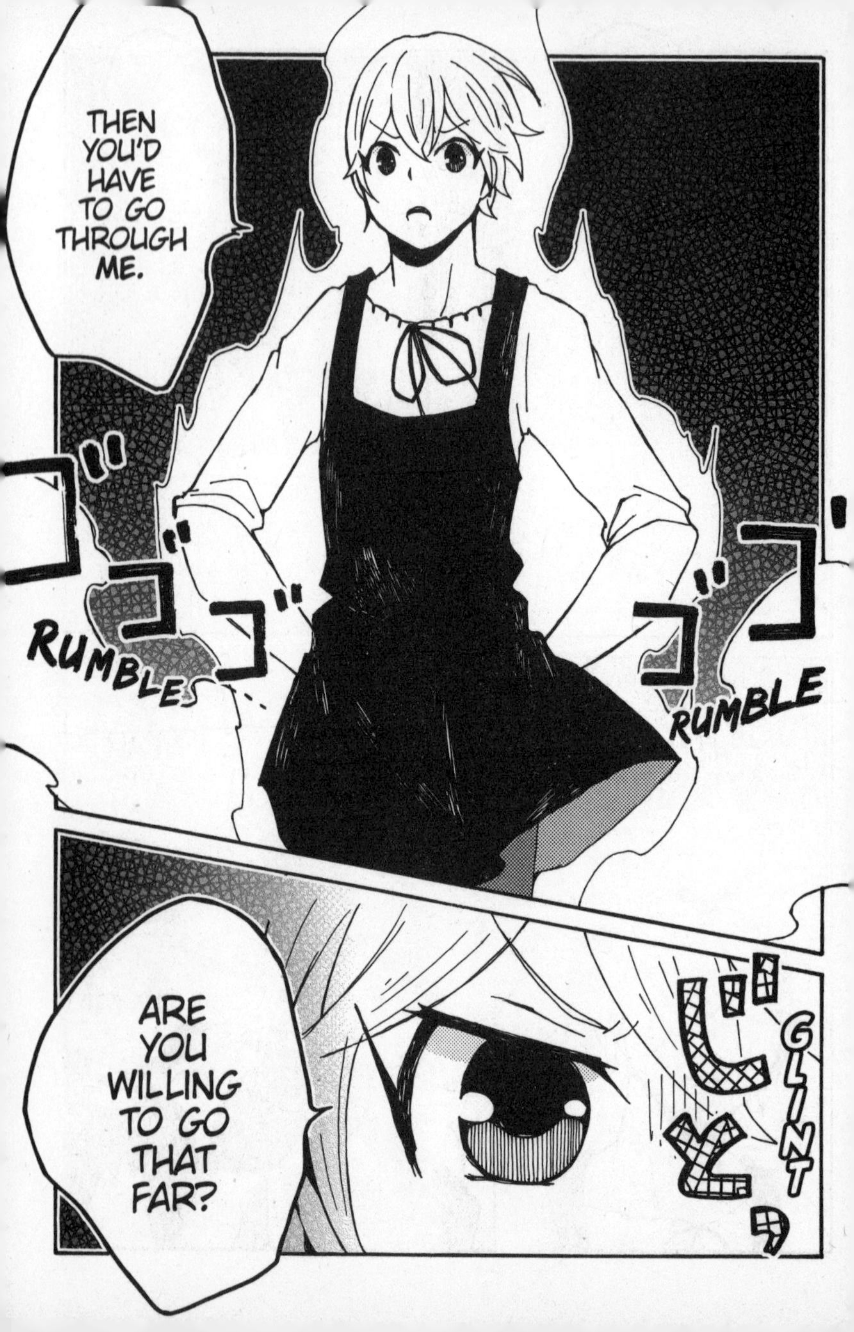
THEN YOU'D HAVE TO GO THROUGH ME.
RUMBLE
RUMBLES
ARE YOU WILLING TO GO THAT FAR?
GLINT

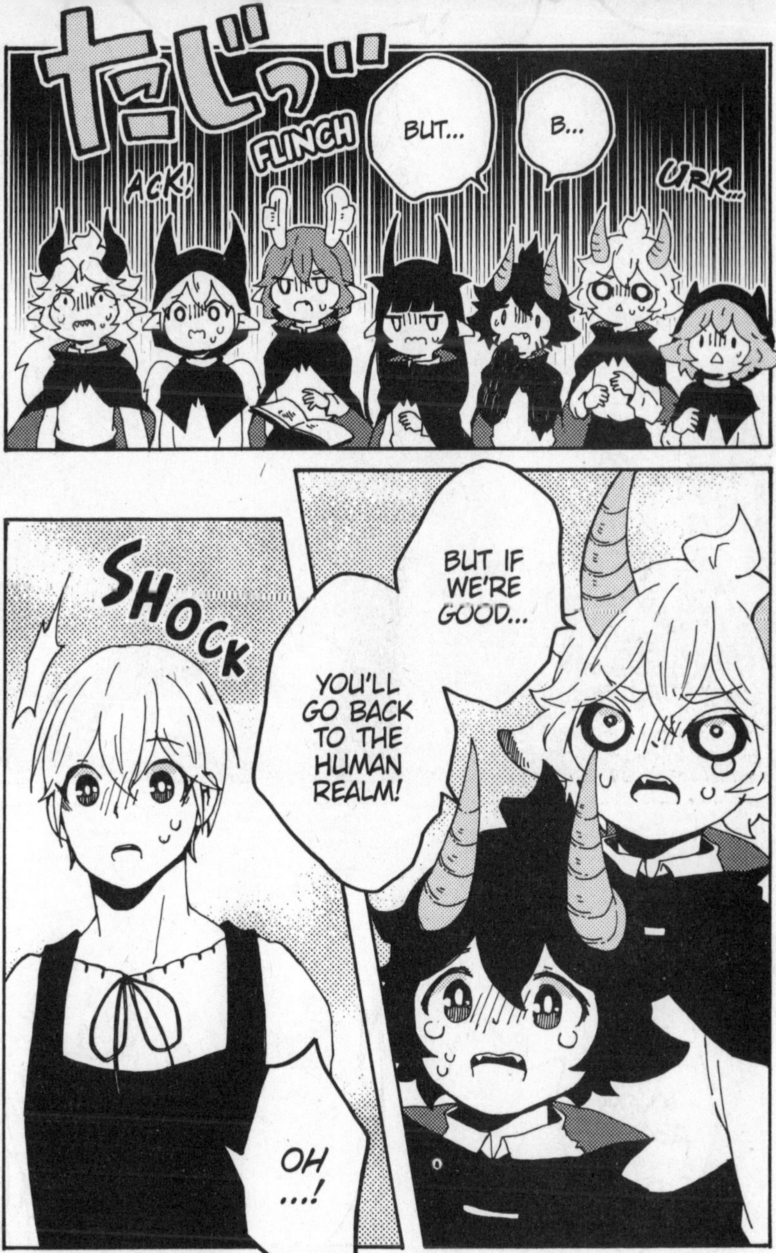
URK...
B...
BUT...
FLINCH
ACK!
BUT IF WE'RE GOOD...
YOU'LL GO BACK TO THE HUMAN REALM!
SHOCK
OH ...!

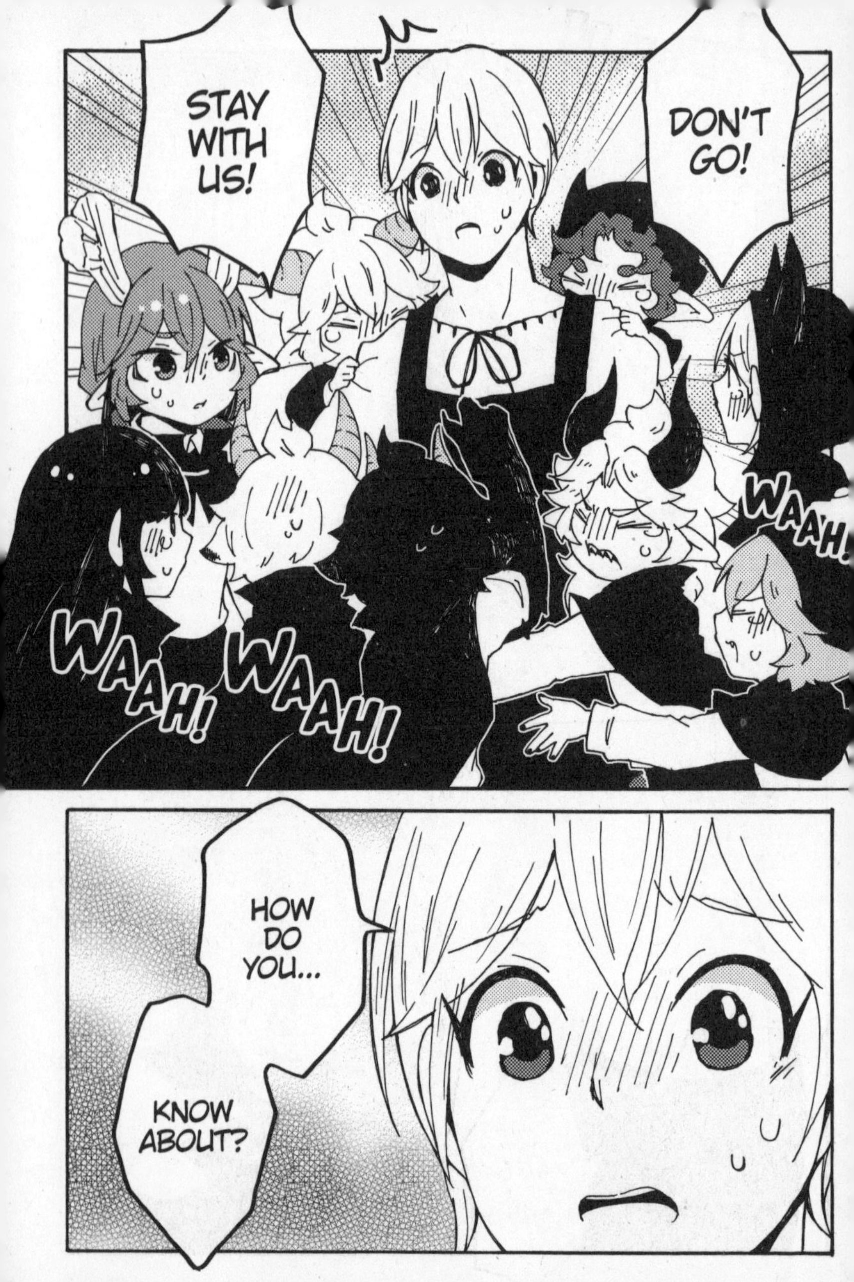
DON'T GO!
STAY WITH US!
WAAH!
WAAH!
WAAH!
HOW DO YOU...
KNOW ABOUT?

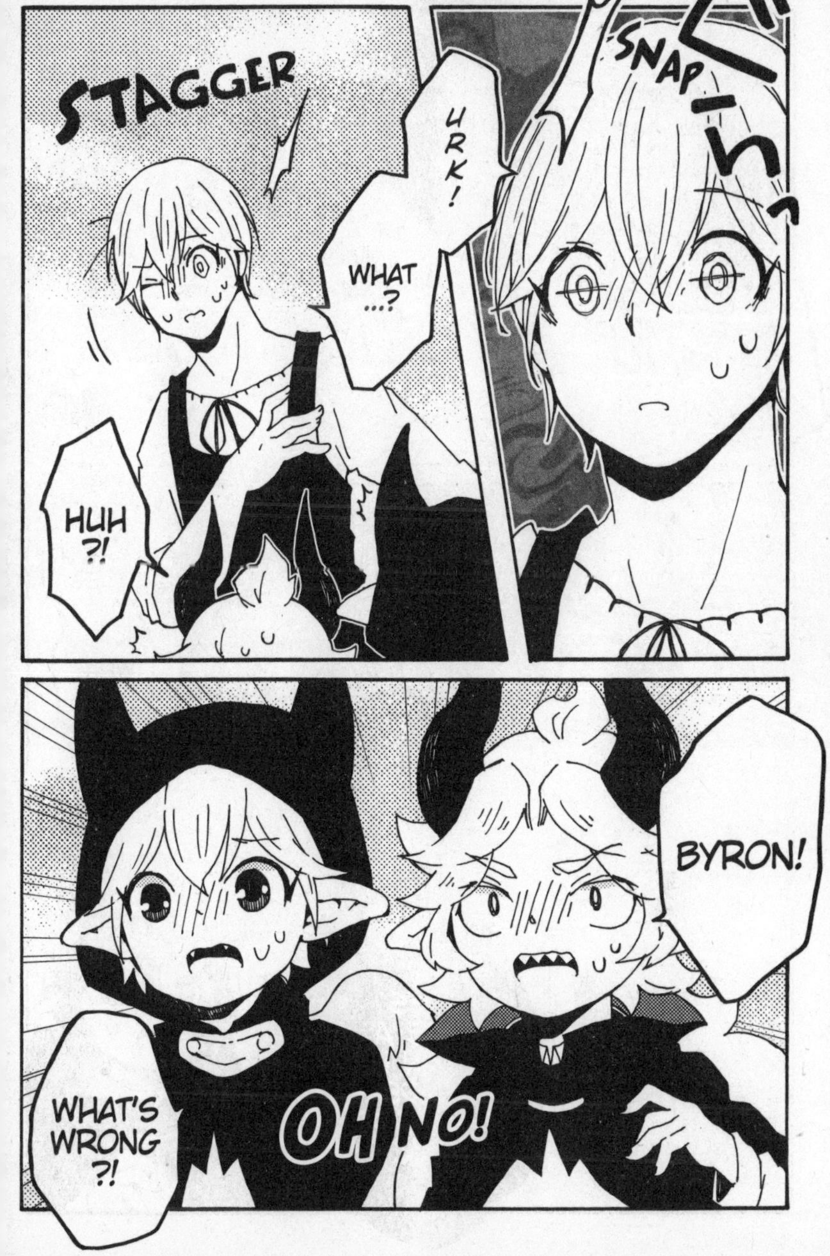
SNAP
URK!
WHAT ...?
STAGGER
HUH ?!
BYRON!
OH NO!
WHAT'S WRONG ?!

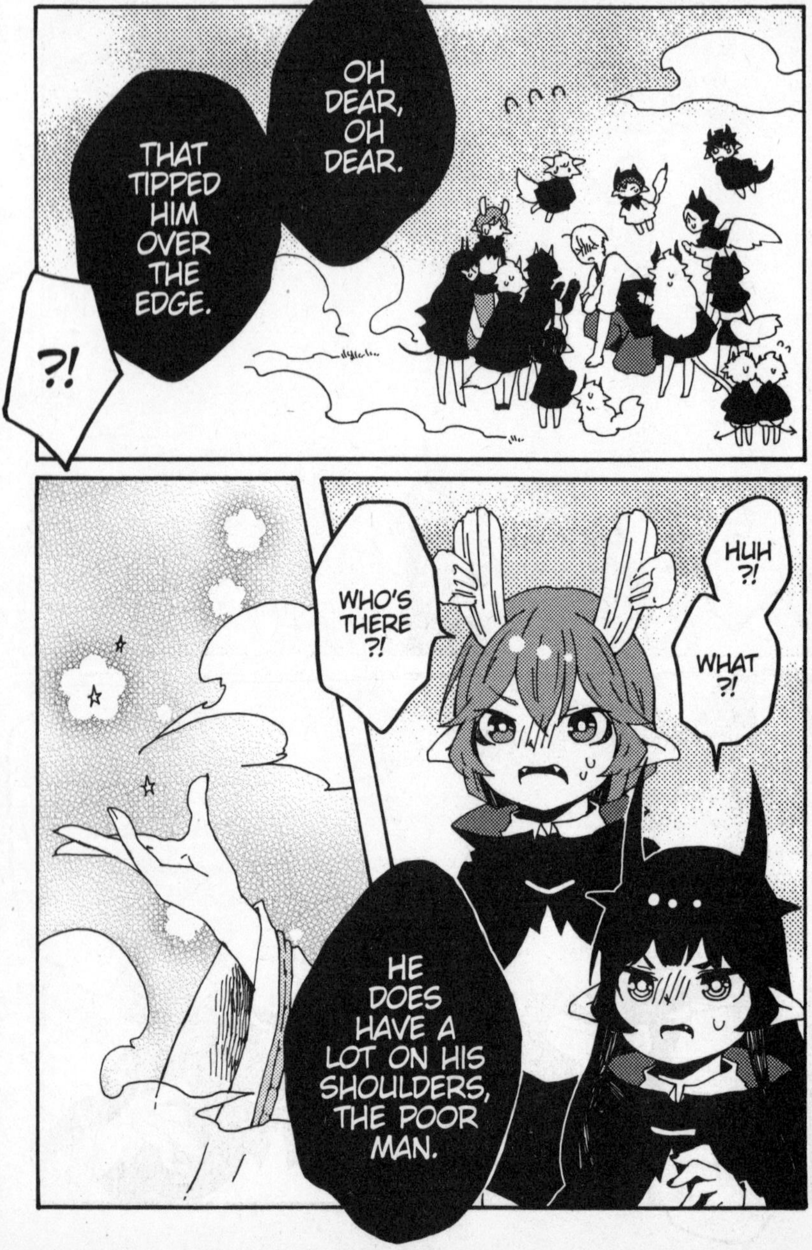
OH DEAR, OH DEAR.
THAT TIPPED HIM OVER THE EDGE.
?!
HUH?!
WHAT?!
WHO'S THERE?!
HE DOES HAVE A LOT ON HIS SHOULDERS, THE POOR MAN.

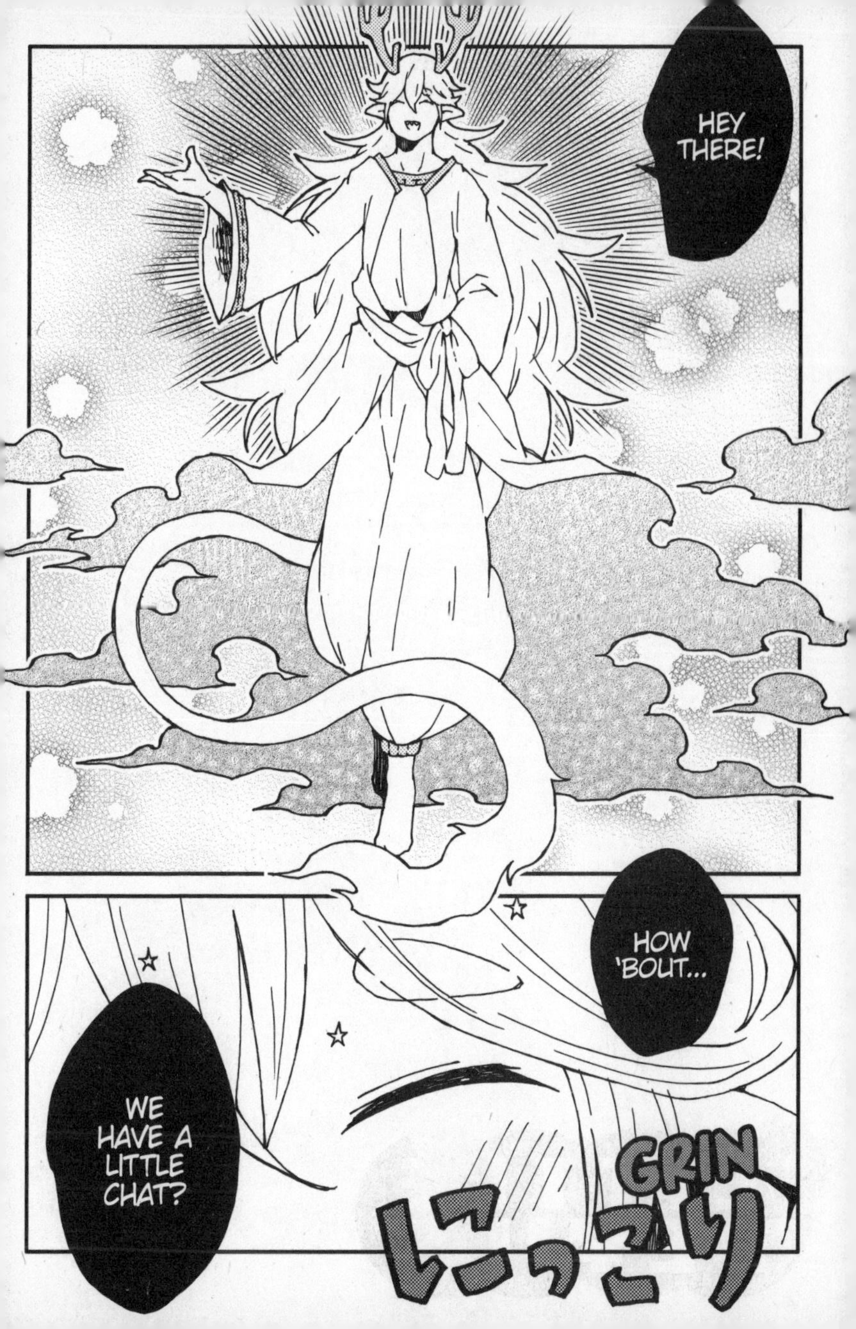
HEY THERE!
HOW 'BOUT...
WE HAVE A LITTLE CHAT?
GRIN
にっこり

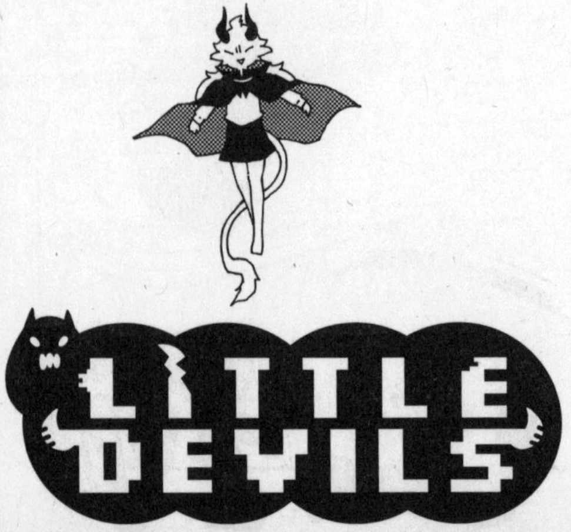

LITTLE DEVILS

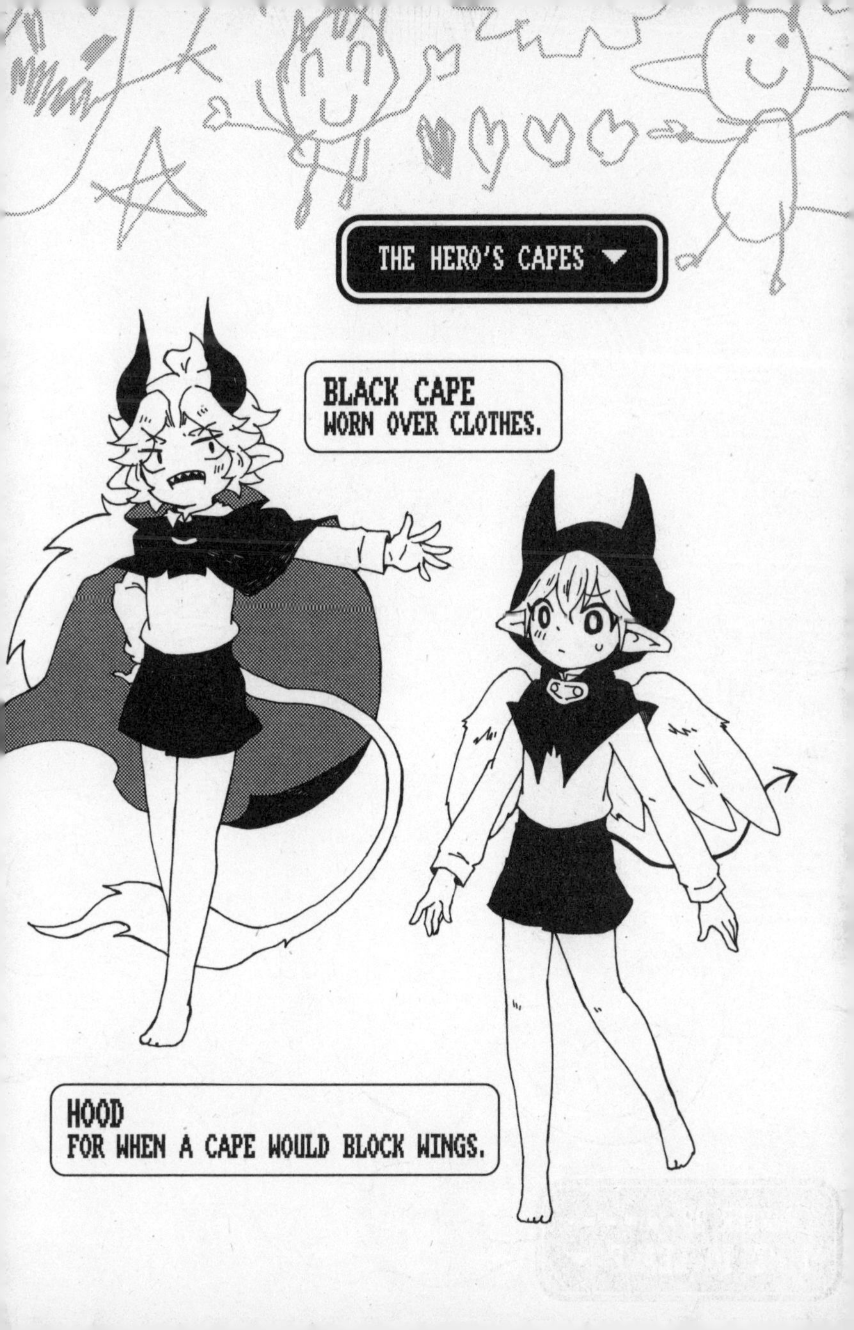
THE HERO'S CAPES
BLACK CAPE
WORN OVER CLOTHES.
HOOD
FOR WHEN A CAPE WOULD BLOCK WINGS.

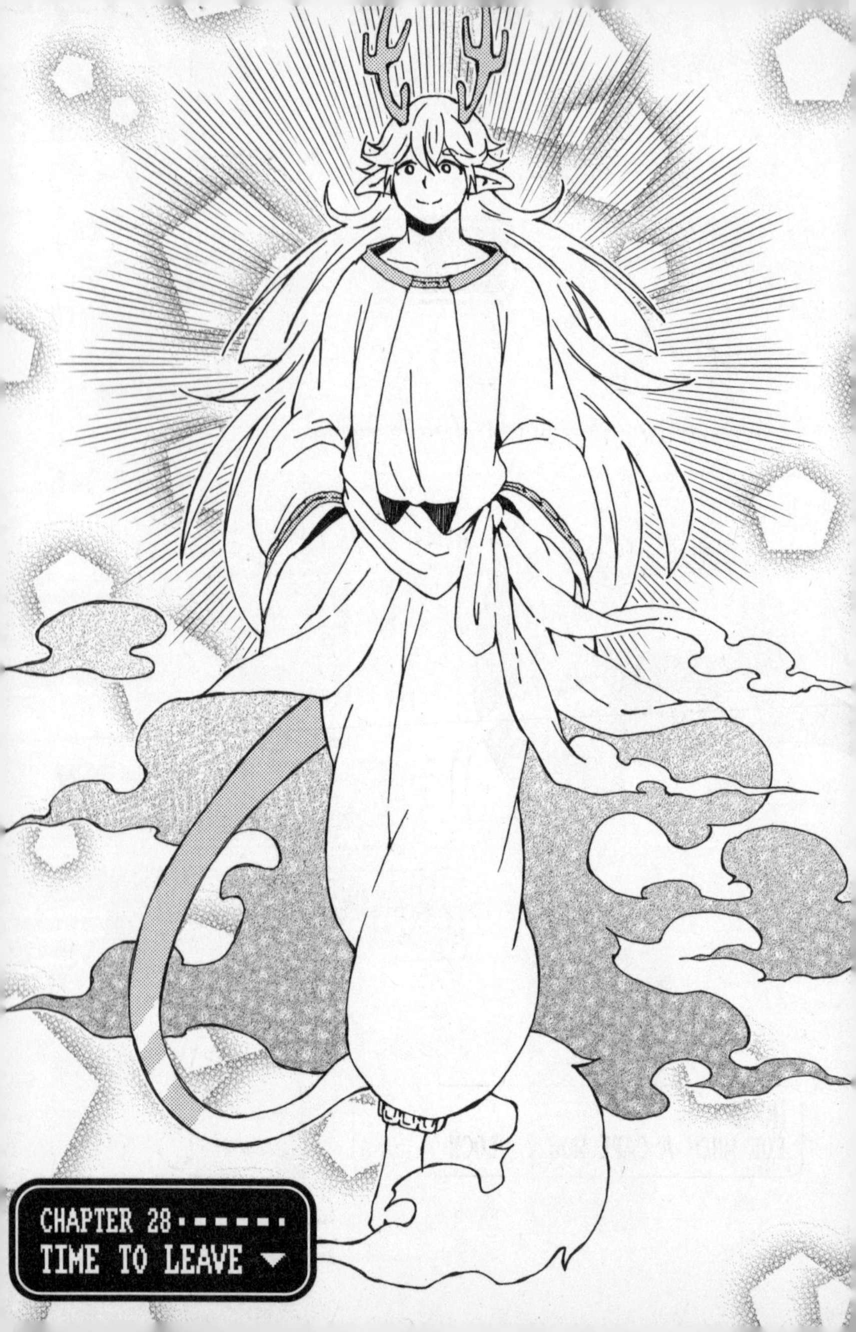
CHAPTER 28
TIME TO LEAVE

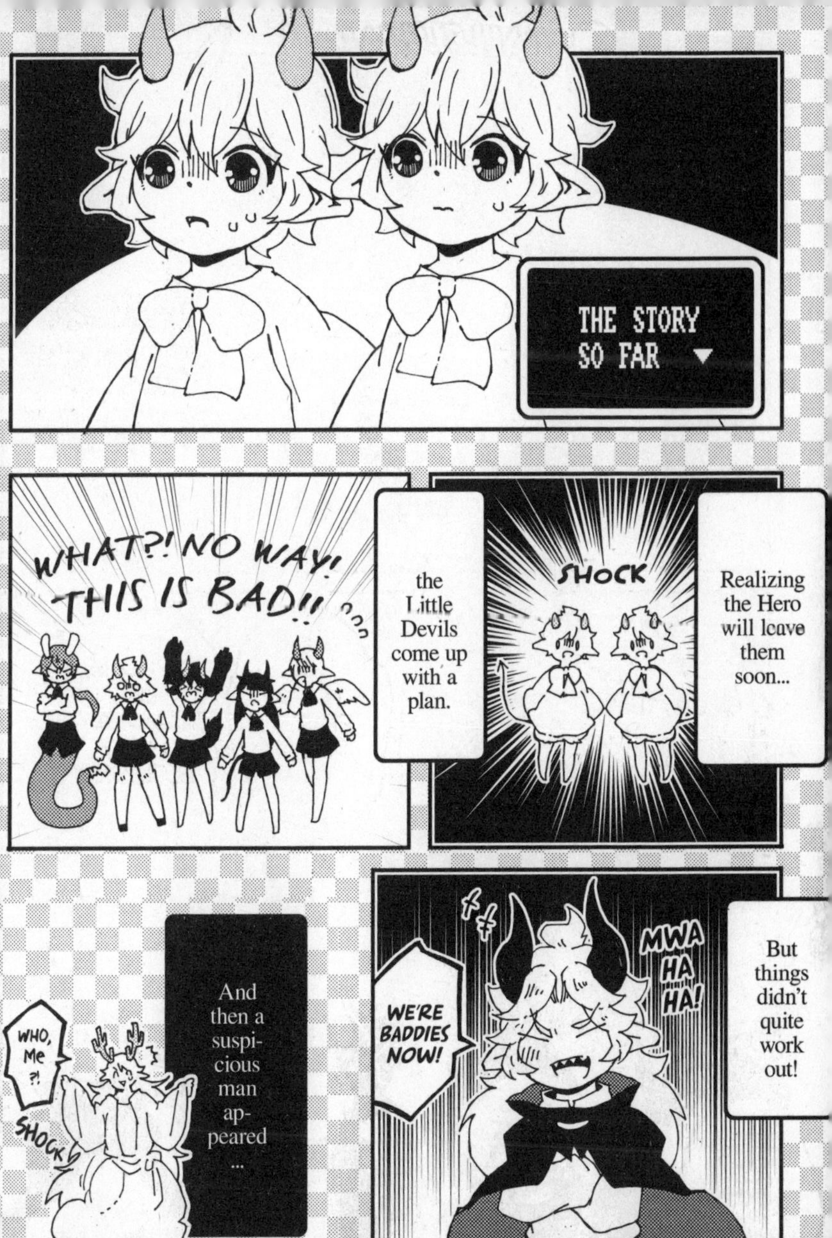
THE STORY SO FAR ▼
Realizing the Hero will leave them soon...
SHOCK
the Little Devils come up with a plan.
WHAT?! NO WAY! THIS IS BAD!!
But things didn't quite work out!
MWA HA HA!
WE'RE BADDIES NOW!
And then a suspicious man appeared...
WHO, Me ?!
SHOCK

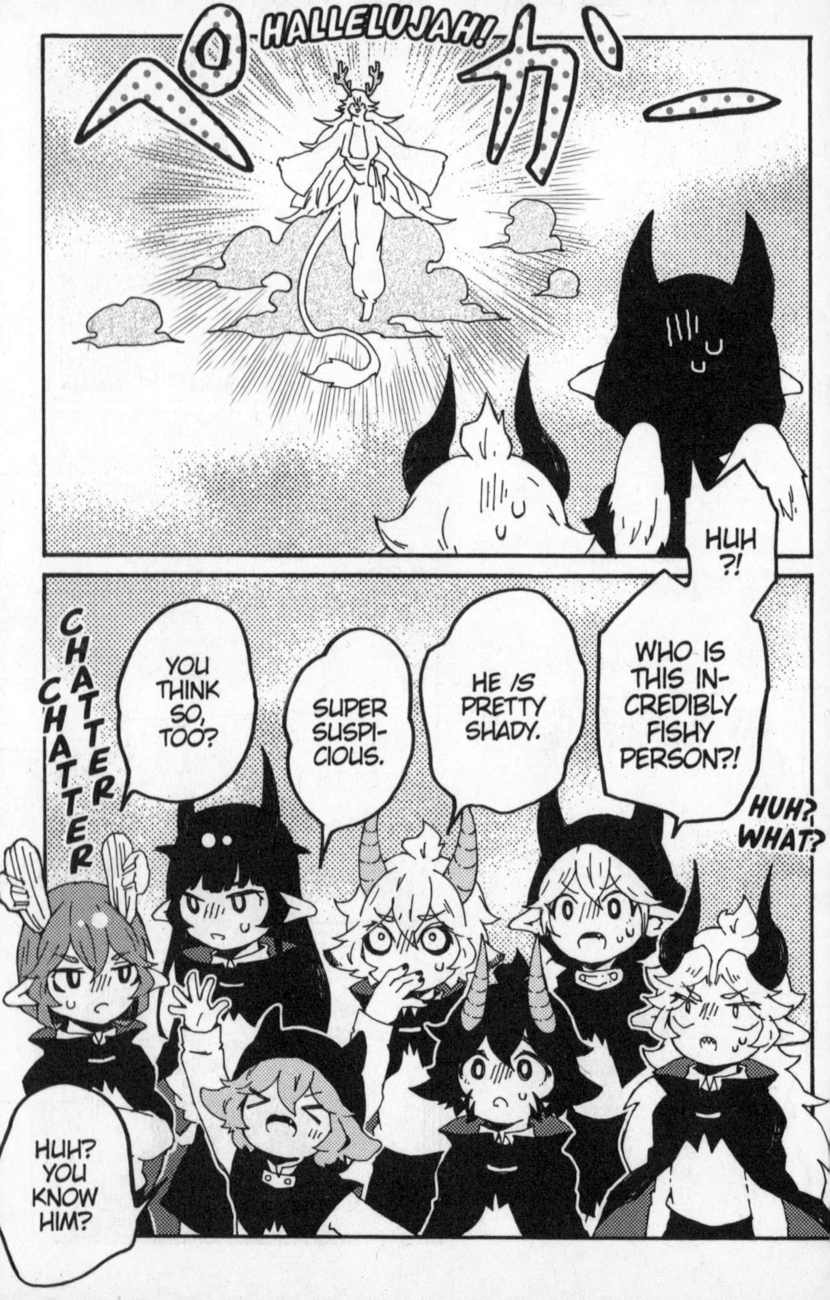
HALLELUJAH!
HUH?!
WHO IS THIS IN-CREDIBLY FISHY PERSON?!
HUH? WHAT?
HE IS PRETTY SHADY.
SUPER SUSPI-CIOUS.
YOU THINK SO, TOO?
CHATTER CHATTER
HUH? YOU KNOW HIM?

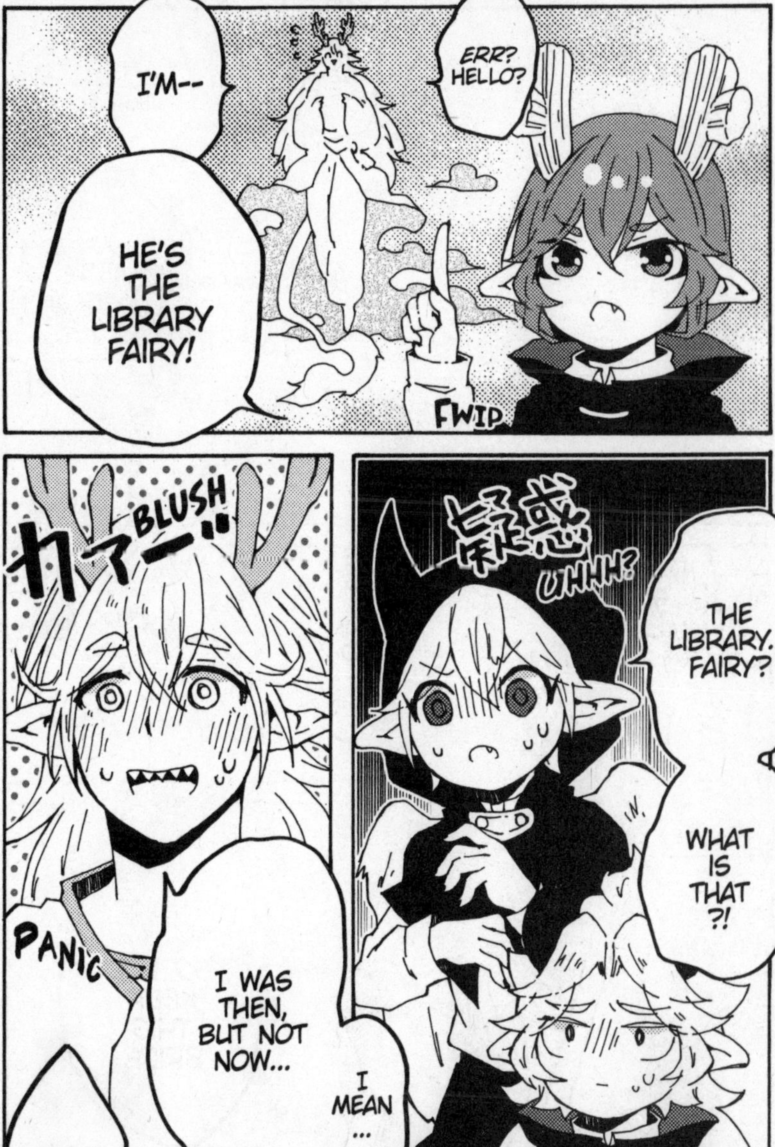
ERR? HELLO?
I'M--
HE'S THE LIBRARY FAIRY!
FWIP
疑惑
UHHH?
THE LIBRARY... FAIRY?
WHAT IS THAT?!
I MEAN ... Wait!
カァー
BLUSH
PANIC
I WAS THEN, BUT NOT NOW...
uu
HUH?

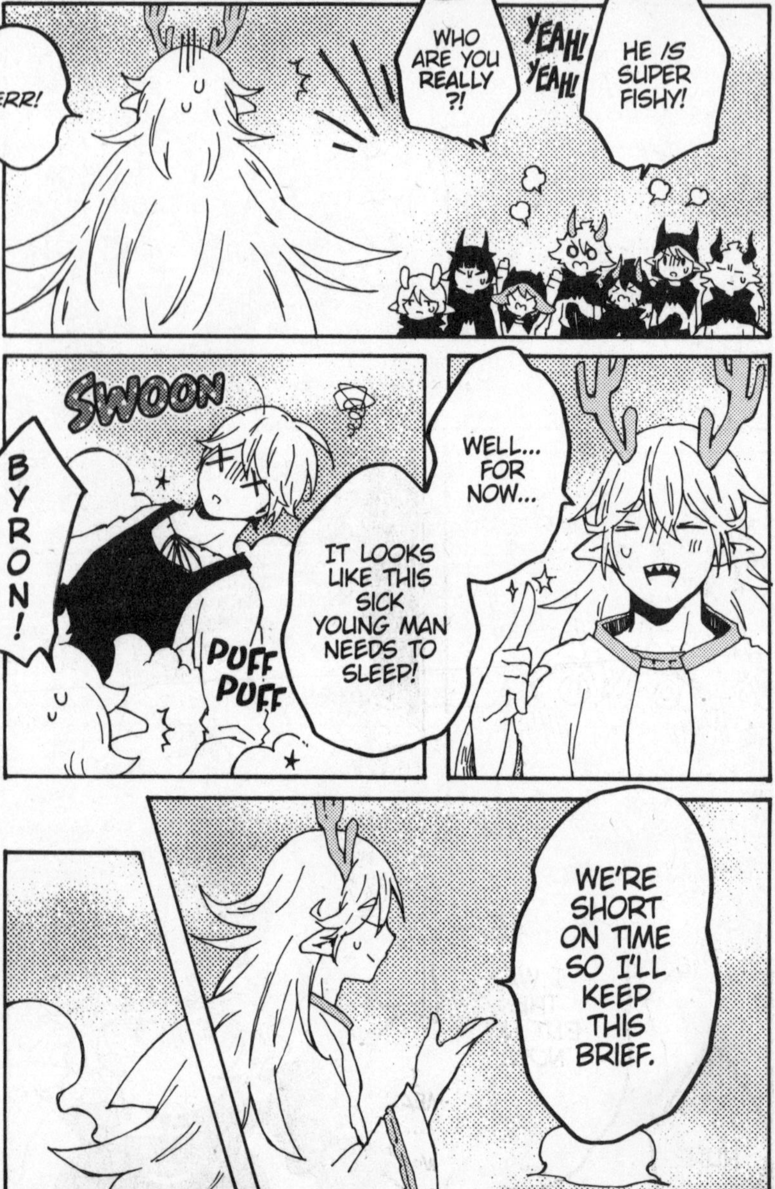
HE IS SUPER FISHY!
YEAH! YEAH!
WHO ARE YOU REALLY ?!
ERR!
WELL... FOR NOW...
IT LOOKS LIKE THIS SICK YOUNG MAN NEEDS TO SLEEP!
SWOON
BYRON!
PUFF PUFF
WE'RE SHORT ON TIME SO I'LL KEEP THIS BRIEF.

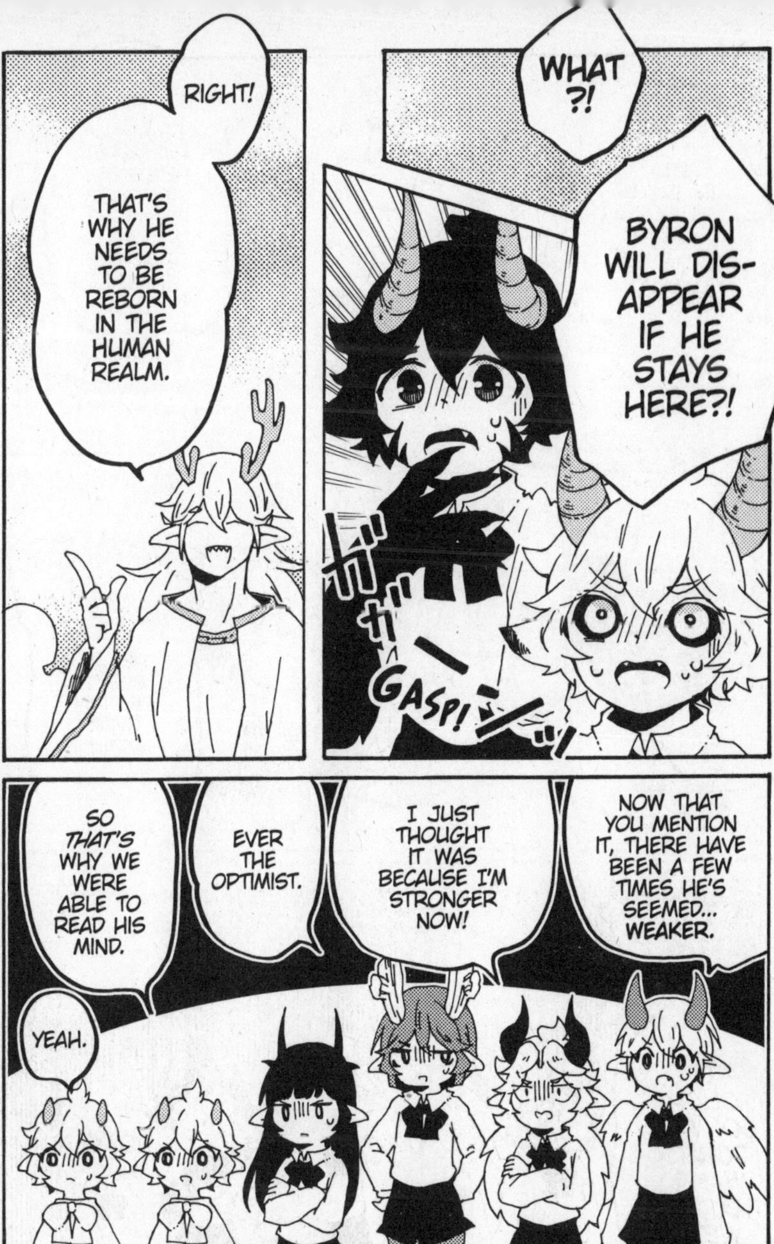
WHAT ?!
BYRON WILL DIS-APPEAR IF HE STAYS HERE?!
GASP!
RIGHT!
THAT'S WHY HE NEEDS TO BE REBORN IN THE HUMAN REALM.
NOW THAT YOU MENTION IT, THERE HAVE BEEN A FEW TIMES HE'S SEEMED... WEAKER.
I JUST THOUGHT IT WAS BECAUSE I'M STRONGER NOW!
EVER THE OPTIMIST.
SO *THAT'S* WHY WE WERE ABLE TO READ HIS MIND.
YEAH.

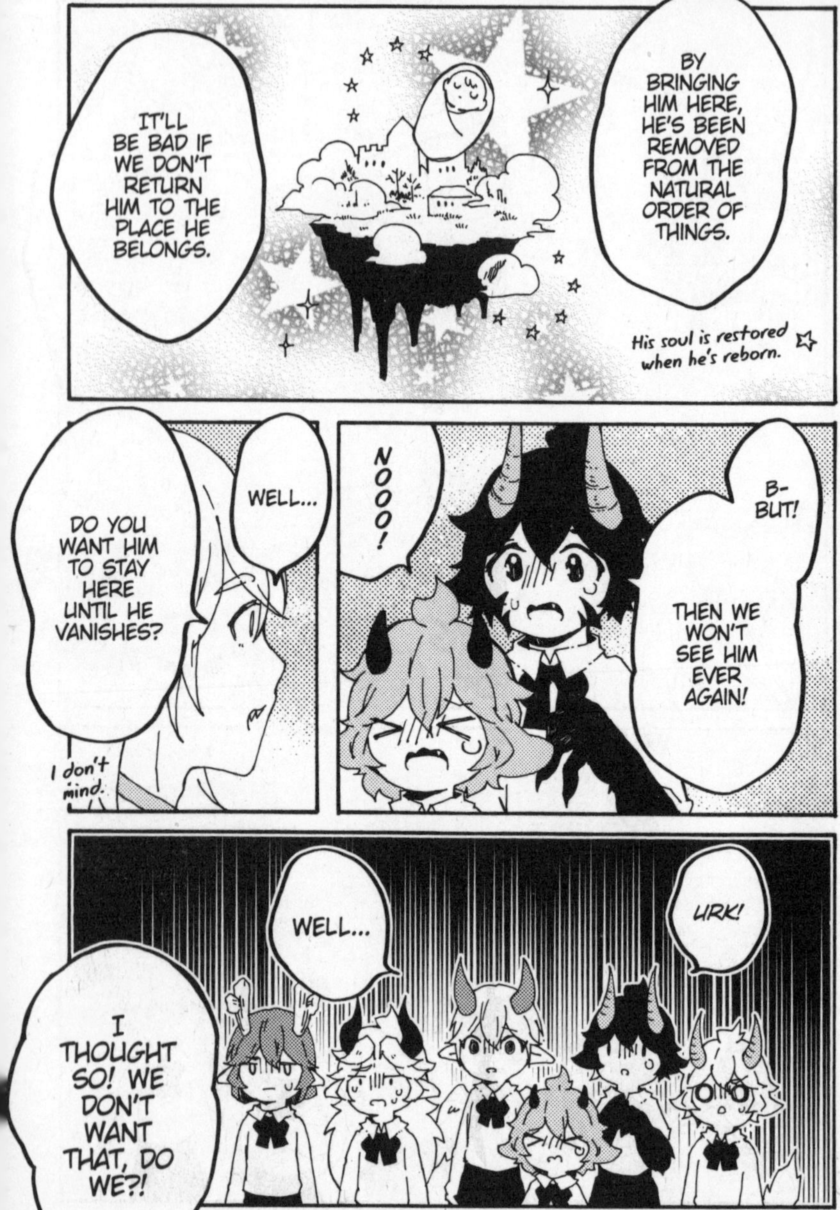
BY BRINGING HIM HERE, HE'S BEEN REMOVED FROM THE NATURAL ORDER OF THINGS.
IT'LL BE BAD IF WE DON'T RETURN HIM TO THE PLACE HE BELONGS.
His soul is restored when he's reborn.
B-BUT!
THEN WE WON'T SEE HIM EVER AGAIN!
NOOOO!
WELL...
DO YOU WANT HIM TO STAY HERE UNTIL HE VANISHES?
I don't mind.
URK!
WELL...
I THOUGHT SO! WE DON'T WANT THAT, DO WE?!

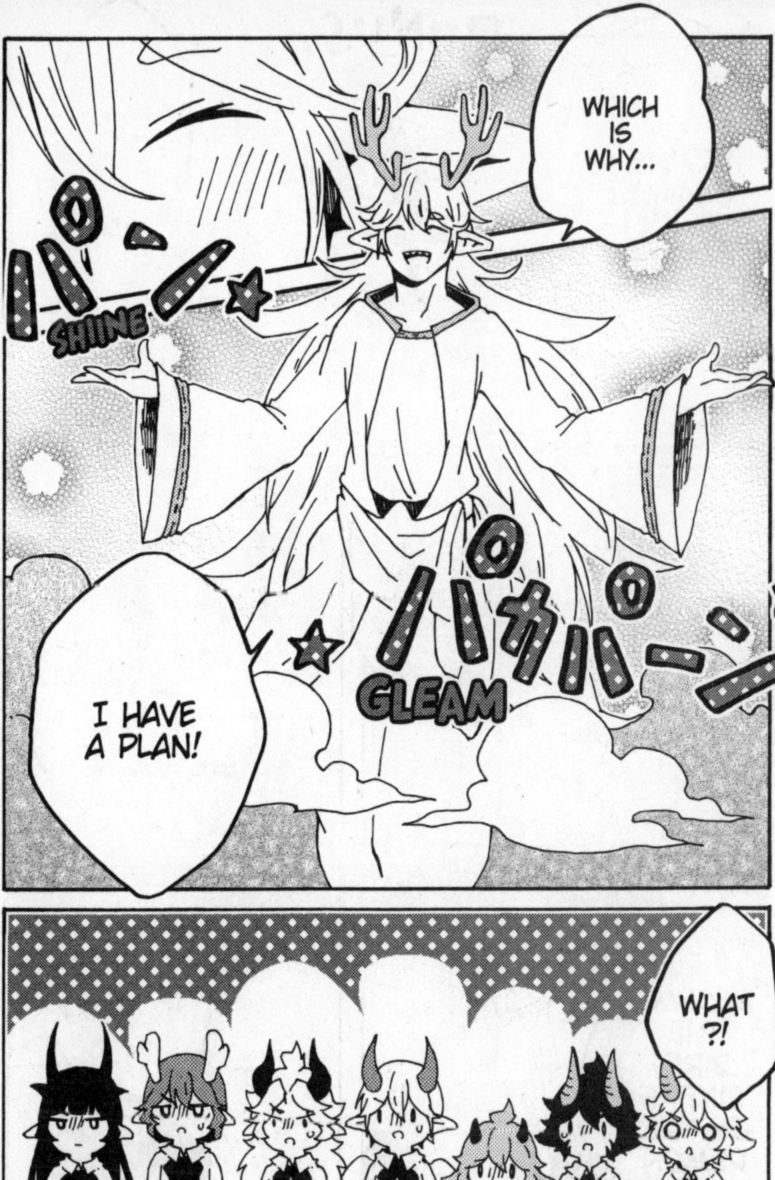
WHICH IS WHY...
SHIINE
GLEAM
I HAVE A PLAN!
WHAT?!

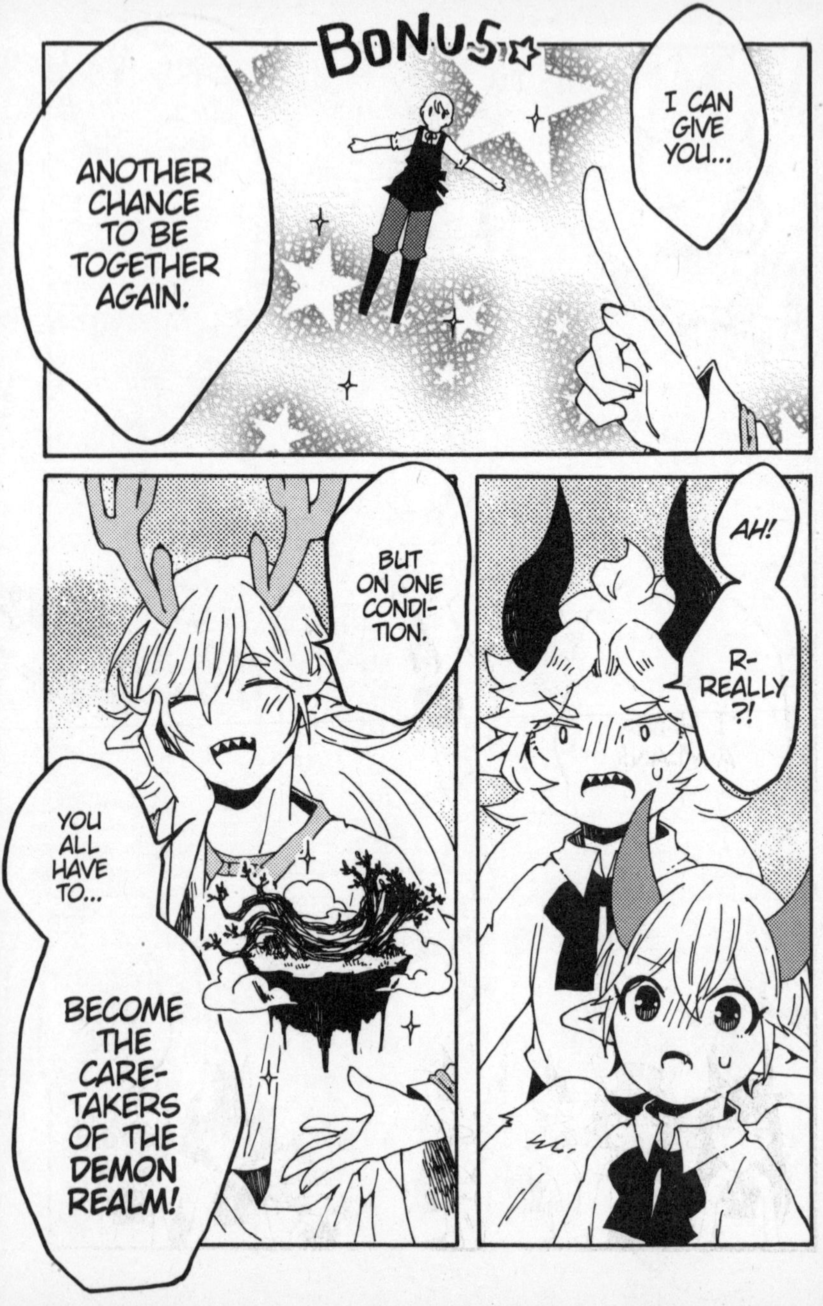
BONUS☆
I CAN GIVE YOU...
ANOTHER CHANCE TO BE TOGETHER AGAIN.
AH!
R-REALLY?!
BUT ON ONE CONDI-TION.
YOU ALL HAVE TO...
BECOME THE CARE-TAKERS OF THE DEMON REALM!

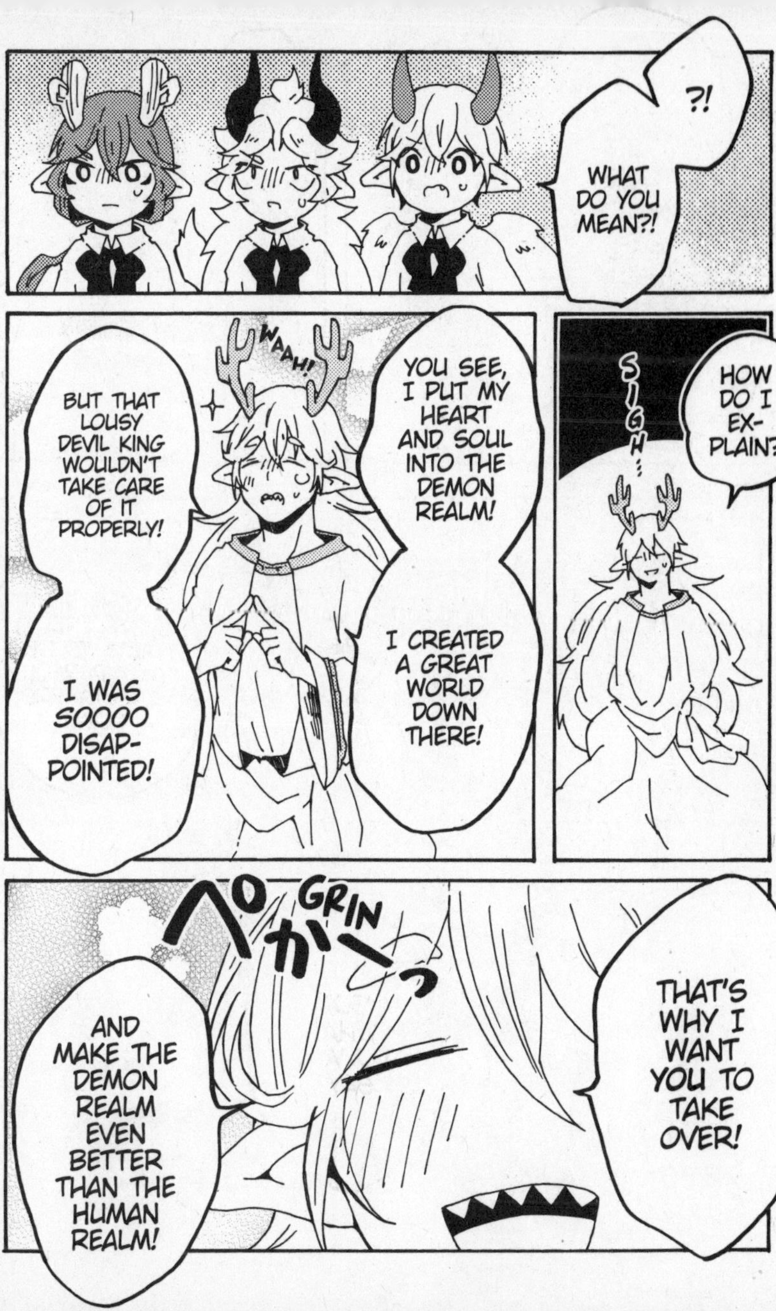
?!
WHAT DO YOU MEAN?!
SIGH...
HOW DO I EX-PLAIN?
WAAH!
YOU SEE, I PUT MY HEART AND SOUL INTO THE DEMON REALM!
I CREATED A GREAT WORLD DOWN THERE!
BUT THAT LOUSY DEVIL KING WOULDN'T TAKE CARE OF IT PROPERLY!
I WAS SOOOO DISAP-POINTED!
ぺかーっ
GRIN
THAT'S WHY I WANT YOU TO TAKE OVER!
AND MAKE THE DEMON REALM EVEN BETTER THAN THE HUMAN REALM!

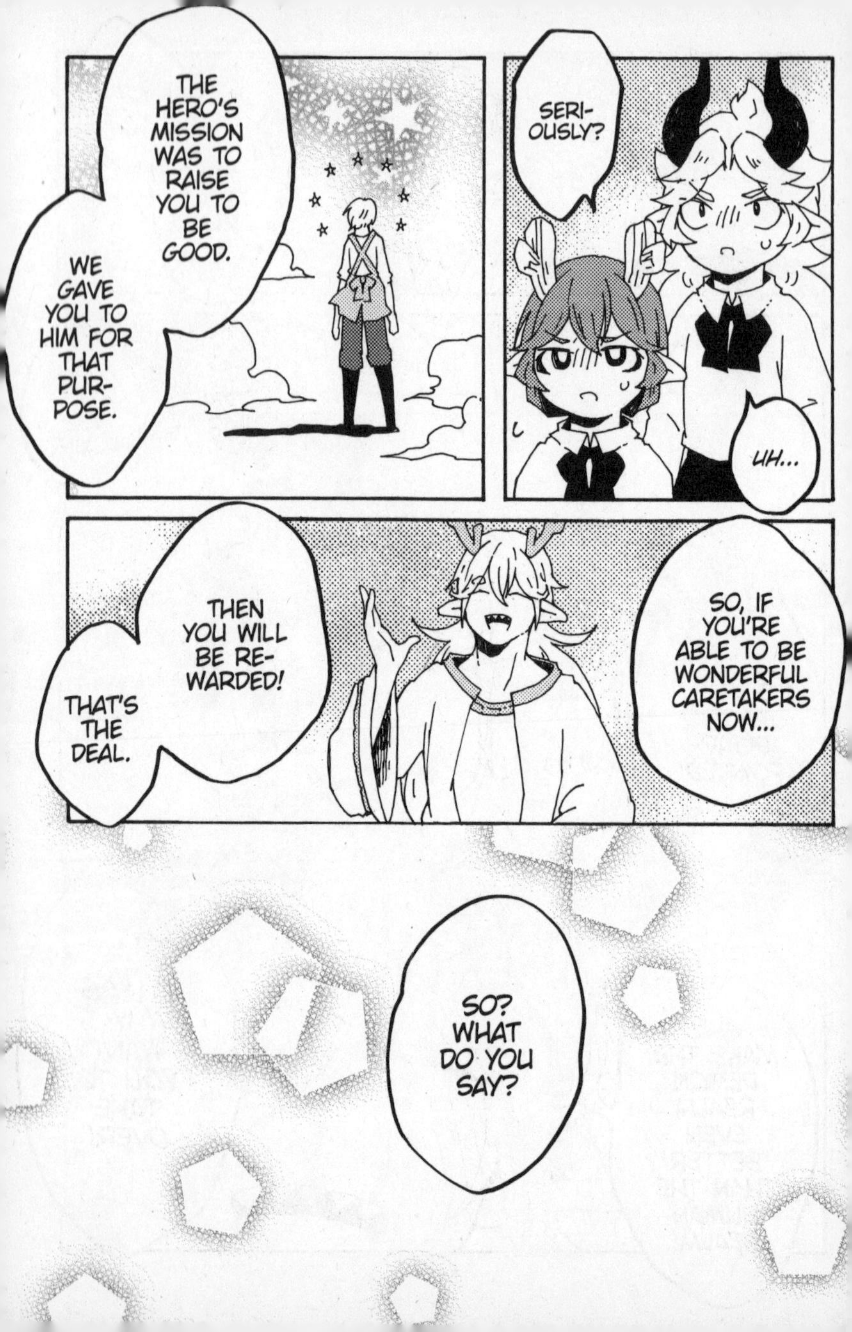
SERI-OUSLY?
UH...
THE HERO'S MISSION WAS TO RAISE YOU TO BE GOOD.
WE GAVE YOU TO HIM FOR THAT PUR-POSE.
SO, IF YOU'RE ABLE TO BE WONDERFUL CARETAKERS NOW...
THEN YOU WILL BE RE-WARDED!
THAT'S THE DEAL.
SO? WHAT DO YOU SAY?

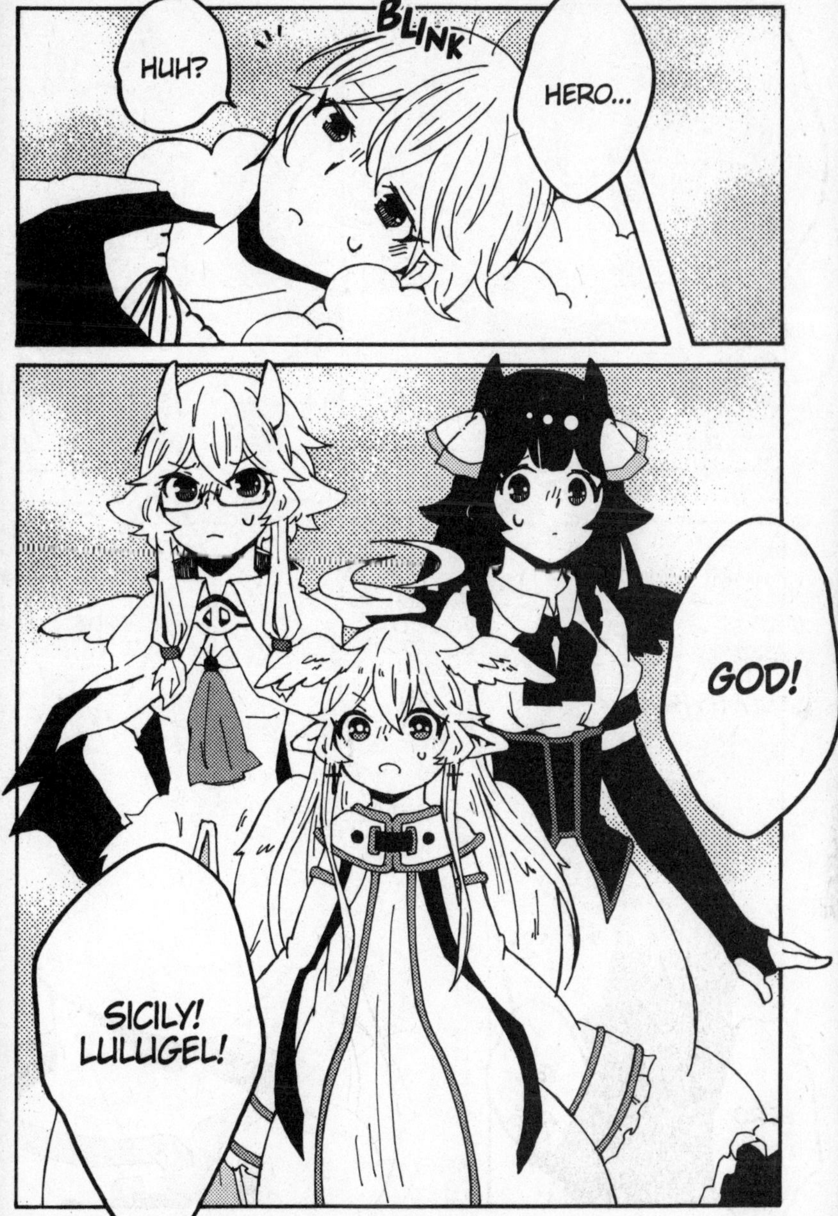
HERO...
BLINK
HUH?
GOD!
SICILY! LULUGEL!

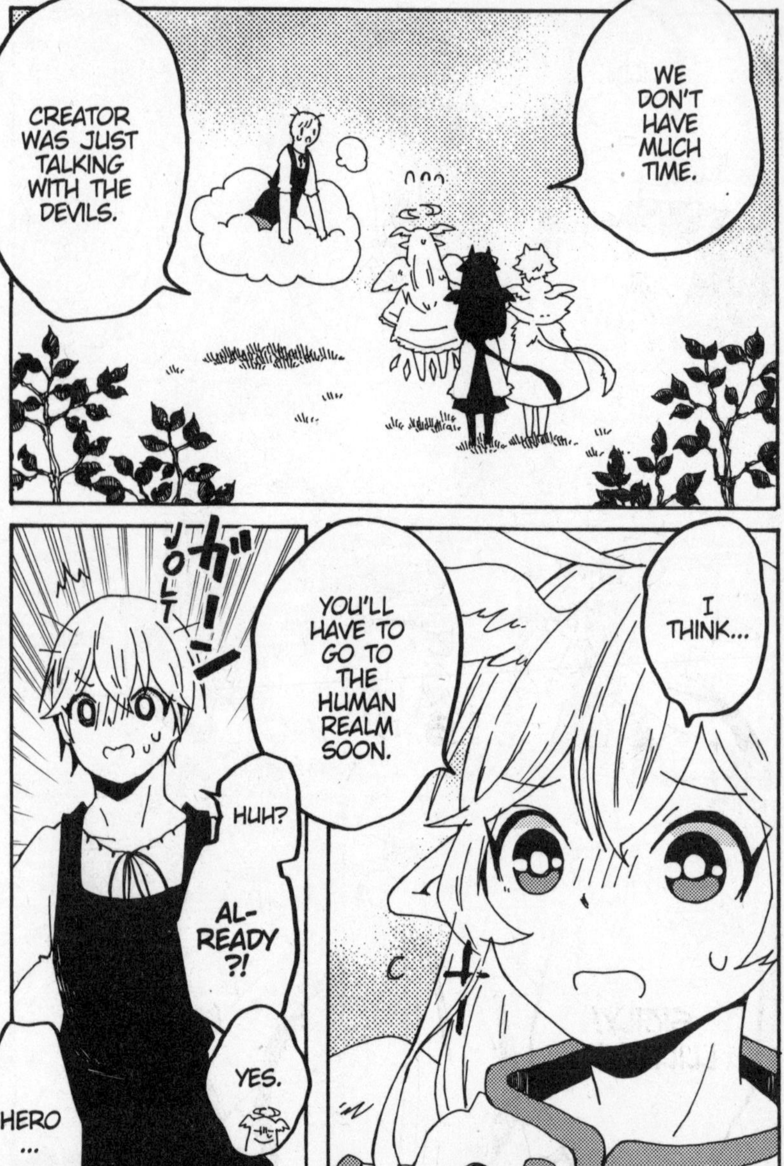
WE DON'T HAVE MUCH TIME.
CREATOR WAS JUST TALKING WITH THE DEVILS.
I THINK...
YOU'LL HAVE TO GO TO THE HUMAN REALM SOON.
JOLT
HUH?
AL-READY?!
YES.
HERO...

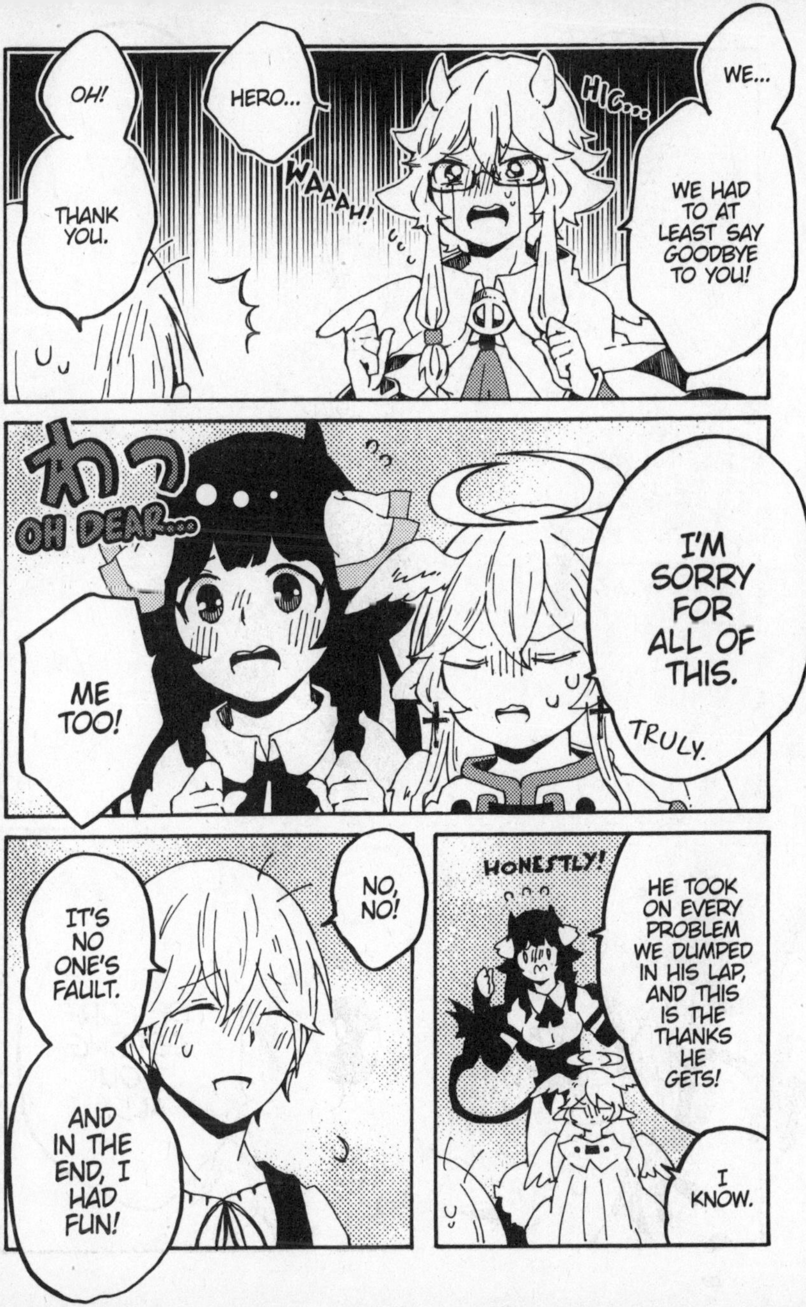
WE...
WE HAD TO AT LEAST SAY GOODBYE TO YOU!
HIC...
WAAAAH!
HERO...
OH!
THANK YOU.
I'M SORRY FOR ALL OF THIS.
TRULY.
わっ
OH DEAR...
ME TOO!
HONESTLY!
HE TOOK ON EVERY PROBLEM WE DUMPED IN HIS LAP, AND THIS IS THE THANKS HE GETS!
I KNOW.
NO, NO!
IT'S NO ONE'S FAULT.
AND IN THE END, I HAD FUN!

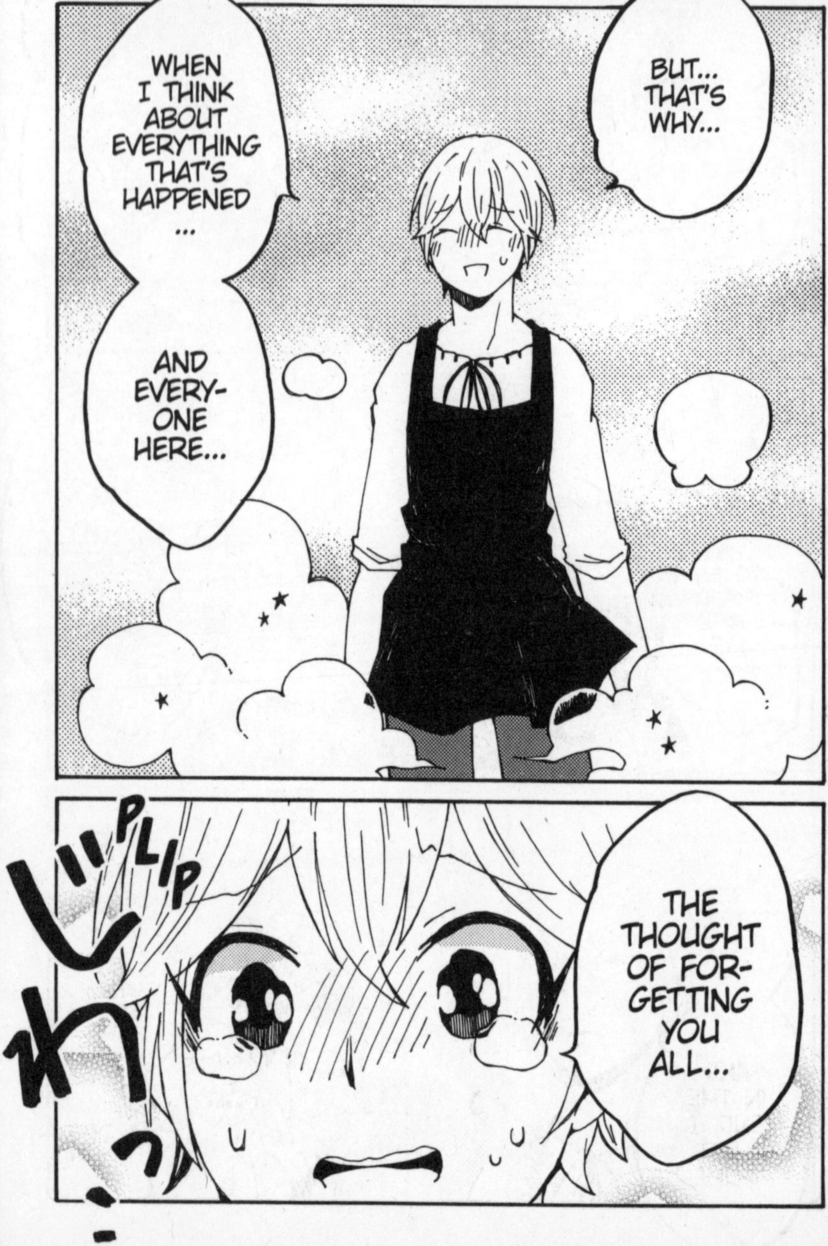
BUT... THAT'S WHY...
WHEN I THINK ABOUT EVERYTHING THAT'S HAPPENED ...
AND EVERY-ONE HERE...
PLIP
じわっ
THE THOUGHT OF FOR-GETTING YOU ALL...

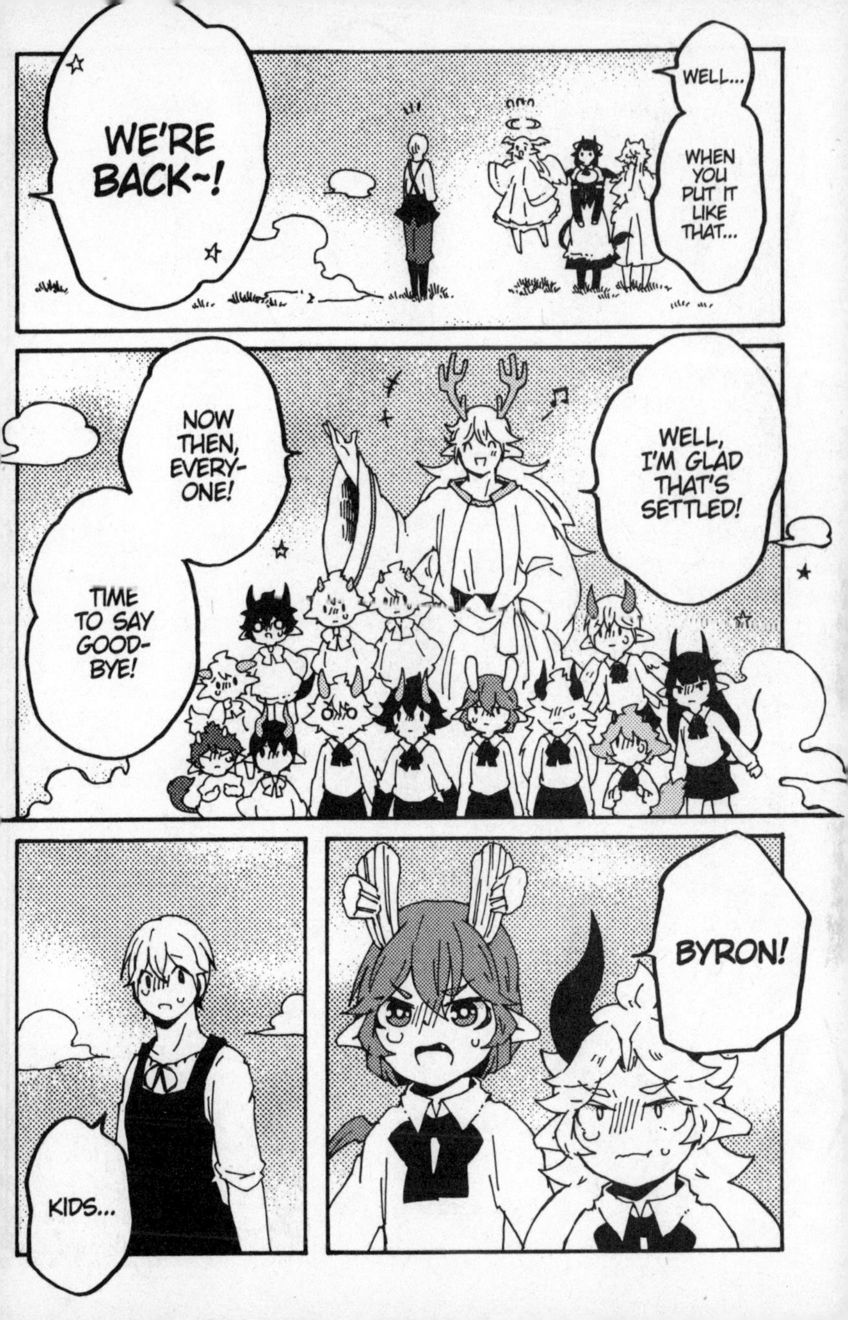
WELL...
WHEN YOU PUT IT LIKE THAT...
WE'RE BACK~!
WELL, I'M GLAD THAT'S SETTLED!
NOW THEN, EVERY-ONE!
TIME TO SAY GOOD-BYE!
BYRON!
KIDS...

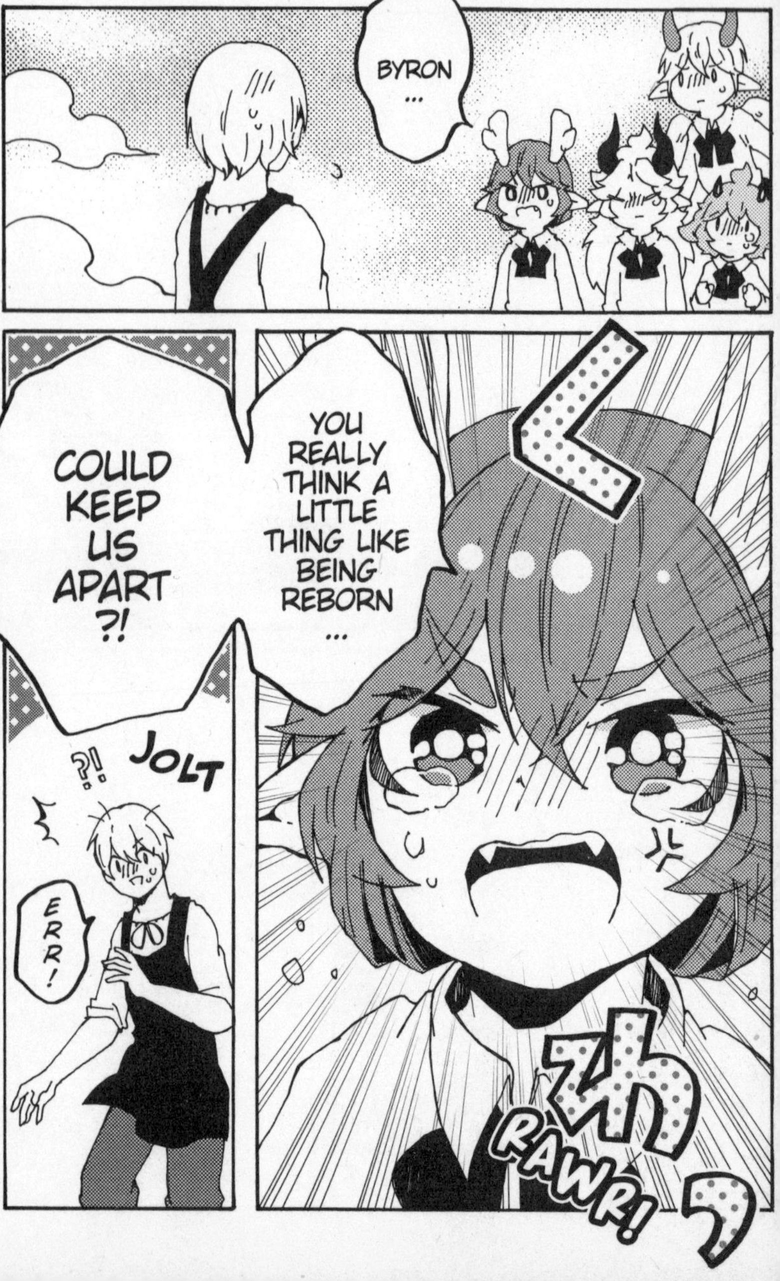
BYRON ...
YOU REALLY THINK A LITTLE THING LIKE BEING REBORN ...
COULD KEEP US APART ?!
RAWR!
?!
JOLT
ERR!

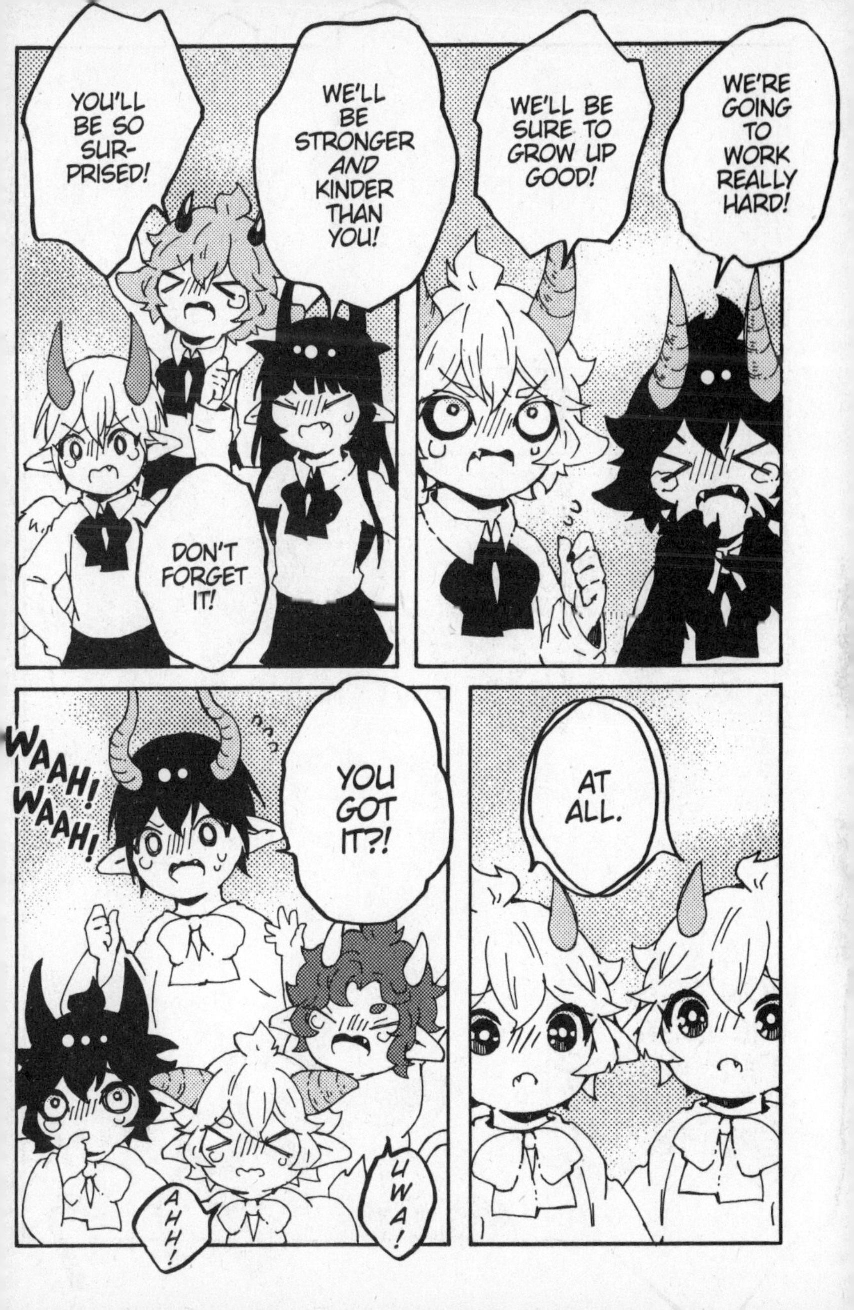
WE'RE GOING TO WORK REALLY HARD!
WE'LL BE SURE TO GROW UP GOOD!
WE'LL BE STRONGER AND KINDER THAN YOU!
YOU'LL BE SO SUR-PRISED!
DON'T FORGET IT!
AT ALL.
YOU GOT IT?!
WAAH! WAAH!
UWA!
AHH!

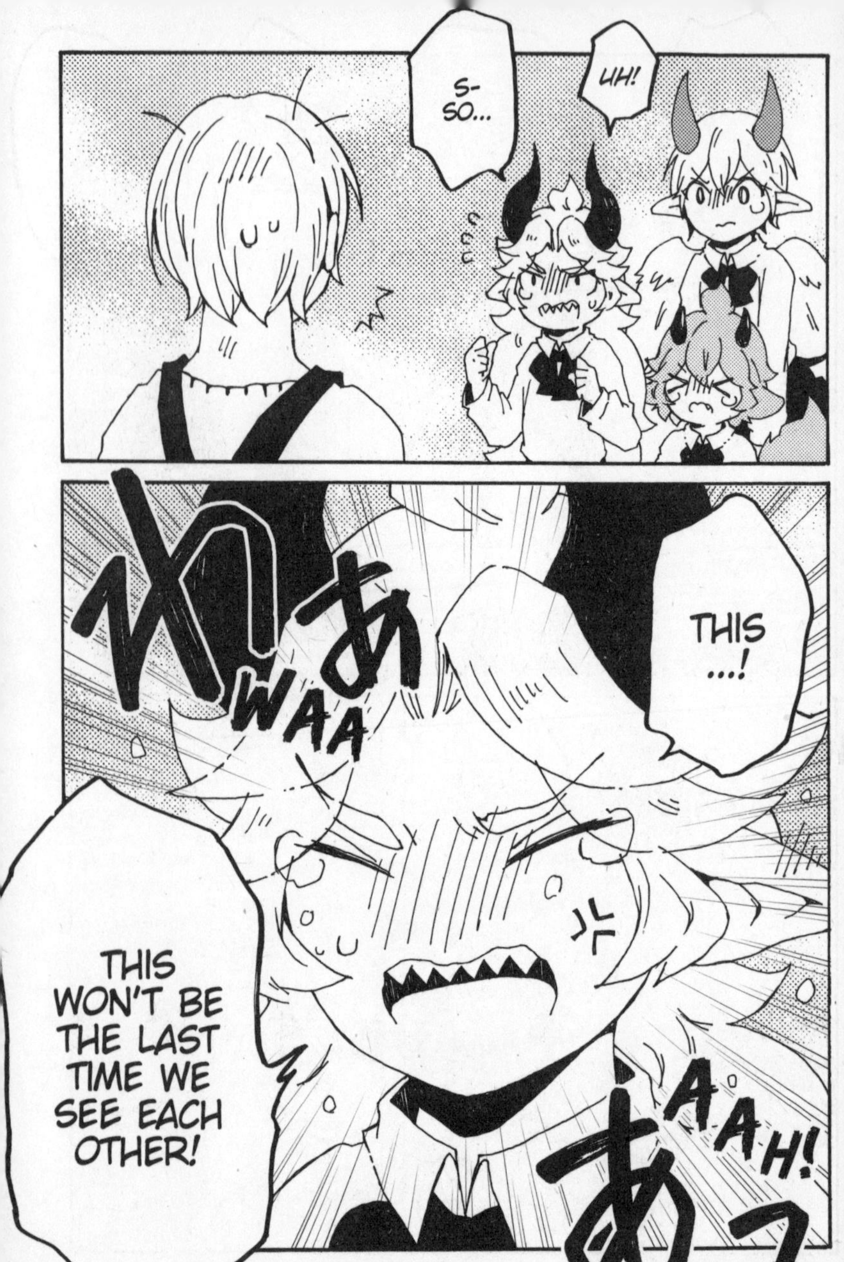
UH!
S- SO...
THIS ...!
わあ WAA
あっ AAH!
THIS WON'T BE THE LAST TIME WE SEE EACH OTHER!

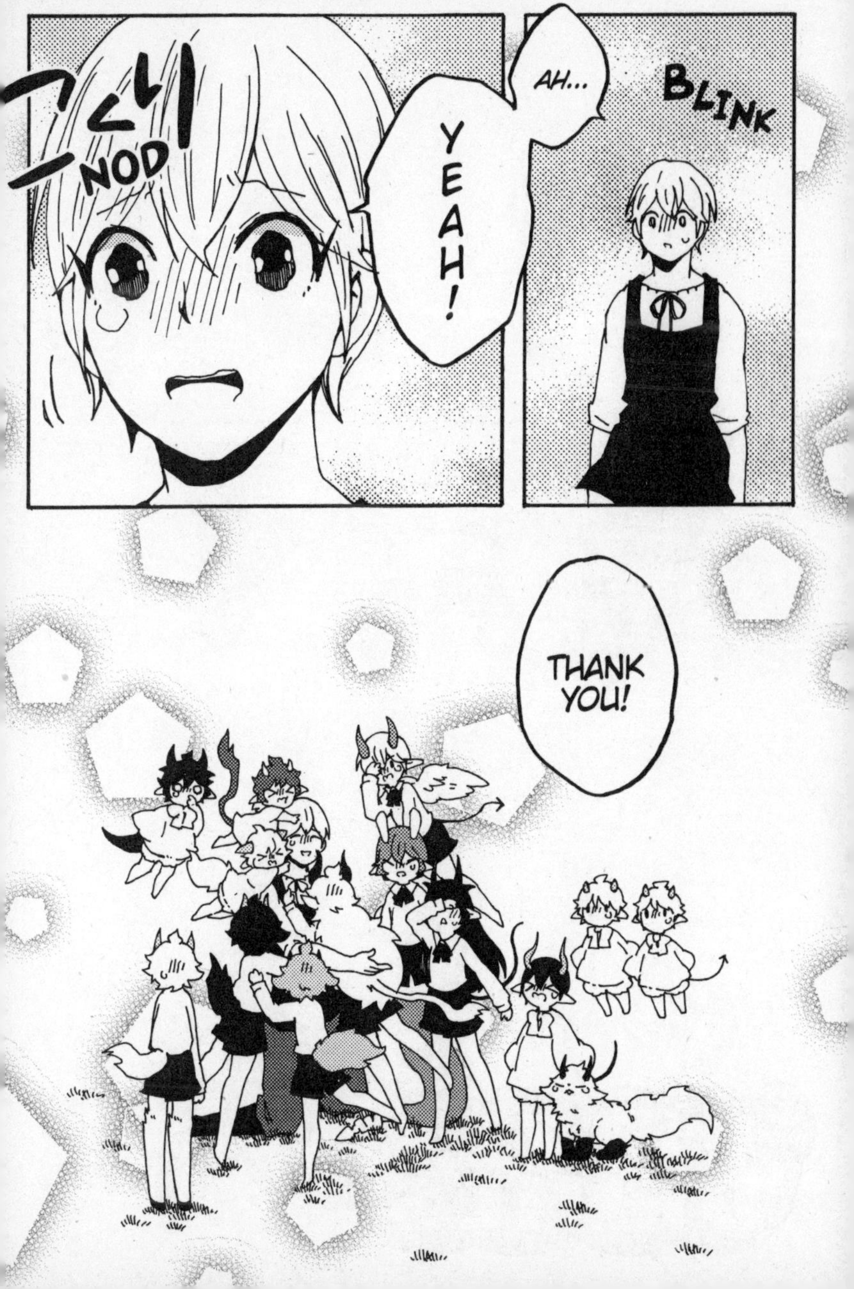
BLINK
AH...
YEAH!
NOD
THANK YOU!

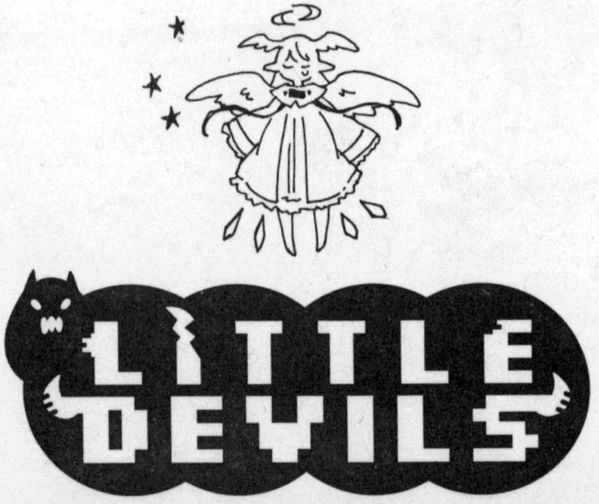

LITTLE DEVILS

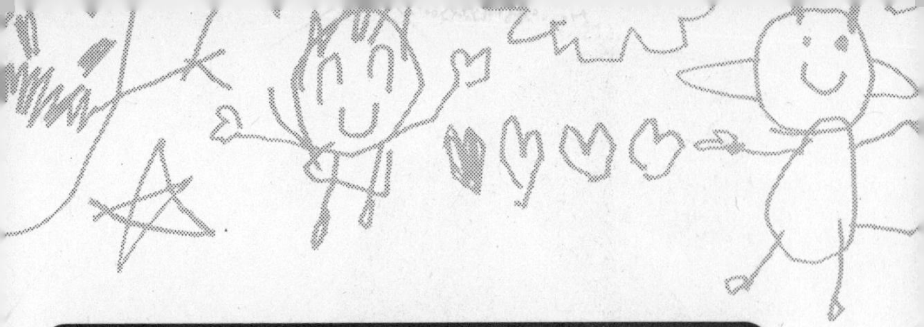

THE SACRED (FLOATING) ISLAND WHERE THE HERO AND THE LITTLE DEVILS SPENT THEIR DAYS

WITH THE TOUGH SOIL NOW CULTIVATED AND THE ADDITION OF MR. TREE AND THE SECRET BASE, THE ISLAND SLOWLY BECAME A HOME EVERYONE COULD LIVE IN HAPPILY.

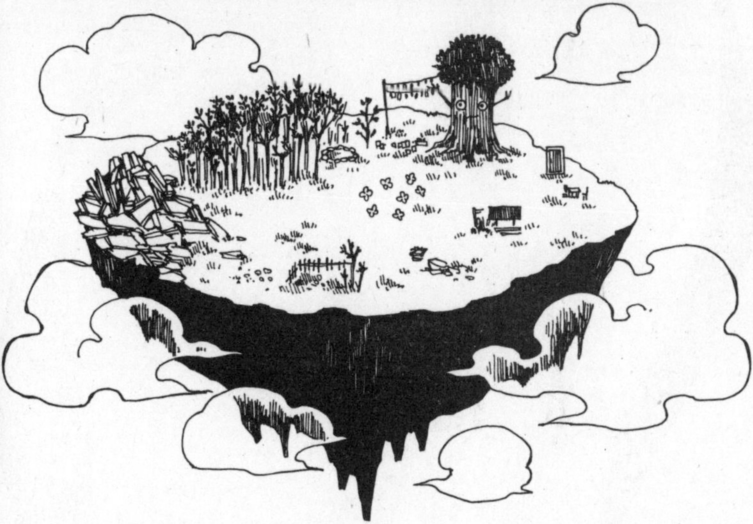

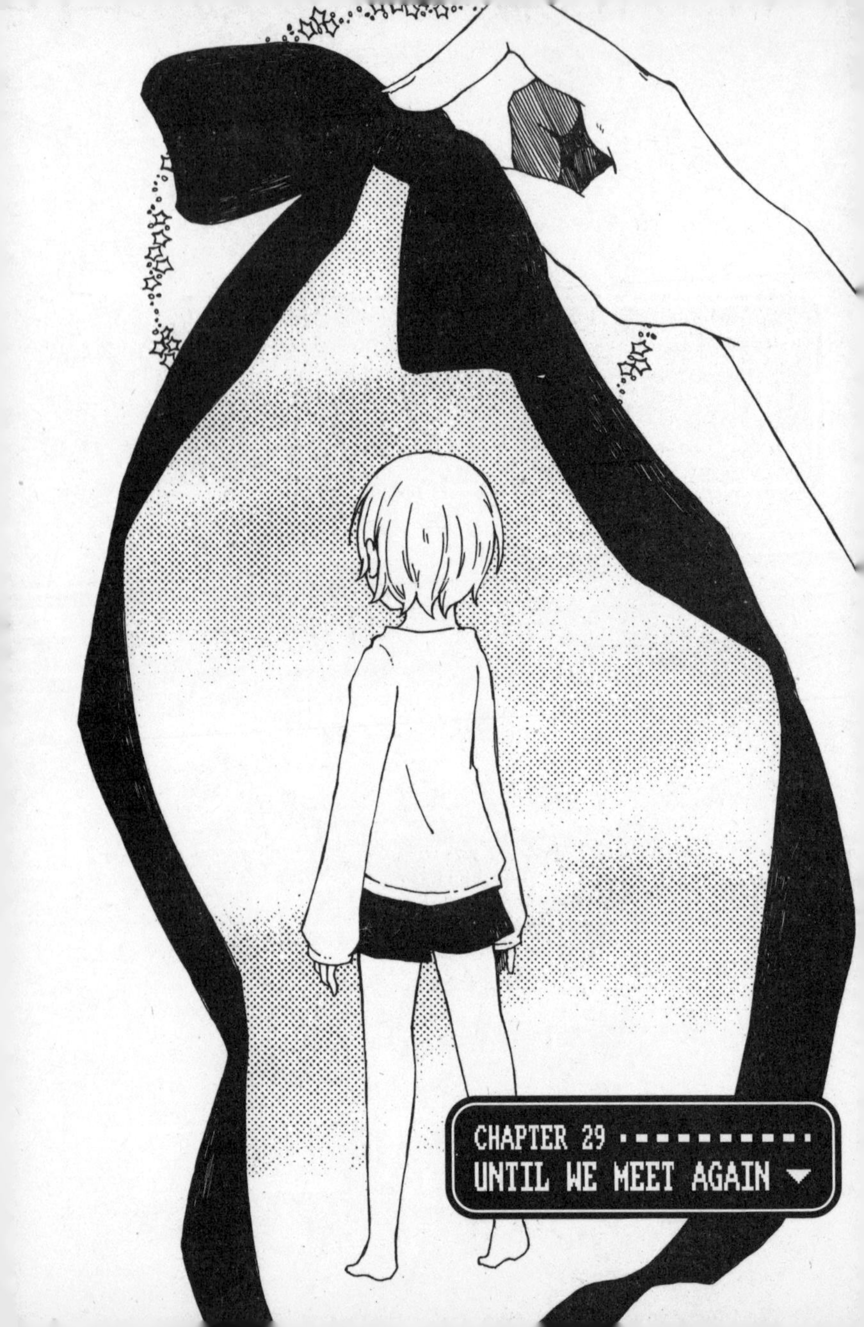
CHAPTER 29
UNTIL WE MEET AGAIN

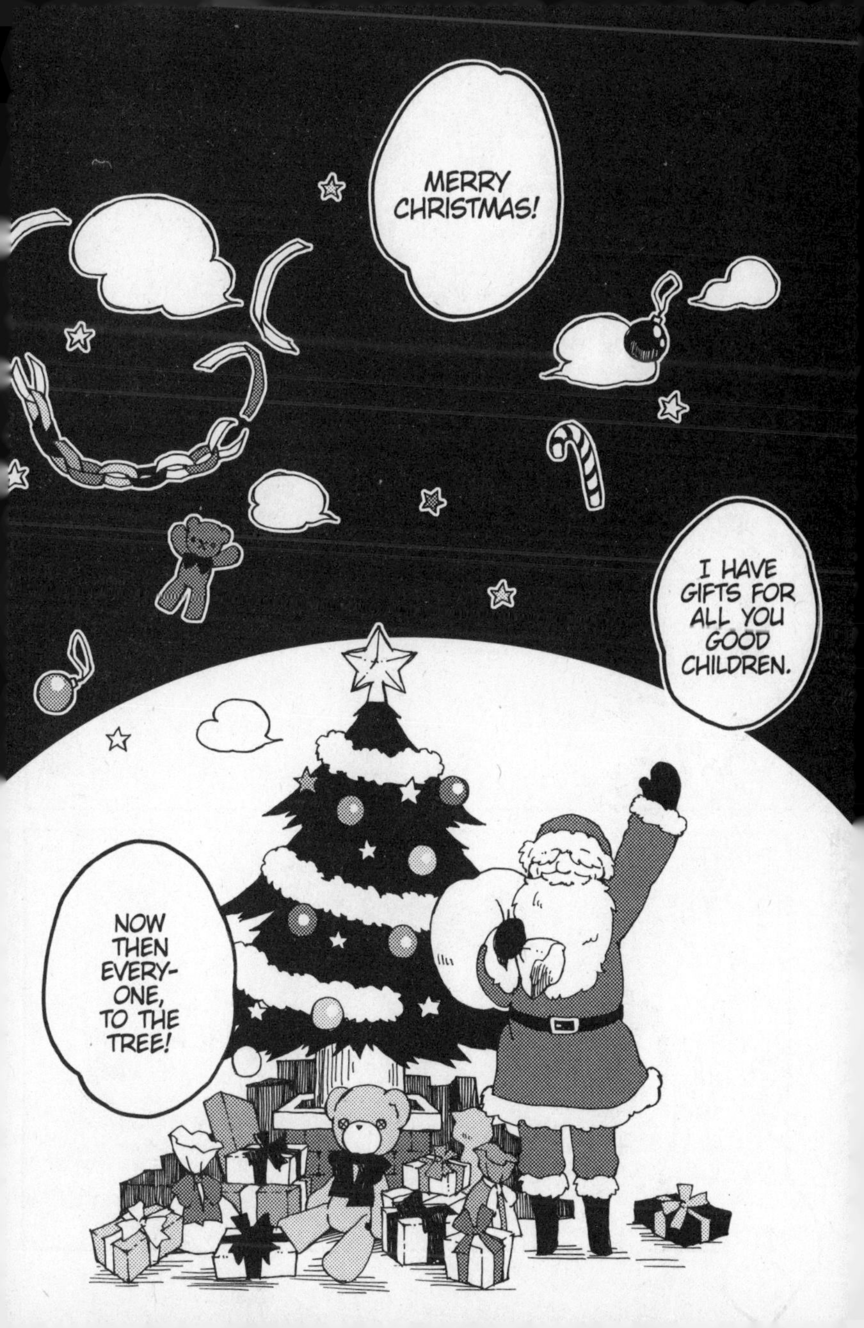
MERRY CHRISTMAS!
I HAVE GIFTS FOR ALL YOU GOOD CHILDREN.
NOW THEN EVERY-ONE, TO THE TREE!

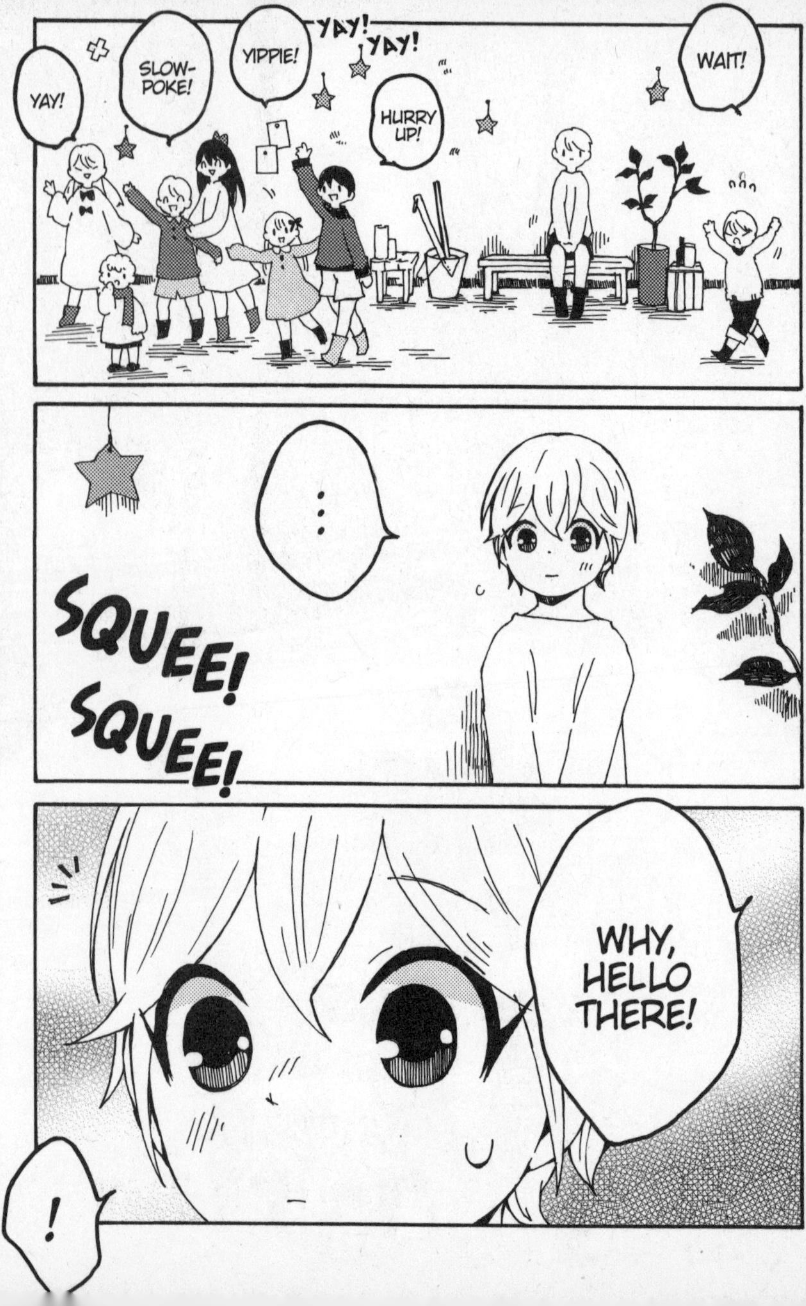
WAIT!
YAY! YAY!
HURRY UP!
YIPPIE!
SLOW-POKE!
YAY!
...
SQUEE! SQUEE!
WHY, HELLO THERE!
!

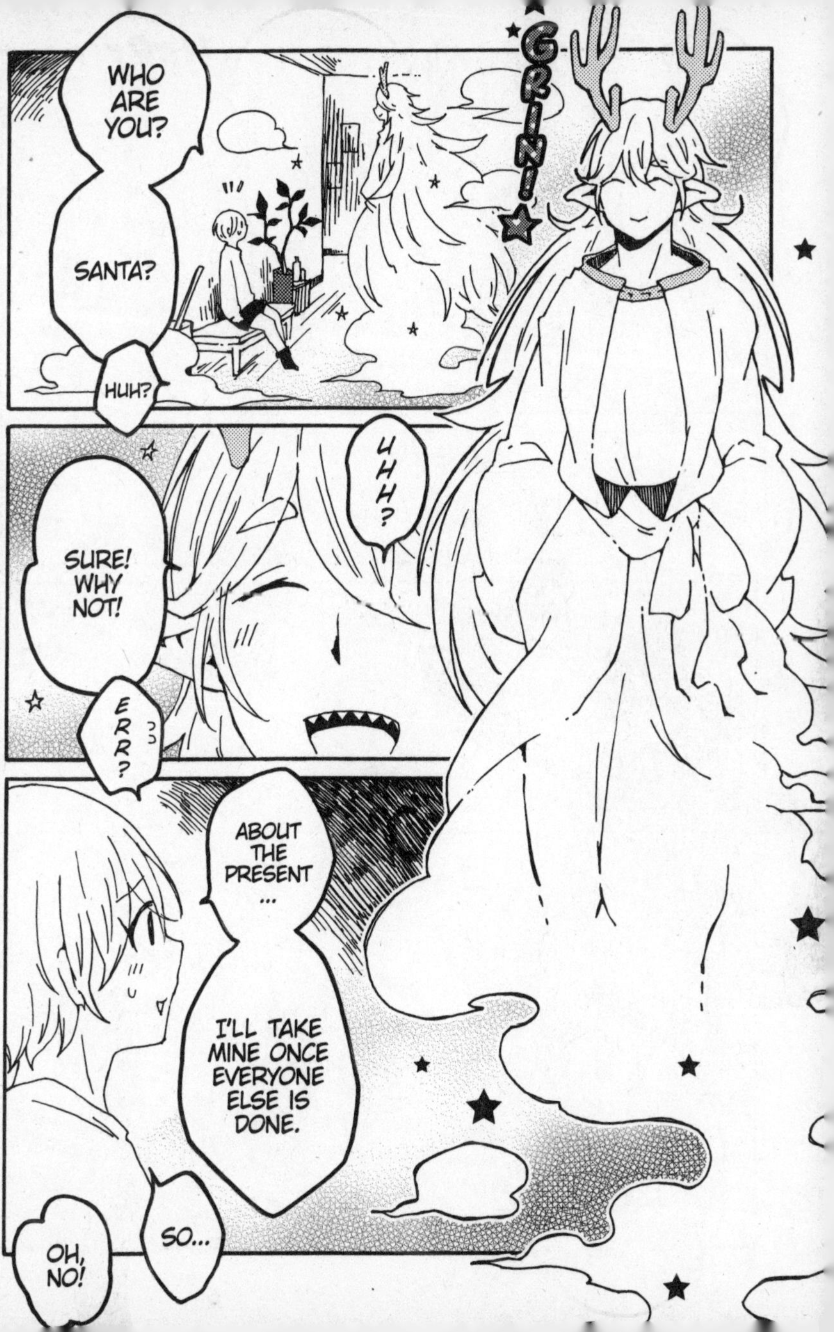
GRIN!
WHO ARE YOU?
SANTA?
HUH?
UHHH?
SURE! WHY NOT!
ERR?
ABOUT THE PRESENT...
I'LL TAKE MINE ONCE EVERYONE ELSE IS DONE.
SO...
OH, NO!

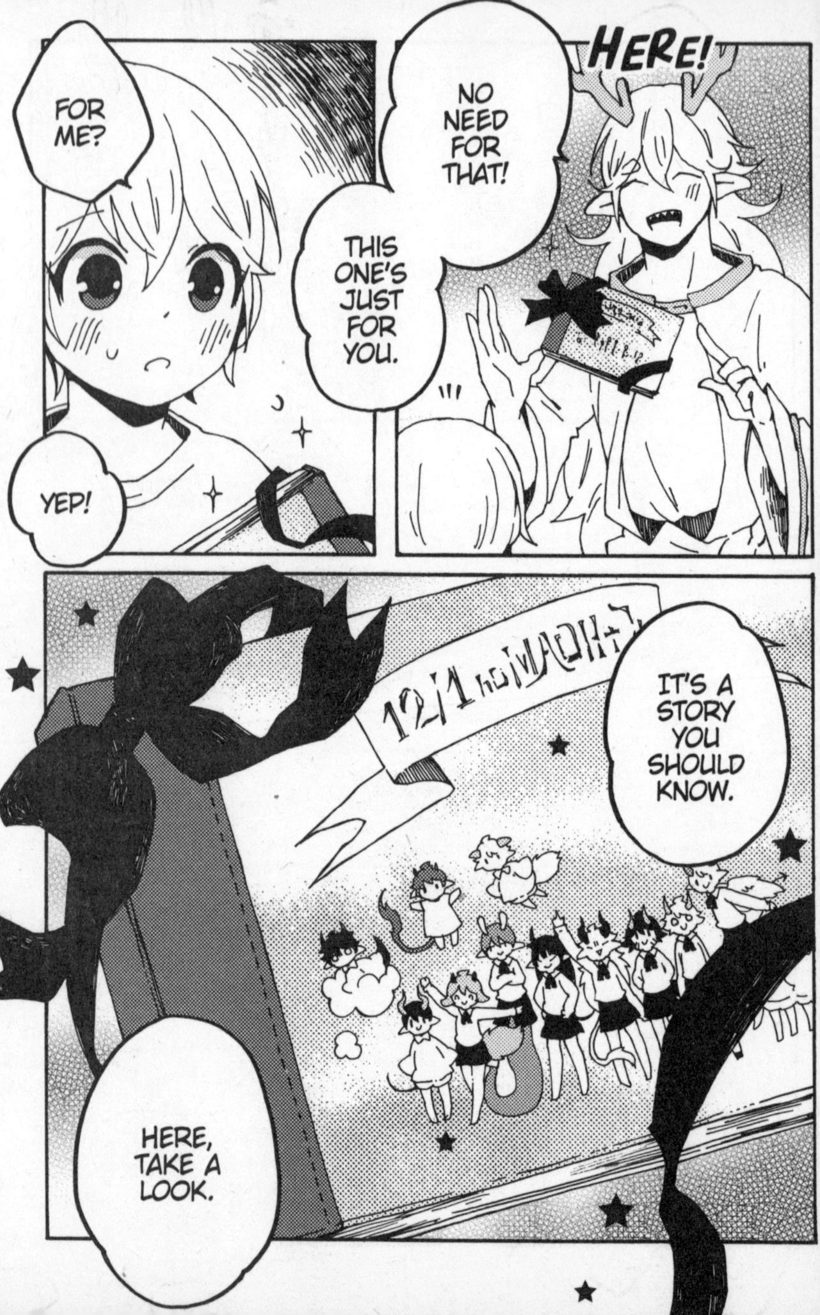
HERE!
NO NEED FOR THAT!
THIS ONE'S JUST FOR YOU.
FOR ME?
YEP!
IT'S A STORY YOU SHOULD KNOW.
HERE, TAKE A LOOK.

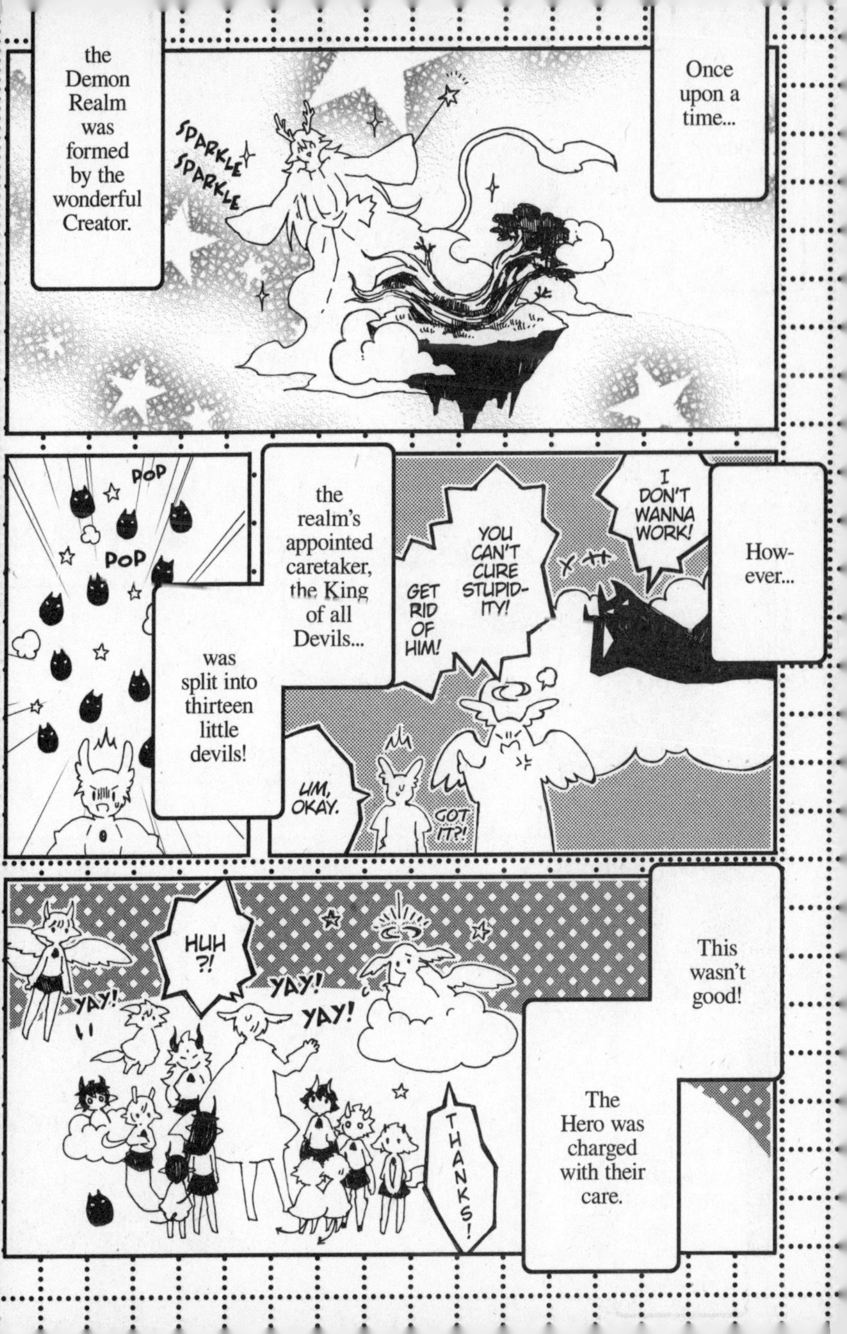
Once upon a time...
the Demon Realm was formed by the wonderful Creator.
SPARKLE SPARKLE
How-ever...
I DON'T WANNA WORK!
YOU CAN'T CURE STUPID-ITY!
GET RID OF HIM!
GOT IT?!
UM, OKAY.
the realm's appointed caretaker, the King of all Devils...
was split into thirteen little devils!
POP
POP
This wasn't good!
The Hero was charged with their care.
THANKS!
YAY!
YAY!
HUH?!
YAY!

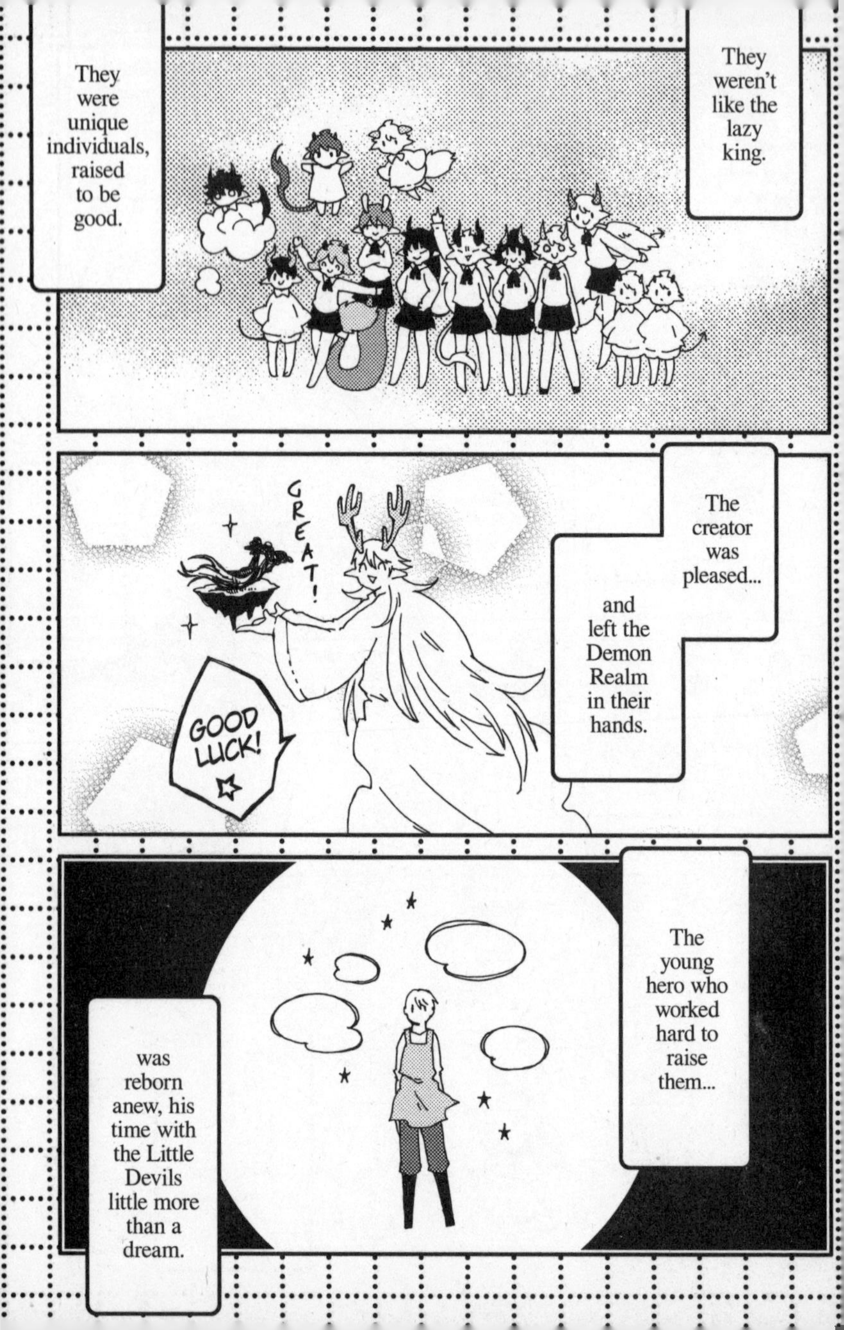
They weren't like the lazy king.
They were unique individuals, raised to be good.
The creator was pleased...
and left the Demon Realm in their hands.
GREAT!
GOOD LUCK!
The young hero who worked hard to raise them...
was reborn anew, his time with the Little Devils little more than a dream.

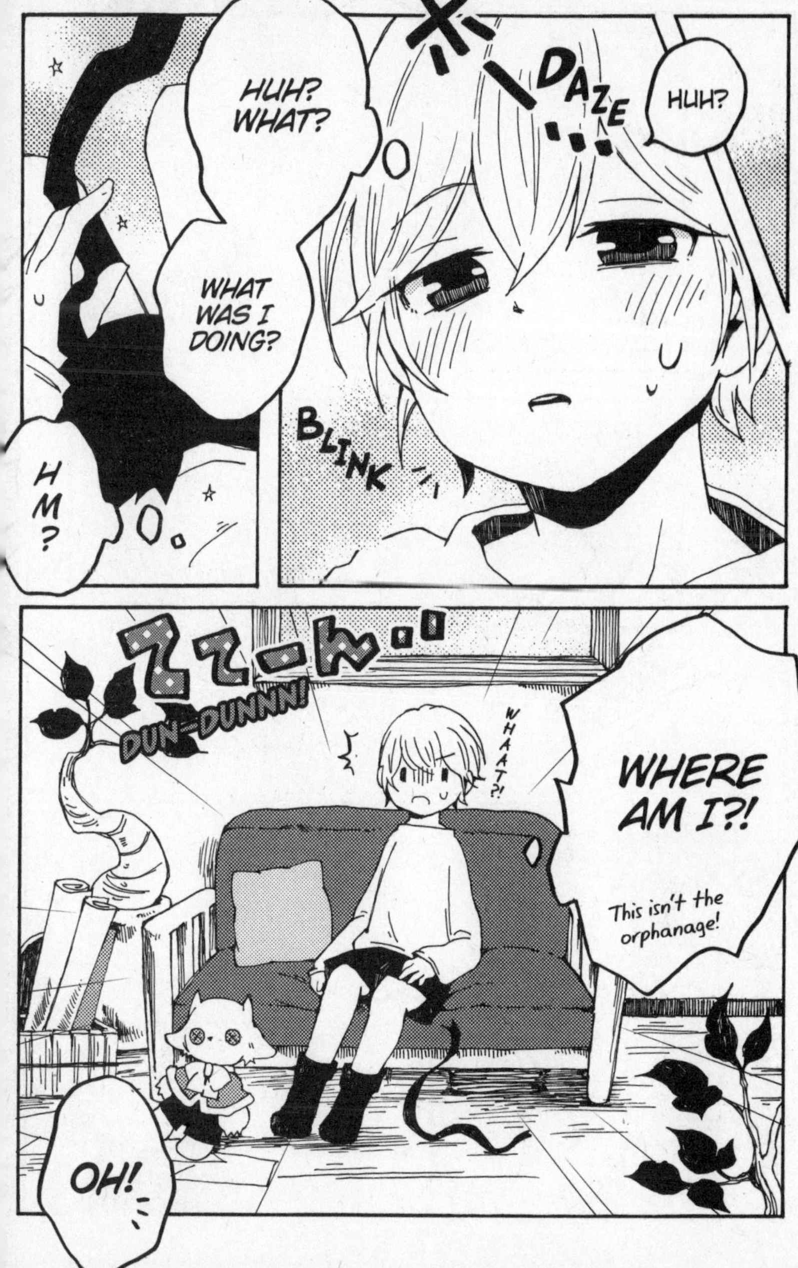
HUH?
DAZE
HUH? WHAT?
WHAT WAS I DOING?
BLINK
HM?
DUN-DUNNN!
WHERE AM I?!
This isn't the orphanage!
WHAAAT?!
OH!

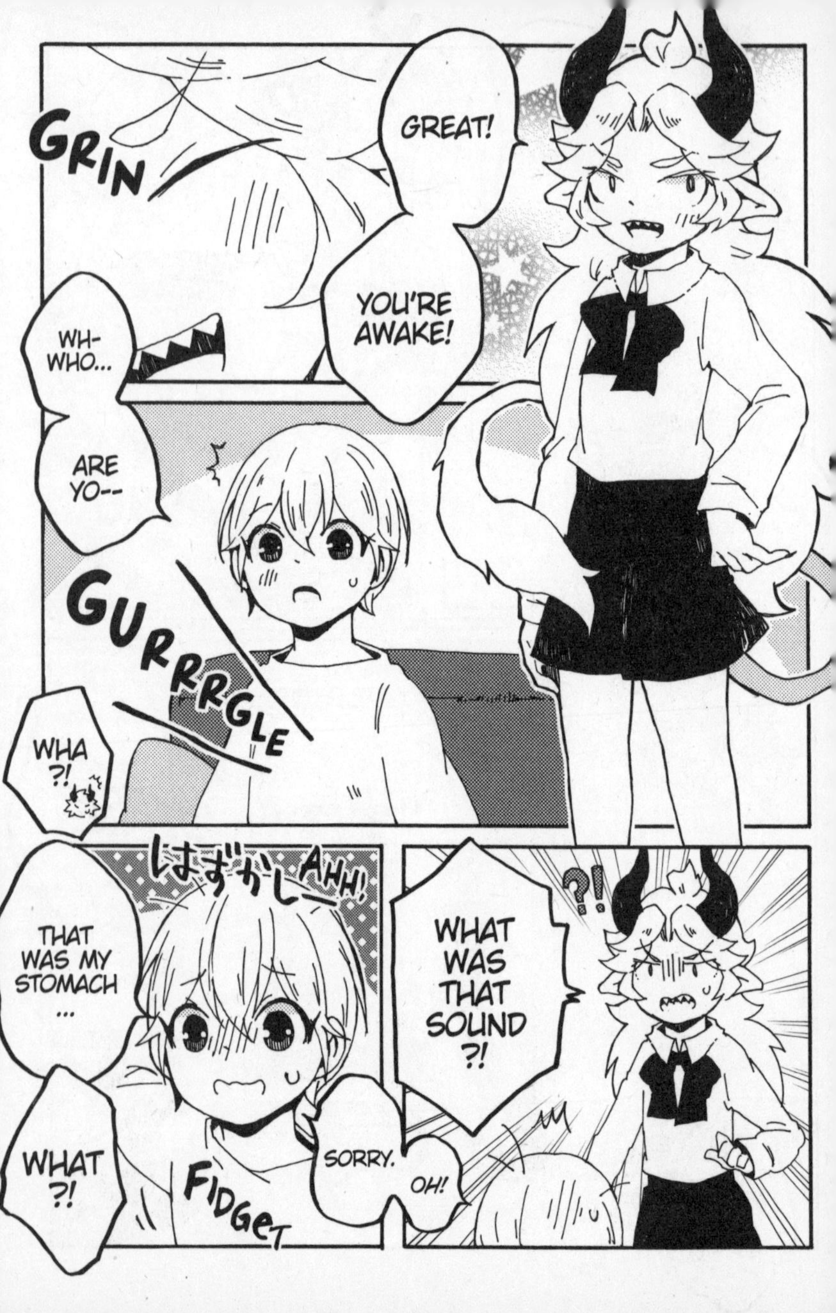
GREAT!
YOU'RE AWAKE!
GRIN
WH- WHO...
ARE YO--
GURRRRGLE
WHA ?!
?!
WHAT WAS THAT SOUND ?!
OH!
はずかしーAHH!
THAT WAS MY STOMACH ...
SORRY.
FIDGET
WHAT ?!

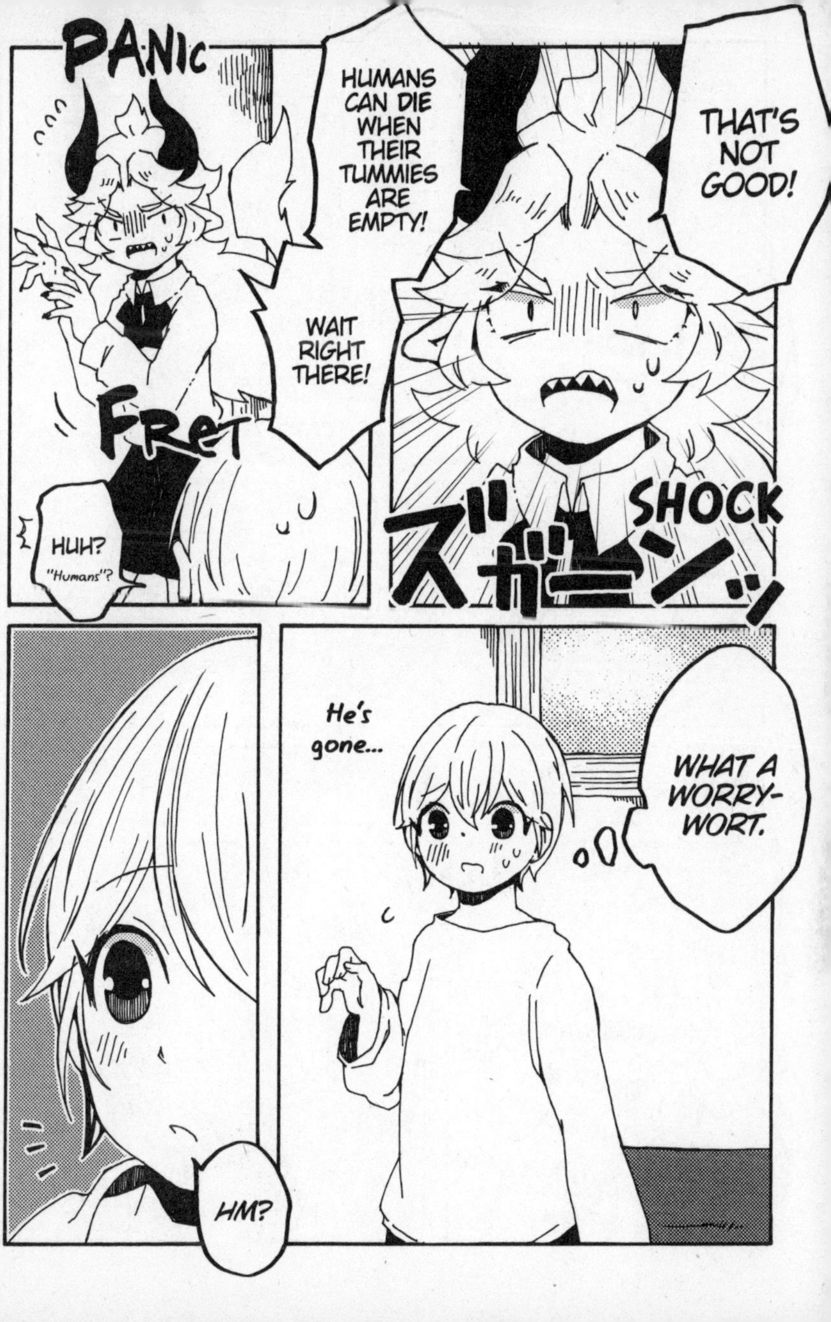

THAT'S NOT GOOD!
SHOCK
ズガーンッ
HUMANS CAN DIE WHEN THEIR TUMMIES ARE EMPTY!
WAIT RIGHT THERE!
PANIC
FRET
HUH? "Humans"?
WHAT A WORRY-WORT.
He's gone...
HM?

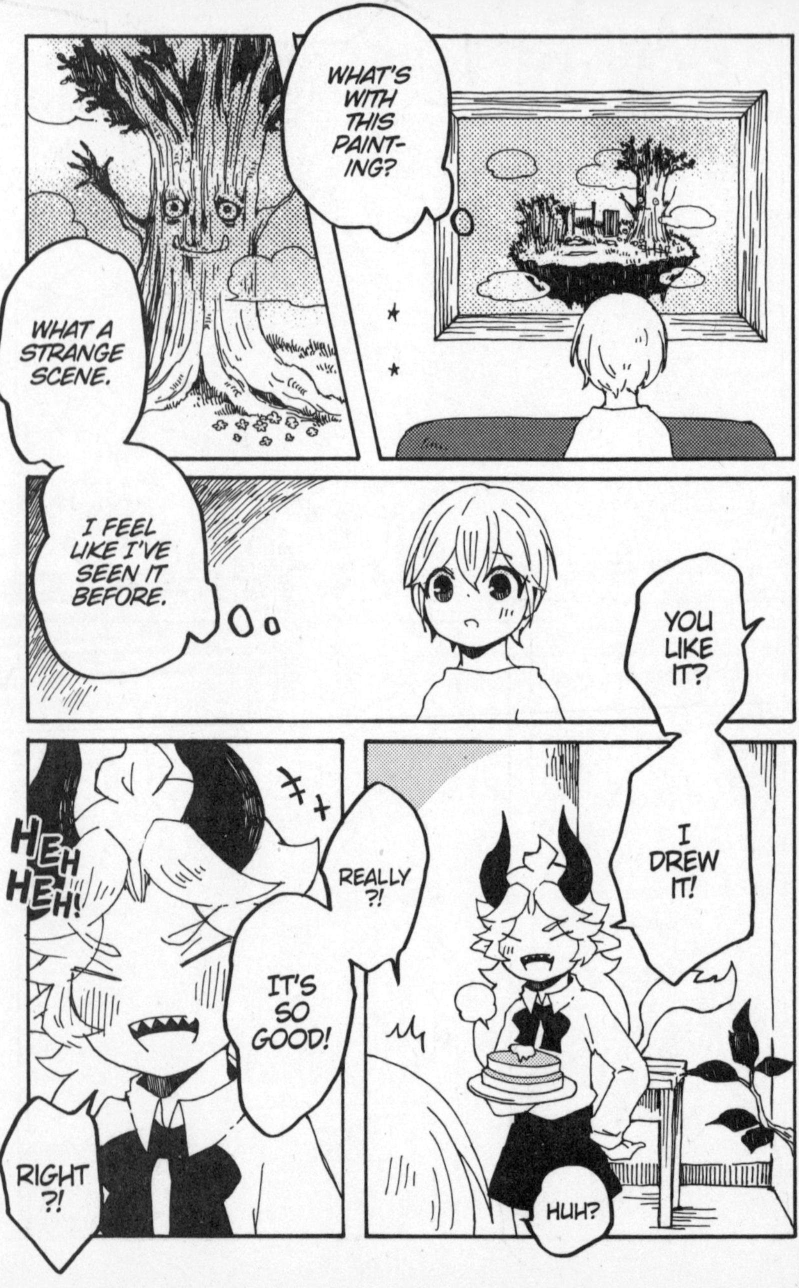
WHAT'S WITH THIS PAINTING?
WHAT A STRANGE SCENE.
I FEEL LIKE I'VE SEEN IT BEFORE.
YOU LIKE IT?
I DREW IT!
HUH?
REALLY?!
IT'S SO GOOD!
HEH HEH!
RIGHT?!

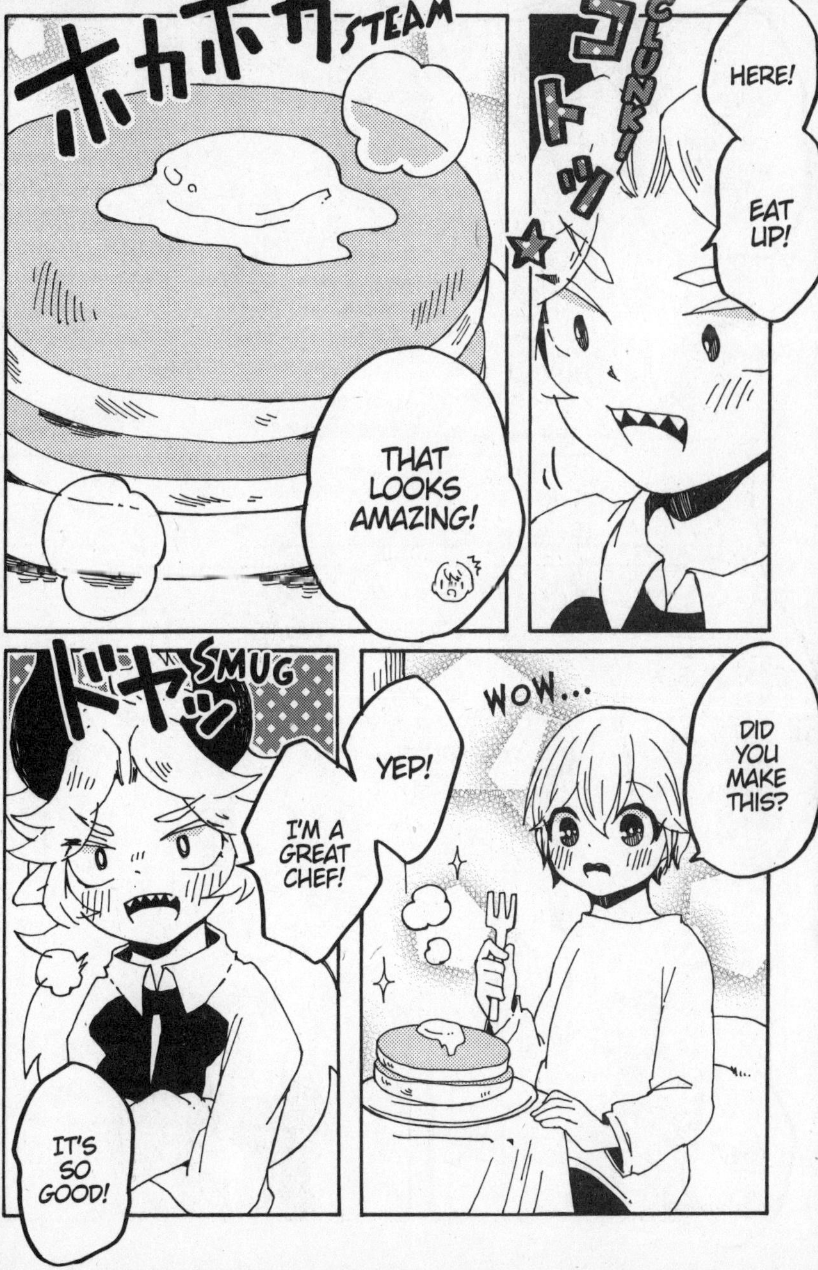
HERE!
EAT UP!
コトッ
CLUNK!
ホカホカ
STEAM
THAT LOOKS AMAZING!
DID YOU MAKE THIS?
WOW...
ドヤッ
SMUG
YEP!
I'M A GREAT CHEF!
IT'S SO GOOD!

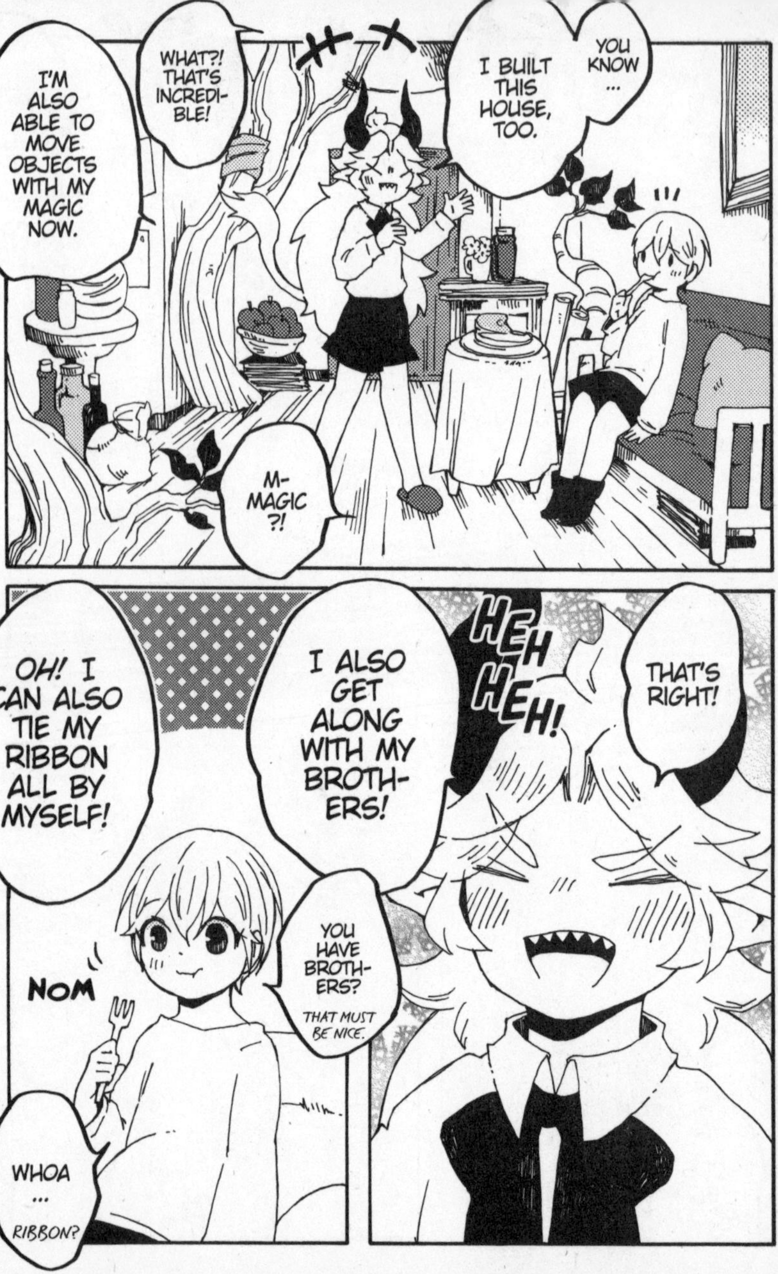
YOU KNOW ...
I BUILT THIS HOUSE, TOO.
WHAT?! THAT'S INCREDI-BLE!
I'M ALSO ABLE TO MOVE OBJECTS WITH MY MAGIC NOW.
M-MAGIC?!
THAT'S RIGHT!
HEH HEH!
I ALSO GET ALONG WITH MY BROTH-ERS!
OH! I CAN ALSO TIE MY RIBBON ALL BY MYSELF!
YOU HAVE BROTH-ERS?
THAT MUST BE NICE.
NOM
WHOA ...
RIBBON?

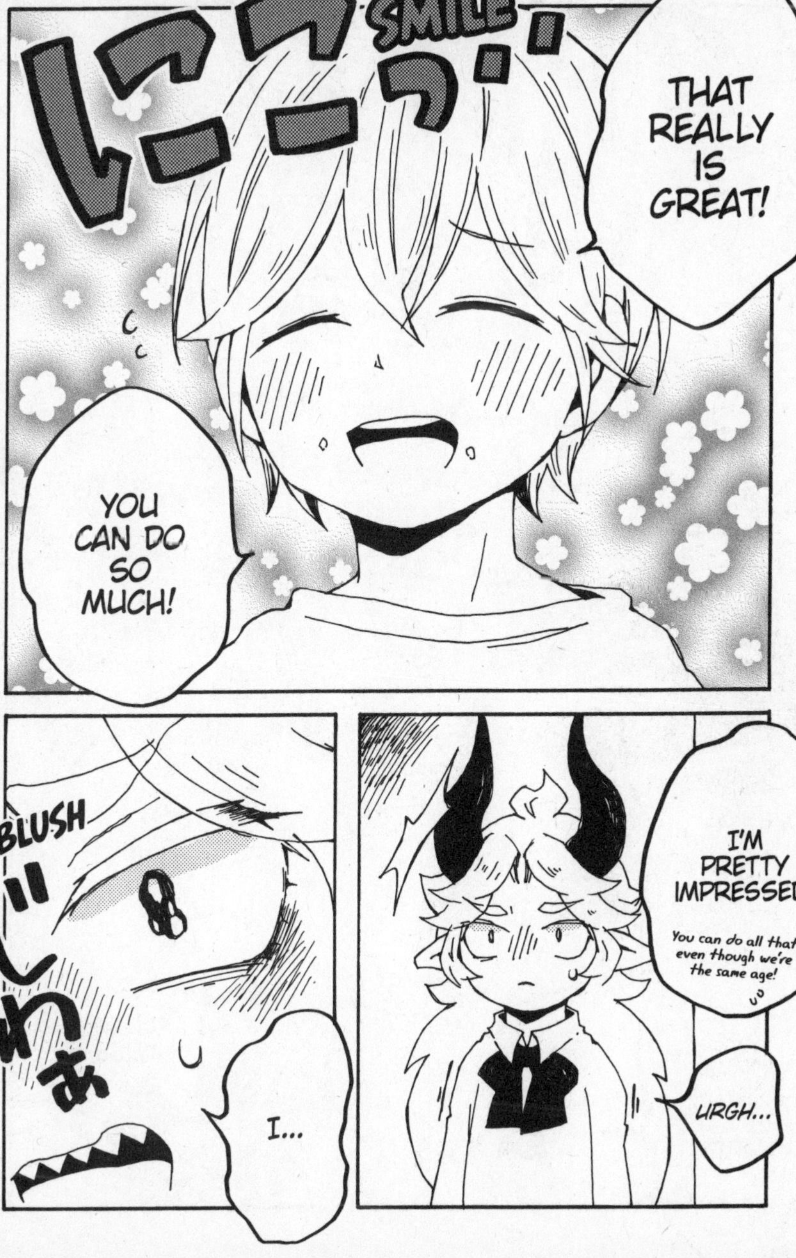
にこっ
SMILE
THAT REALLY IS GREAT!
YOU CAN DO SO MUCH!
I'M PRETTY IMPRESSED!
You can do all that even though we're the same age!
URGH...
じわぁ
BLUSH
I...

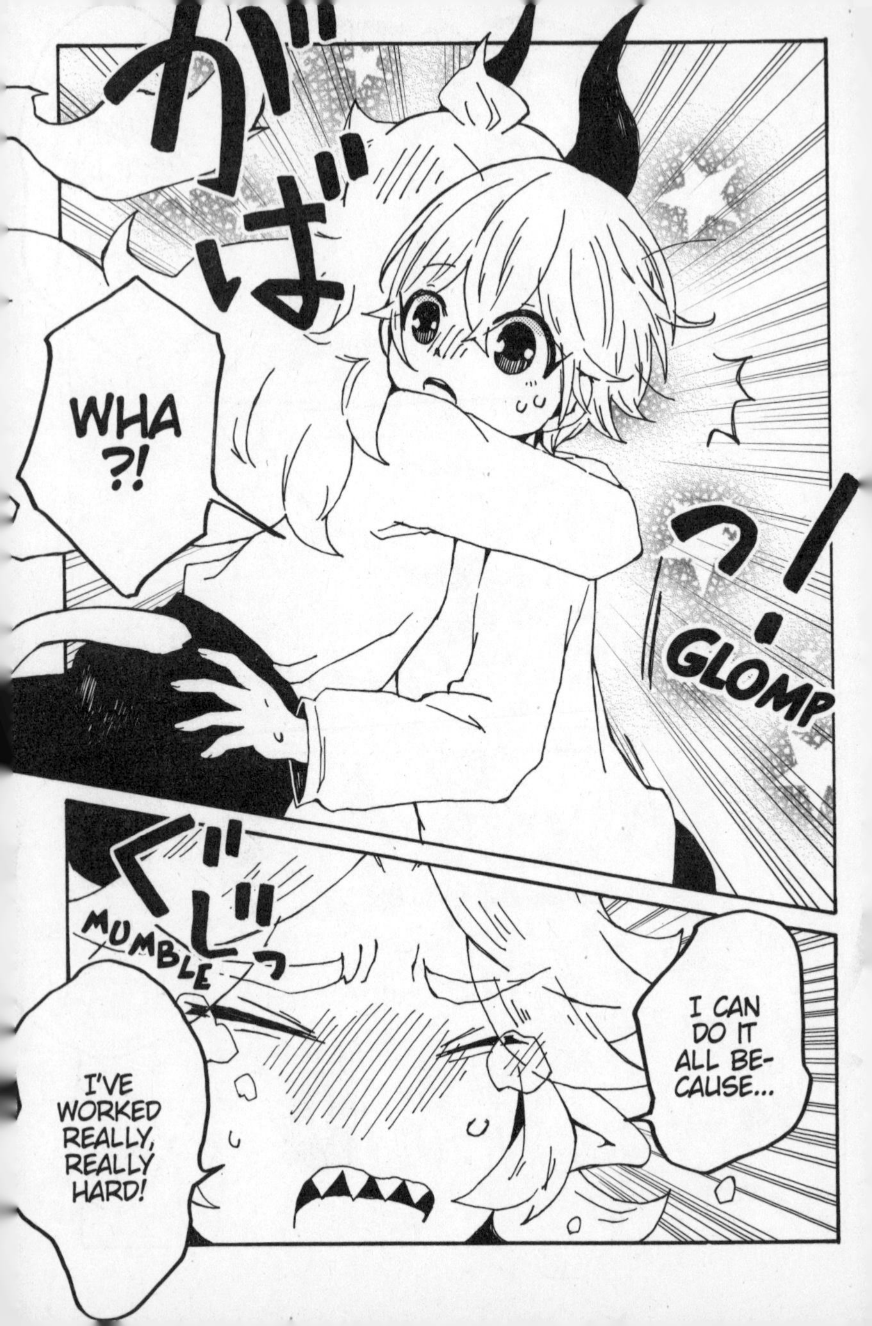

がば
っ！
GLOMP
WHA ?!
I CAN DO IT ALL BE-CAUSE...
くじっ
MUMBLE
I'VE WORKED REALLY, REALLY HARD!

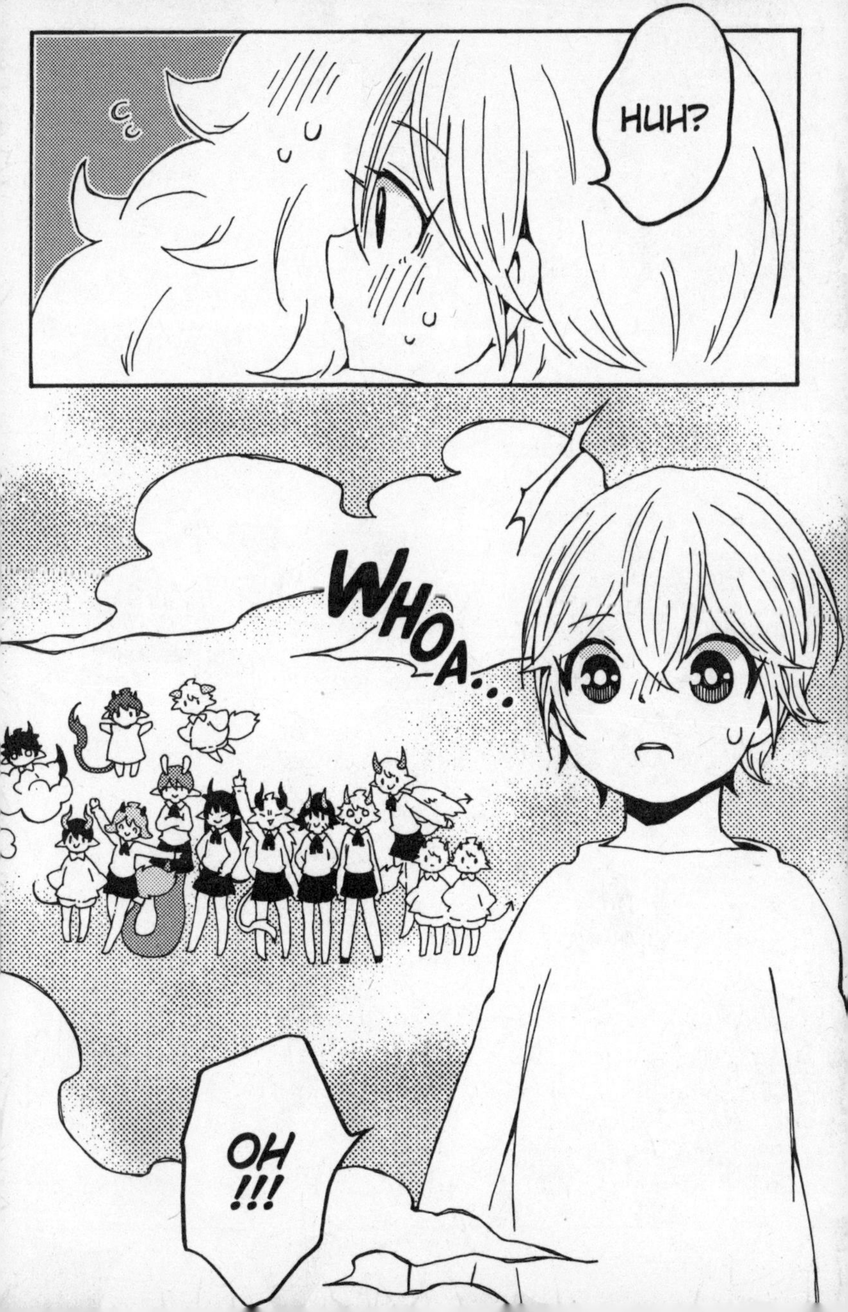
HUH?
WHOA...
OH !!!

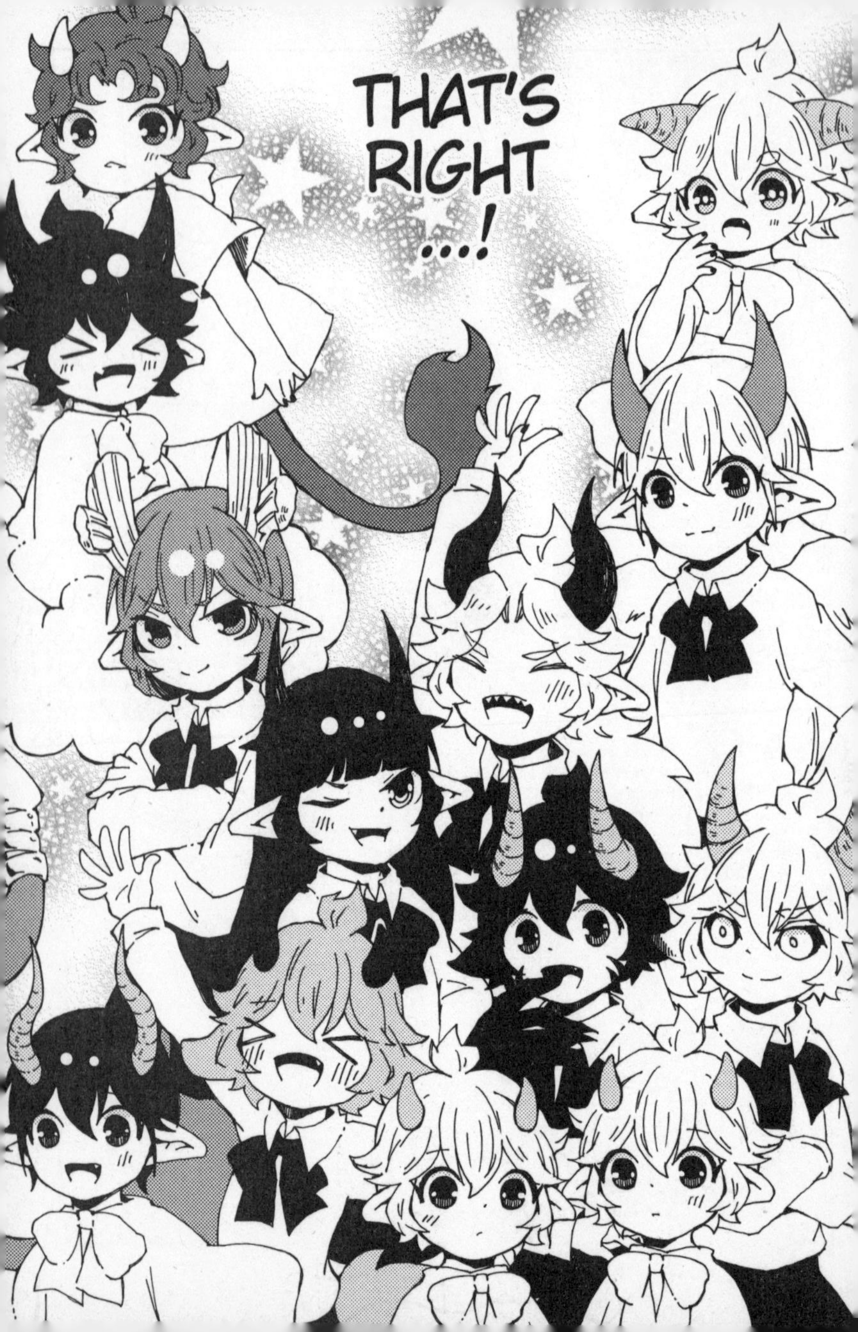
THAT'S RIGHT ...!

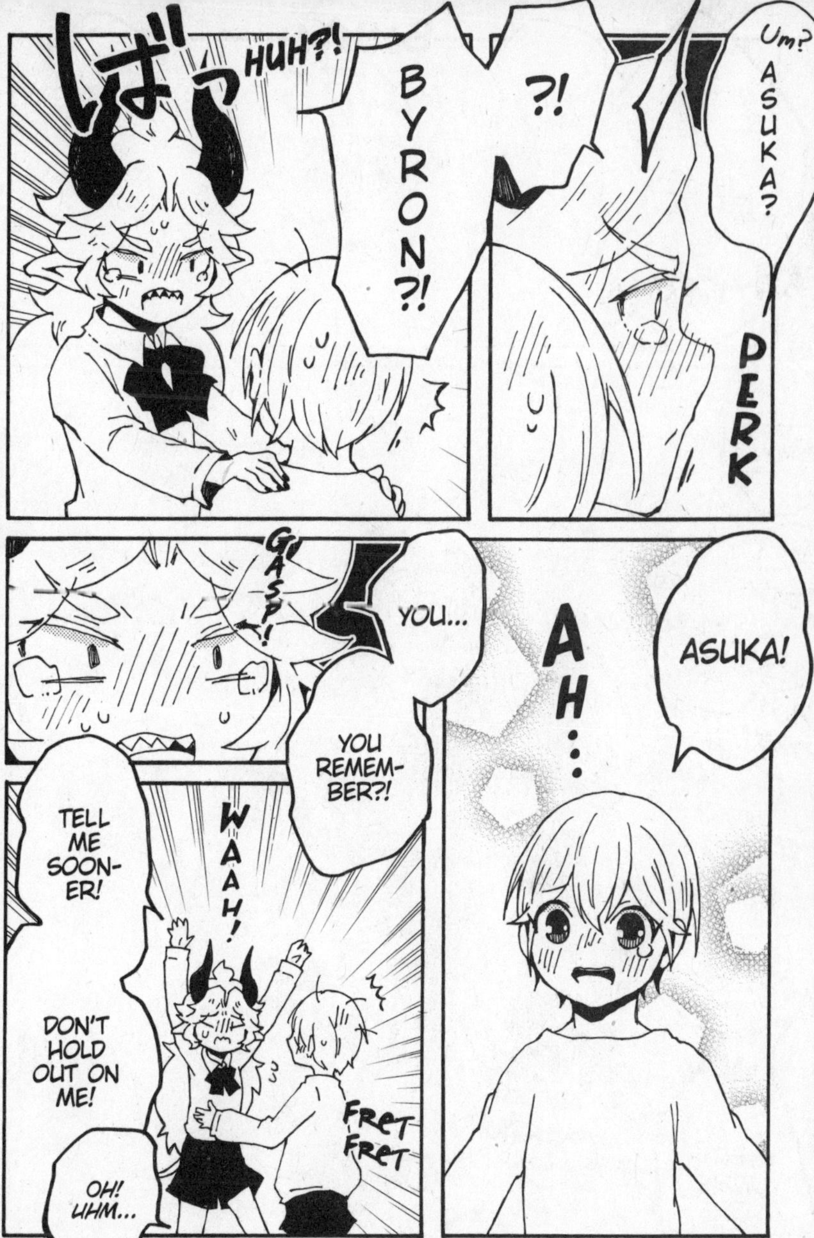
Um? ASUKA?
PERK
?!
BYRON?!
HUH?!
ばっ
ASUKA!
AH...
YOU...
GASP!
YOU REMEMBER?!
WAAAH!
TELL ME SOONER!
DON'T HOLD OUT ON ME!
FRET FRET
OH! UHM...

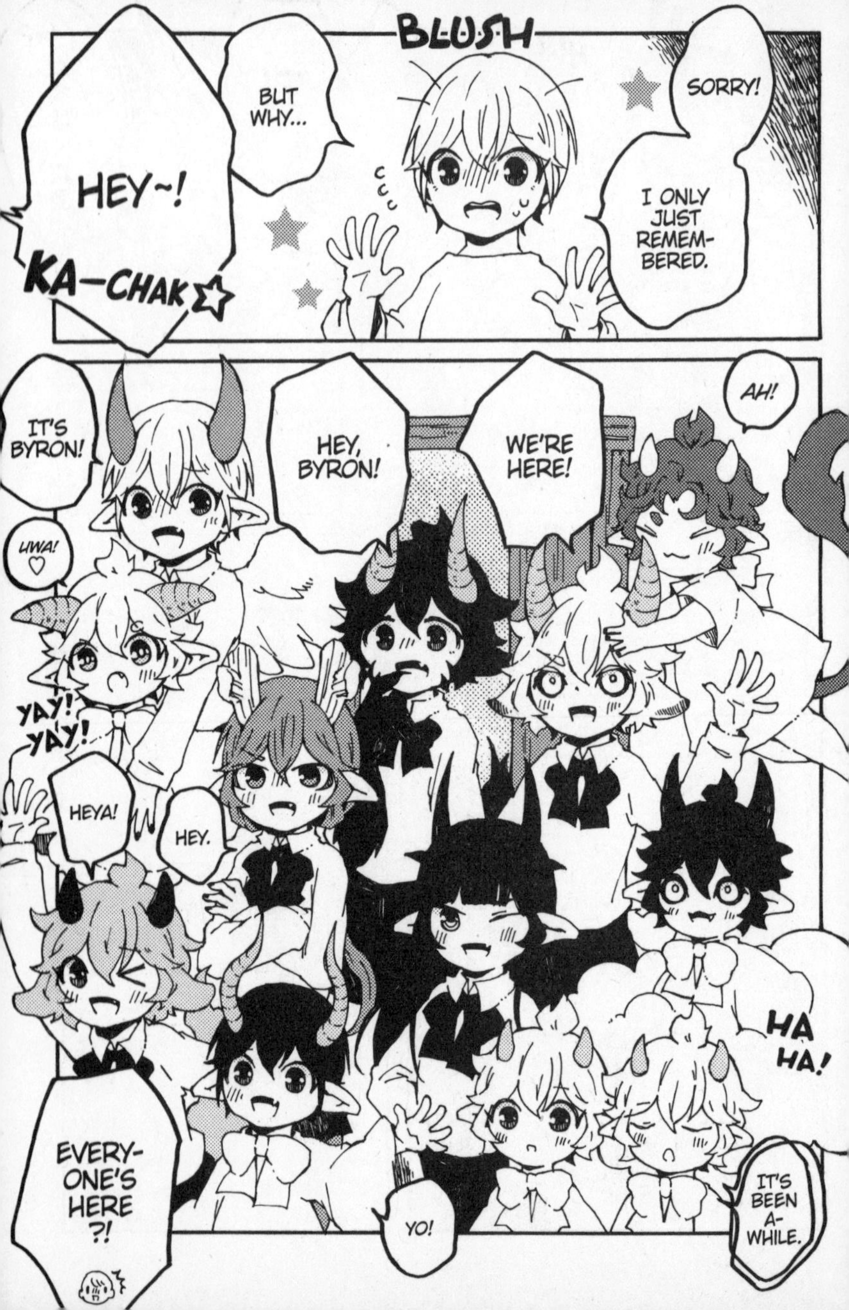
BLUSH
SORRY!
I ONLY JUST REMEMBERED.
BUT WHY...
HEY~!
KA-CHAK☆
AH!
WE'RE HERE!
HEY, BYRON!
IT'S BYRON!
UWA! ♡
HA HA!
YAY! YAY!
HEY.
HEYA!
IT'S BEEN A-WHILE.
YO!
EVERYONE'S HERE?!

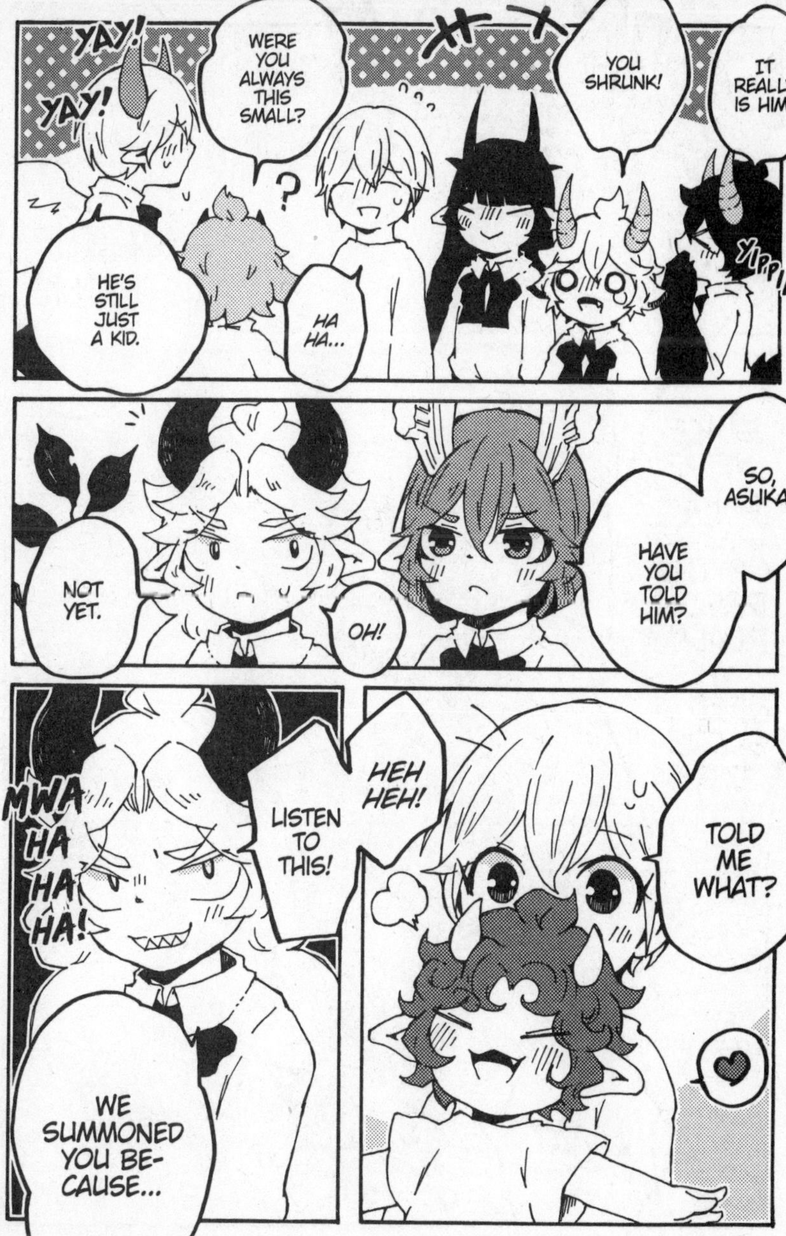
IT REALLY IS HIM!
YOU SHRUNK!
WERE YOU ALWAYS THIS SMALL?
YAY!
YAY!
YIPPIE!
HA HA...
HE'S STILL JUST A KID.
SO, ASUKA.
HAVE YOU TOLD HIM?
OH!
NOT YET.
TOLD ME WHAT?
HEH HEH!
LISTEN TO THIS!
MWA HA HA HA!
WE SUMMONED YOU BE-CAUSE...

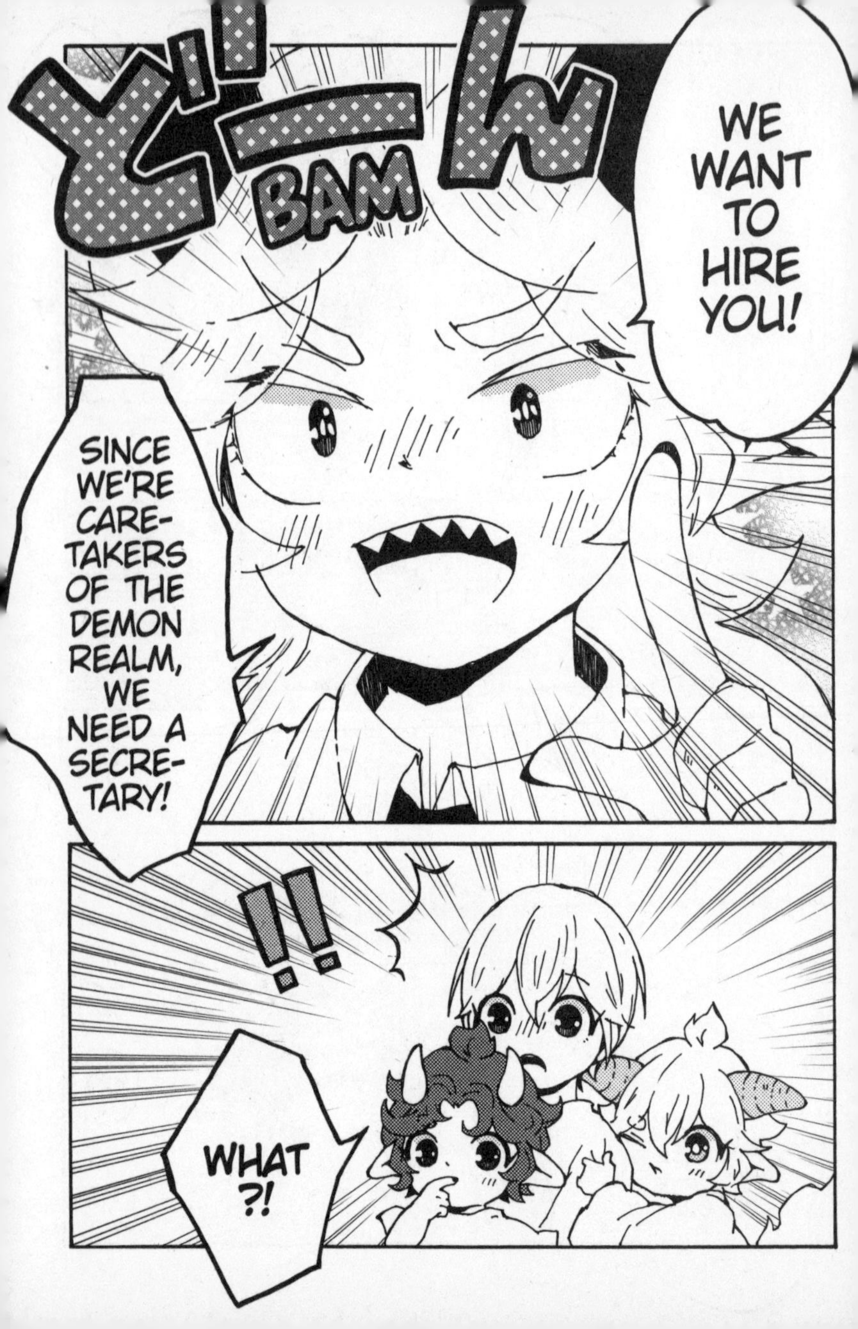
WE WANT TO HIRE YOU!
どーん
BAM
SINCE WE'RE CARE-TAKERS OF THE DEMON REALM, WE NEED A SECRE-TARY!
!!
WHAT?!

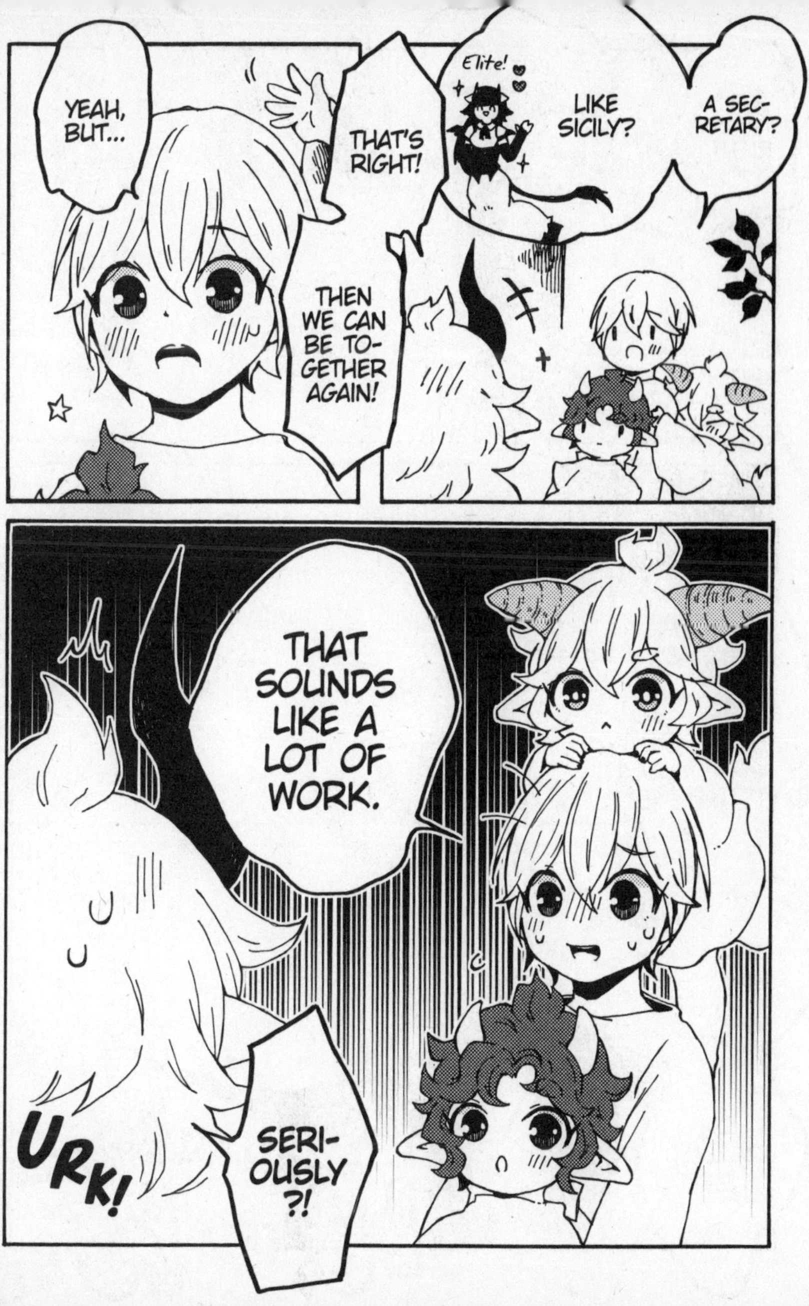
A SEC-RETARY?
LIKE SICILY?
Elite!
THAT'S RIGHT!
THEN WE CAN BE TO-GETHER AGAIN!
YEAH, BUT...
THAT SOUNDS LIKE A LOT OF WORK.
SERI-OUSLY?!
URK!

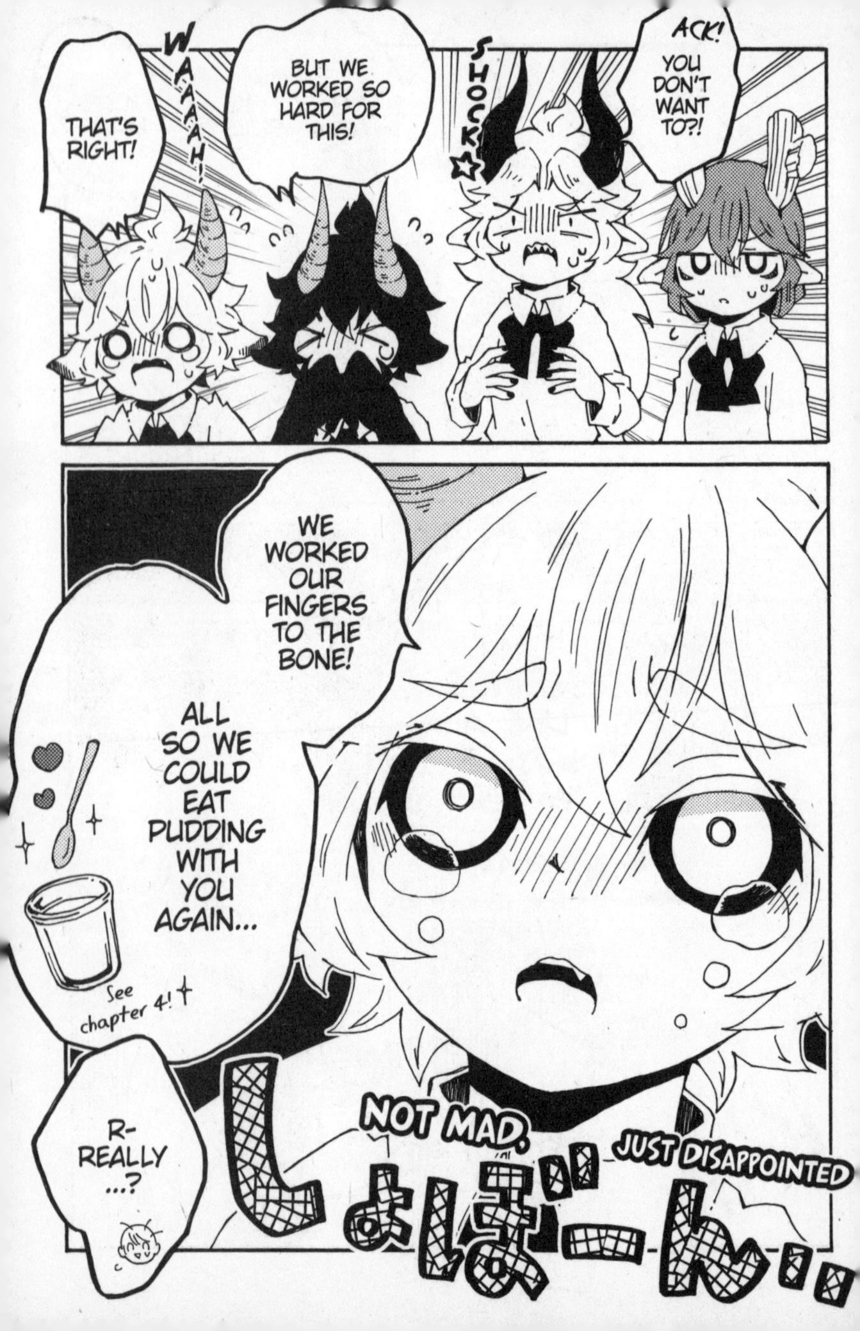
ACK!
YOU DON'T WANT TO?!
SHOCK☆
BUT WE WORKED SO HARD FOR THIS!
WAAAAH!
THAT'S RIGHT!
WE WORKED OUR FINGERS TO THE BONE!
ALL SO WE COULD EAT PUDDING WITH YOU AGAIN...
See chapter 4!
R-REALLY ...?
NOT MAD. JUST DISAPPOINTED
しょぼーん..

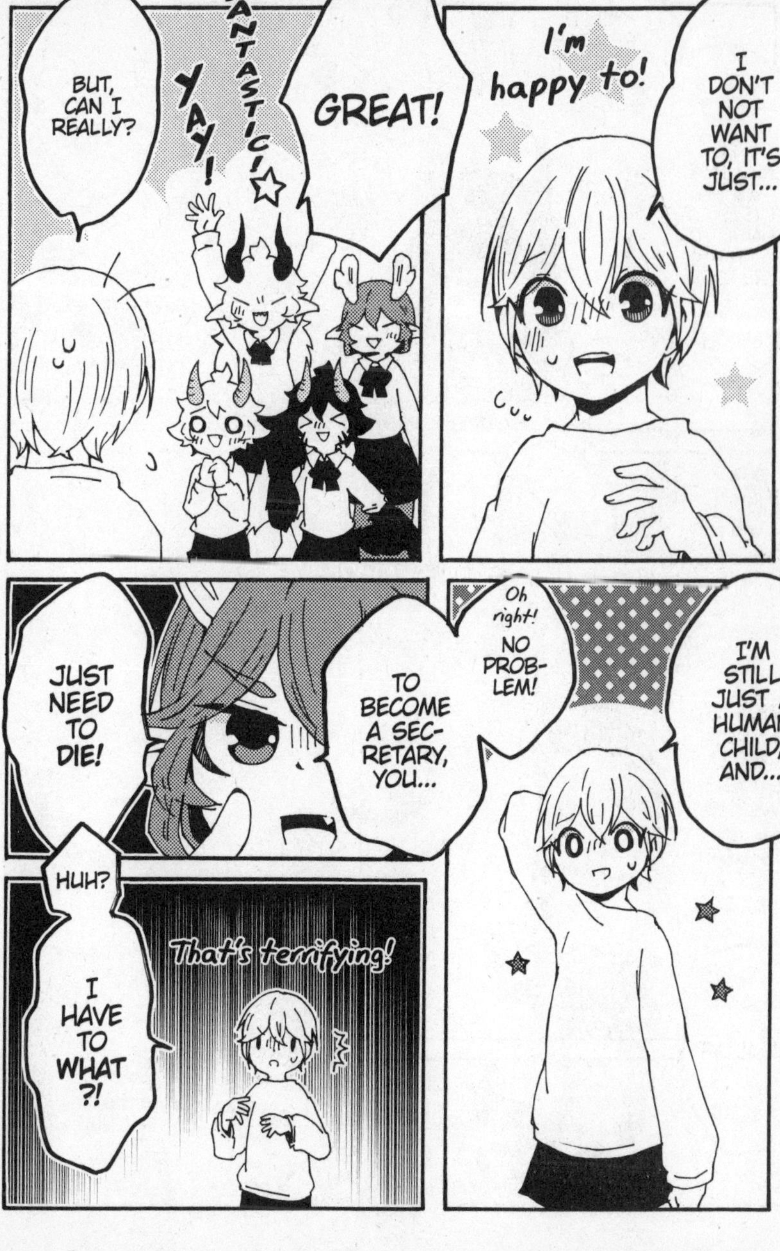
I DON'T NOT WANT TO, IT'S JUST...
I'm happy to!
GREAT!
FANTASTIC!☆
YAY!
BUT, CAN I REALLY?
I'M STILL JUST A HUMAN CHILD, AND...
Oh right! NO PROB-LEM!
TO BECOME A SEC-RETARY, YOU...
JUST NEED TO DIE!
HUH?
I HAVE TO WHAT?!
That's terrifying!

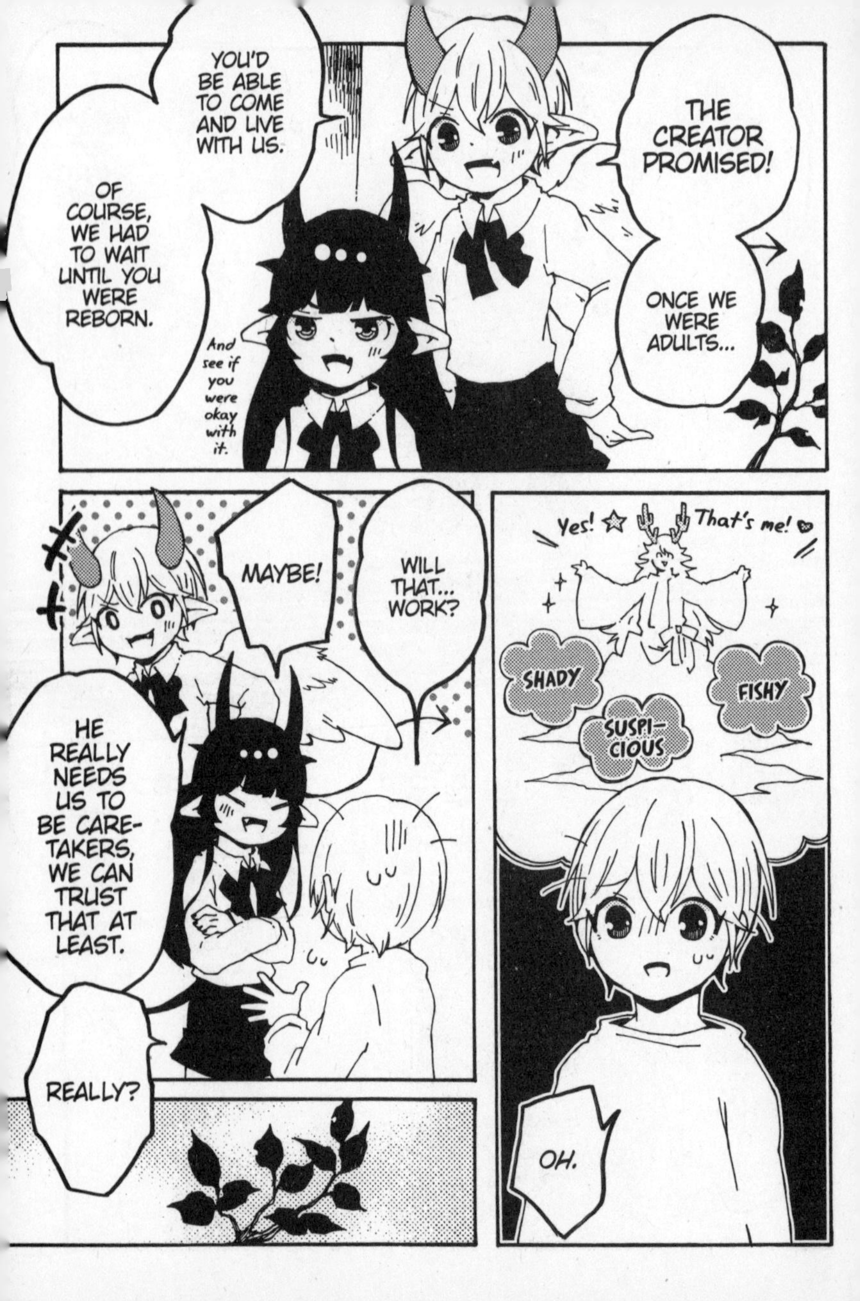
THE CREATOR PROMISED!
ONCE WE WERE ADULTS...
YOU'D BE ABLE TO COME AND LIVE WITH US.
OF COURSE, WE HAD TO WAIT UNTIL YOU WERE REBORN.
And see if you were okay with it.
Yes! ☆ That's me! ♡
SHADY
FISHY
SUSPI-CIOUS
OH.
WILL THAT... WORK?
MAYBE!
HE REALLY NEEDS US TO BE CARE-TAKERS, WE CAN TRUST THAT AT LEAST.
REALLY?

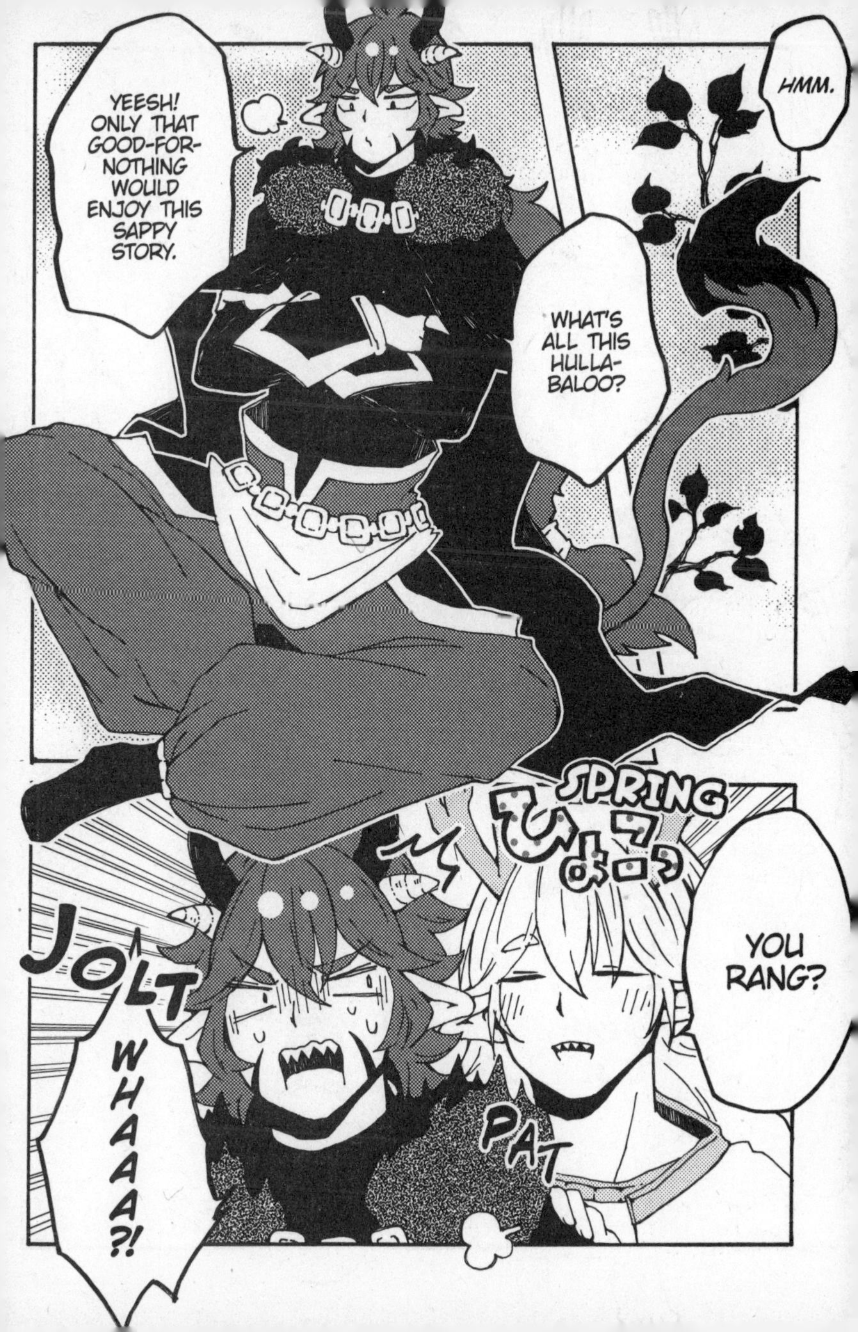
HMM.
WHAT'S ALL THIS HULLA-BALOO?
YEESH! ONLY THAT GOOD-FOR-NOTHING WOULD ENJOY THIS SAPPY STORY.
SPRING
ひょこっ
YOU RANG?
JOLT
WHAAAA?!
PAT

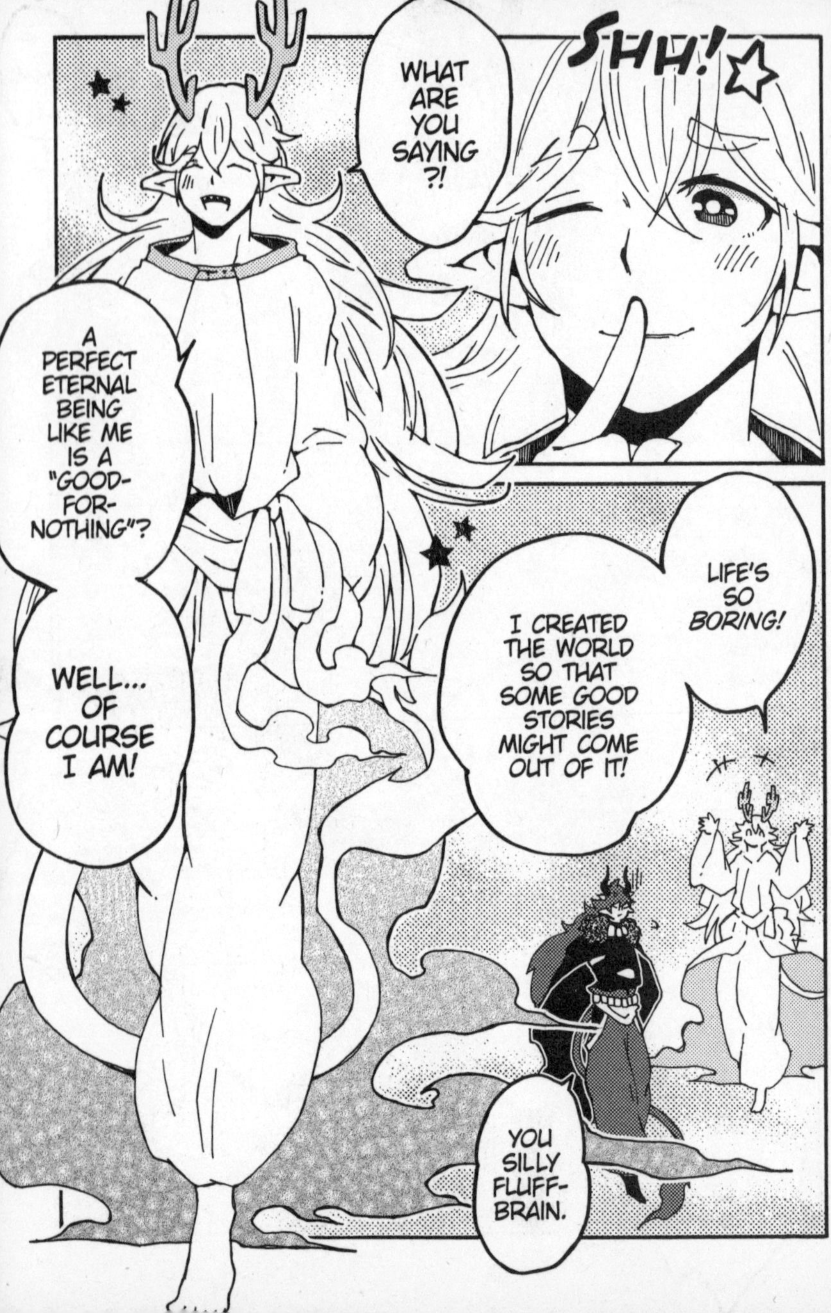
WHAT ARE YOU SAYING?!
A PERFECT ETERNAL BEING LIKE ME IS A "GOOD-FOR-NOTHING"?
WELL... OF COURSE I AM!
SHH!
LIFE'S SO BORING!
I CREATED THE WORLD SO THAT SOME GOOD STORIES MIGHT COME OUT OF IT!
YOU SILLY FLUFF-BRAIN.

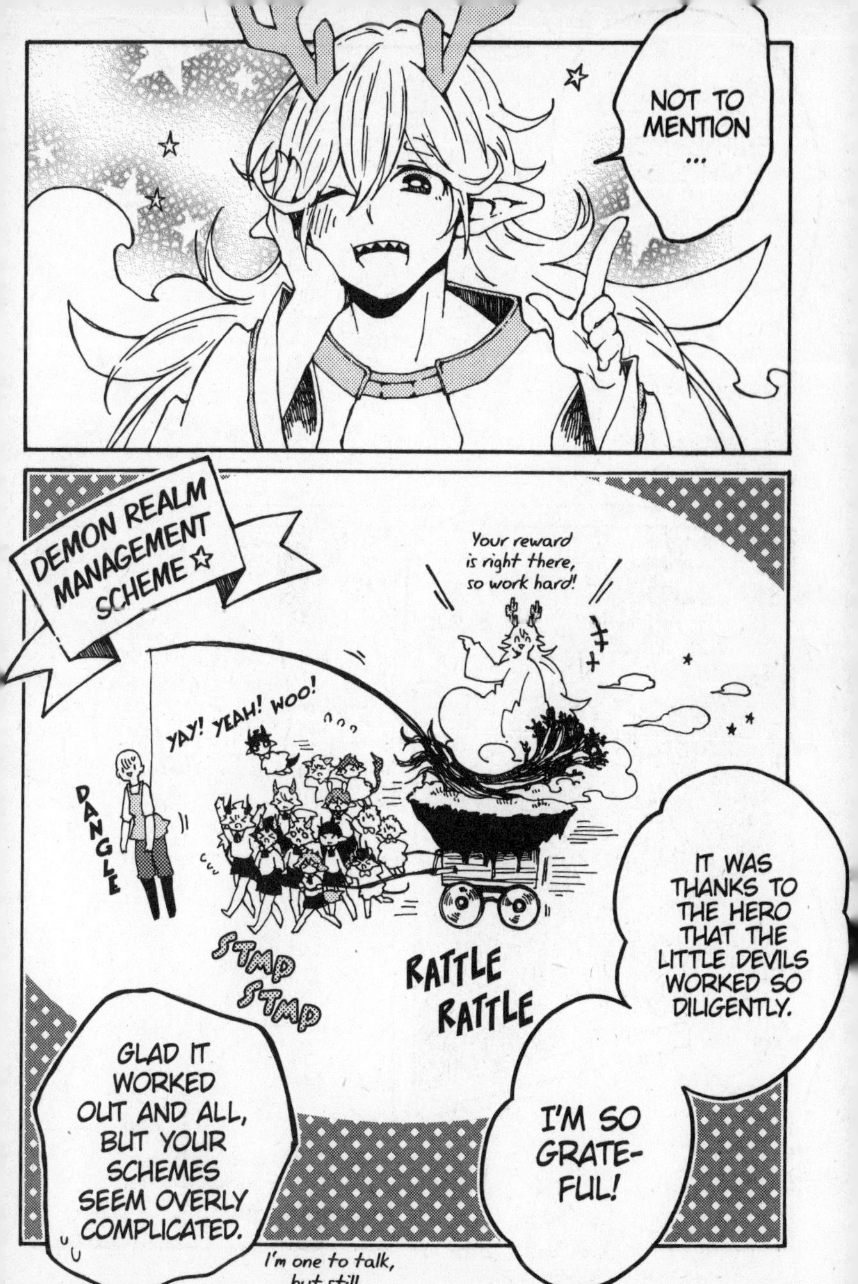
NOT TO MENTION ...
DEMON REALM MANAGEMENT SCHEME☆
Your reward is right there, so work hard!
YAY! YEAH! WOO!
IT WAS THANKS TO THE HERO THAT THE LITTLE DEVILS WORKED SO DILIGENTLY.
RATTLE RATTLE
STMP STMP
DANGLE
I'M SO GRATEFUL!
GLAD IT WORKED OUT AND ALL, BUT YOUR SCHEMES SEEM OVERLY COMPLICATED.
I'm one to talk, but still...

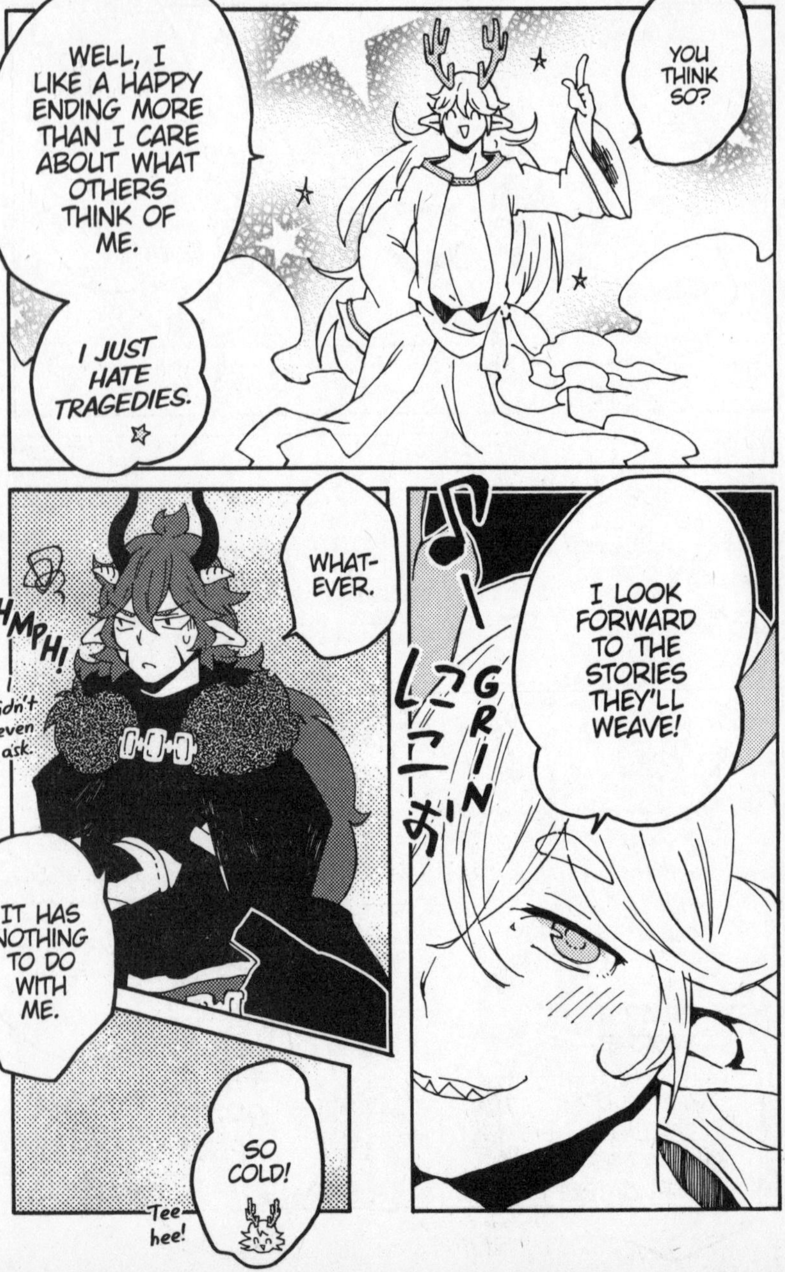
YOU THINK SO?
WELL, I LIKE A HAPPY ENDING MORE THAN I CARE ABOUT WHAT OTHERS THINK OF ME.
I JUST HATE TRAGEDIES.
GRIN
I LOOK FORWARD TO THE STORIES THEY'LL WEAVE!
WHAT-EVER.
HMPH!
I didn't even ask.
IT HAS NOTHING TO DO WITH ME.
SO COLD!
Tee-hee!

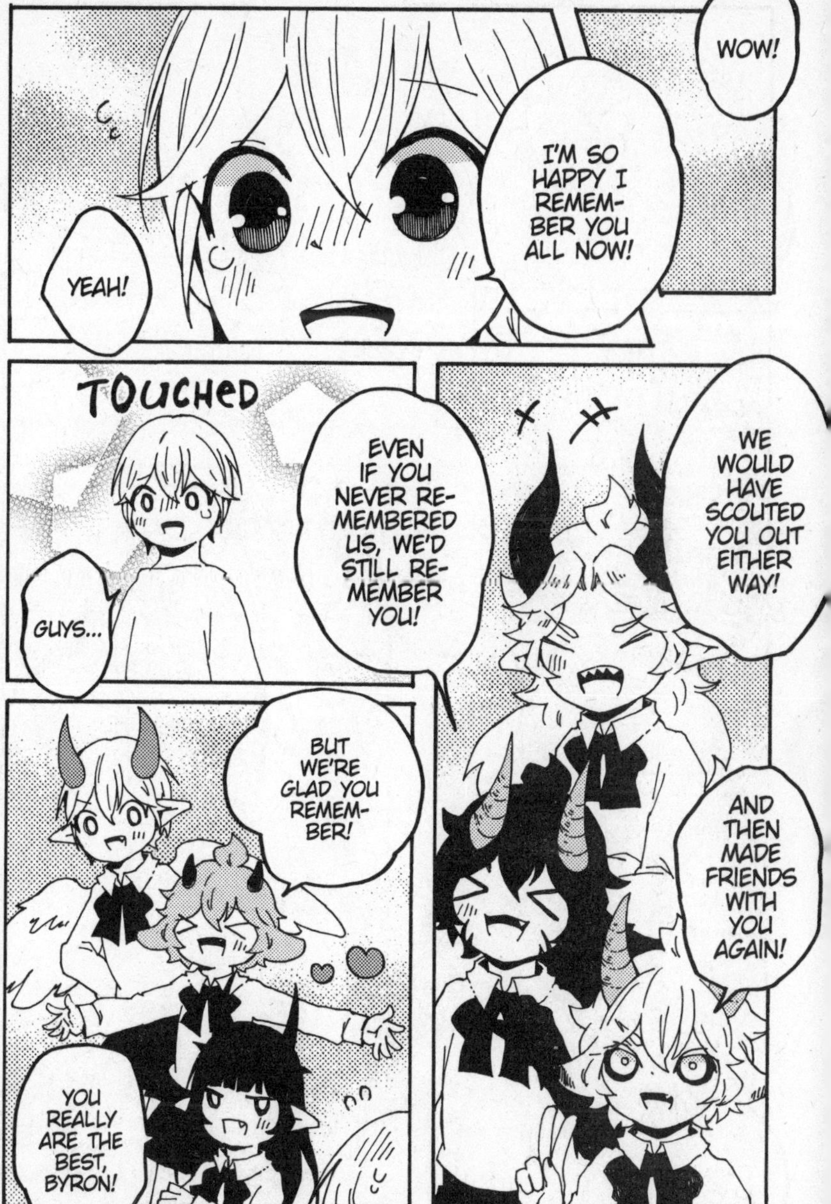
WOW!
I'M SO HAPPY I REMEMBER YOU ALL NOW!
YEAH!
EVEN IF YOU NEVER REMEMBERED US, WE'D STILL REMEMBER YOU!
WE WOULD HAVE SCOUTED YOU OUT EITHER WAY!
AND THEN MADE FRIENDS WITH YOU AGAIN!
TOUCHED
GUYS...
BUT WE'RE GLAD YOU REMEMBER!
YOU REALLY ARE THE BEST, BYRON!

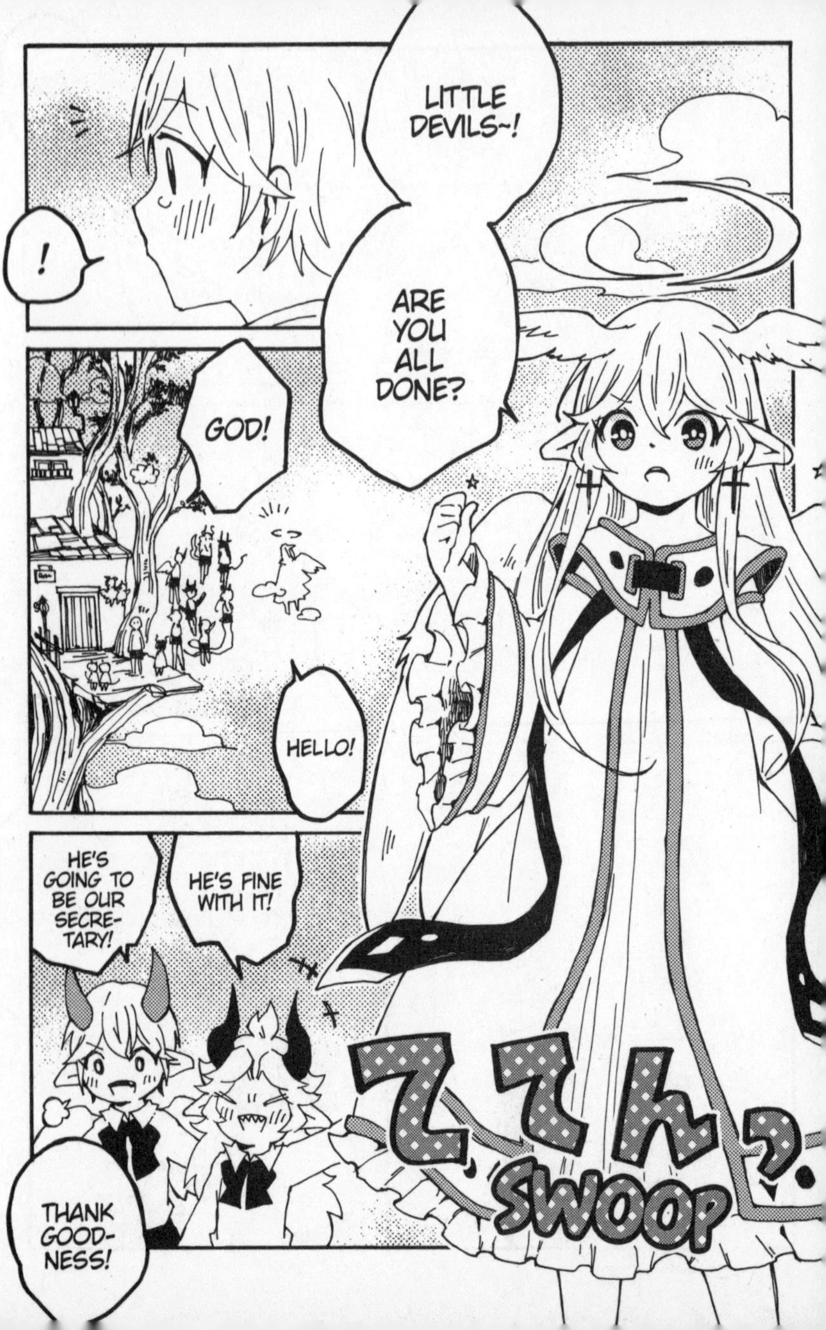

LITTLE DEVILS~!
ARE YOU ALL DONE?
!
GOD!
HELLO!
HE'S FINE WITH IT!
HE'S GOING TO BE OUR SECRE- TARY!
THANK GOOD- NESS!
SWOOP

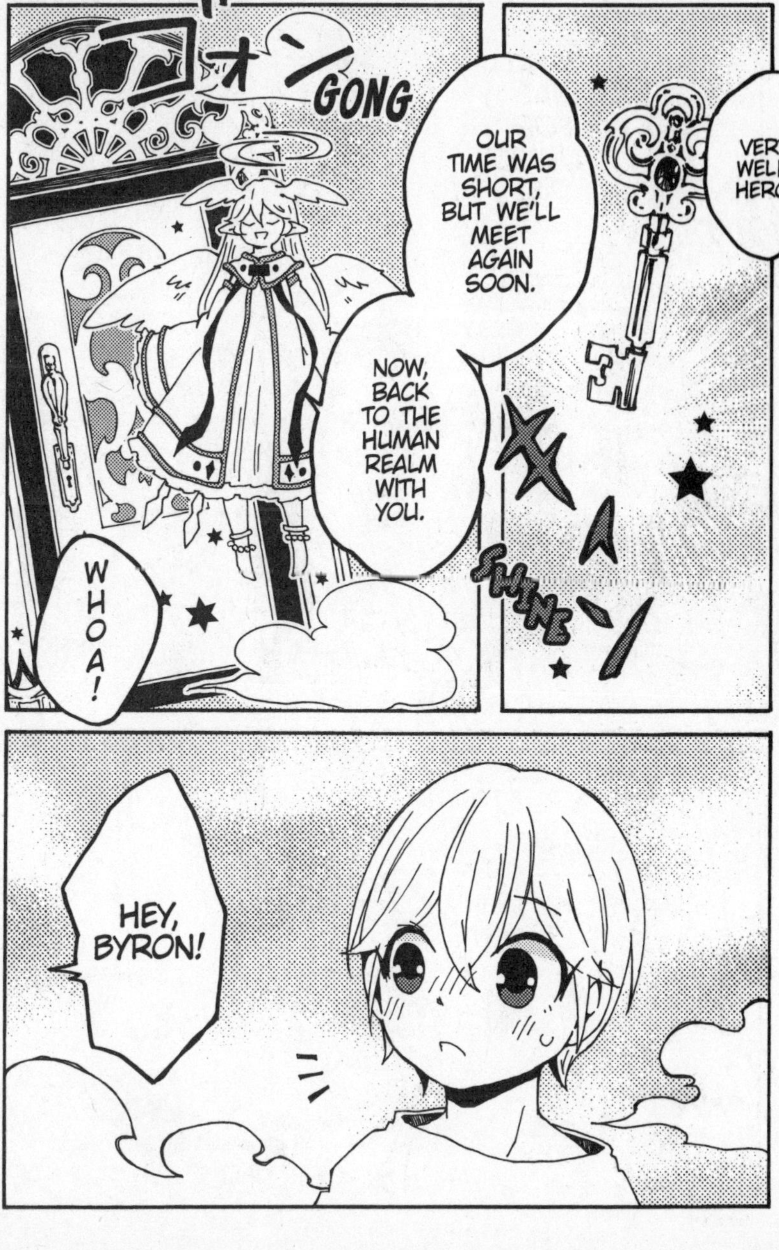
VERY WELL, HERO.
SHINE
GONG
OUR TIME WAS SHORT, BUT WE'LL MEET AGAIN SOON.
NOW, BACK TO THE HUMAN REALM WITH YOU.
WHOA!
HEY, BYRON!

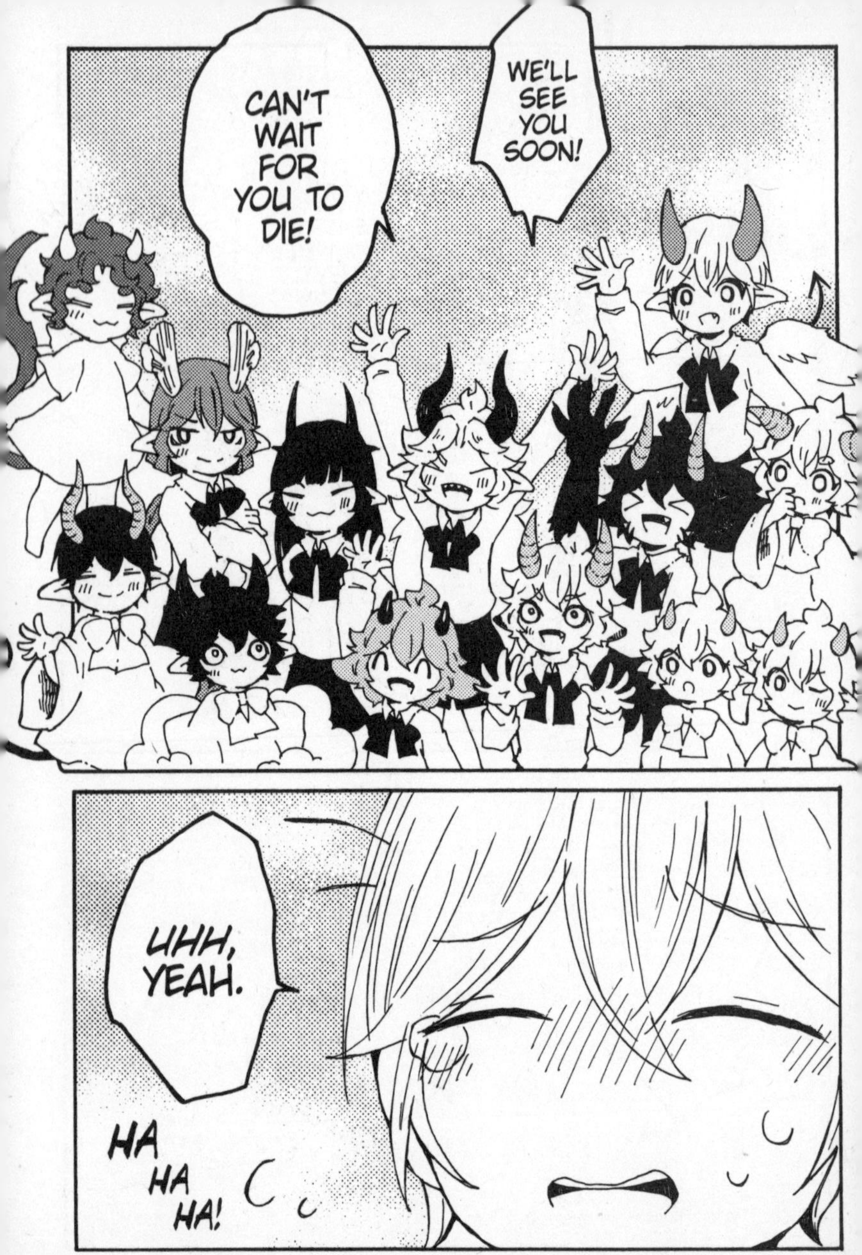
WE'LL SEE YOU SOON!
CAN'T WAIT FOR YOU TO DIE!
UHH, YEAH.
HA HA HA!

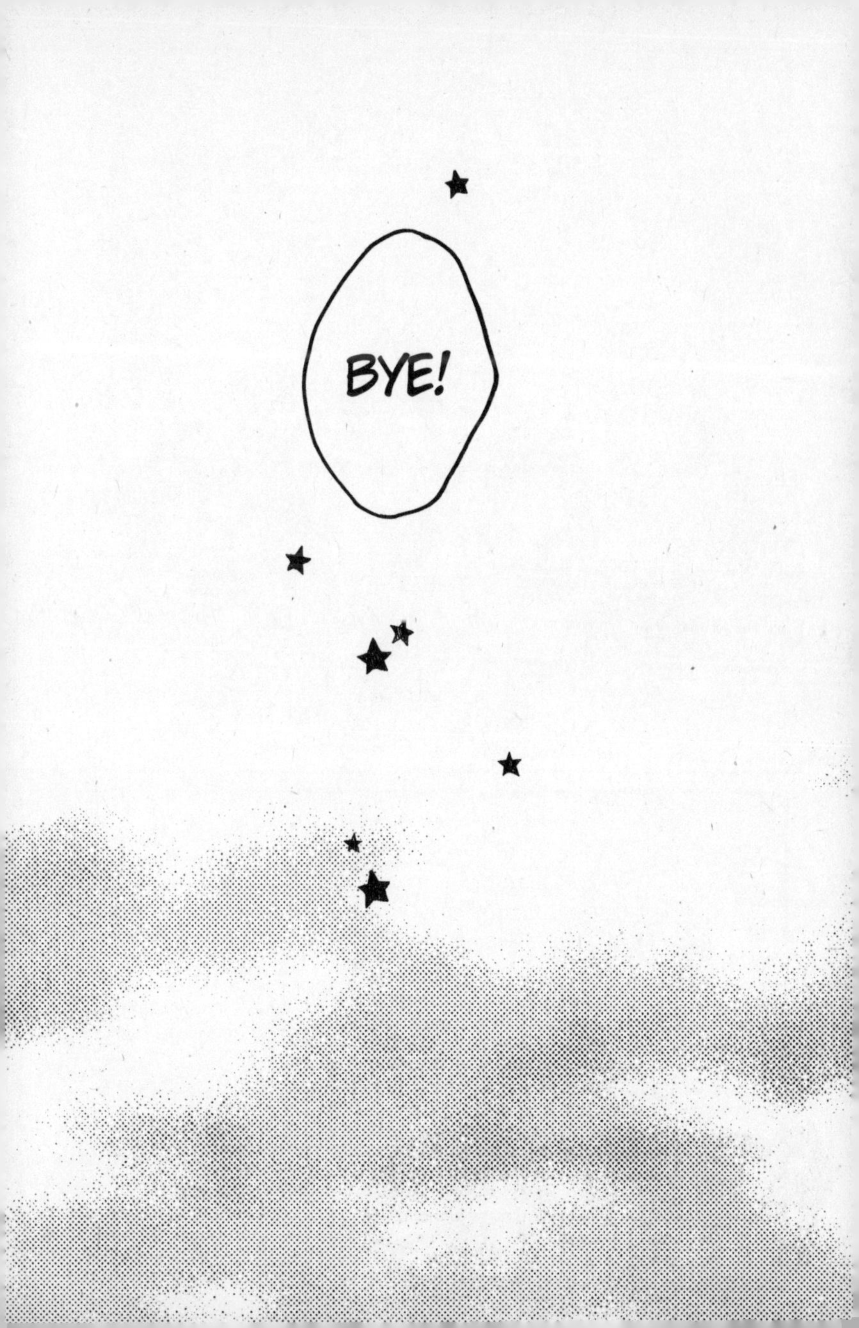
BYE!

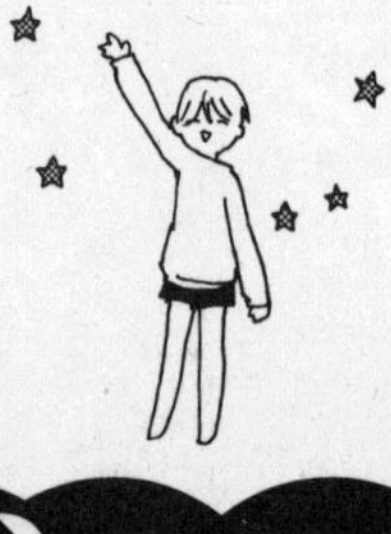

LITTLE DEVILS

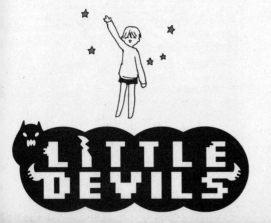

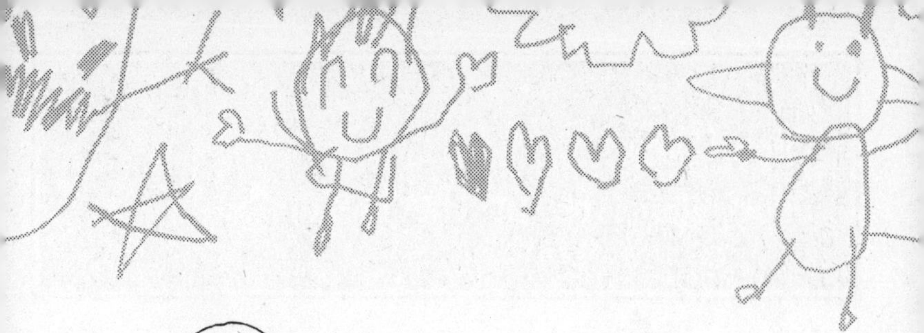

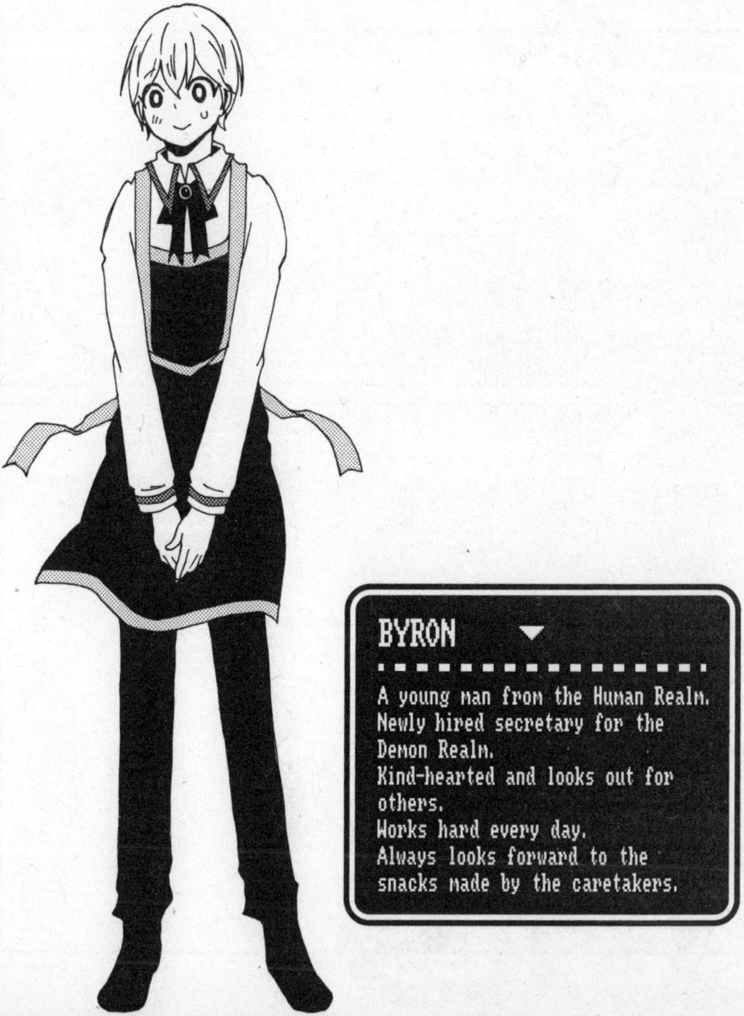

BYRON

A young man from the Human Realm.
Newly hired secretary for the Demon Realm.
Kind-hearted and looks out for others.
Works hard every day.
Always looks forward to the snacks made by the caretakers.

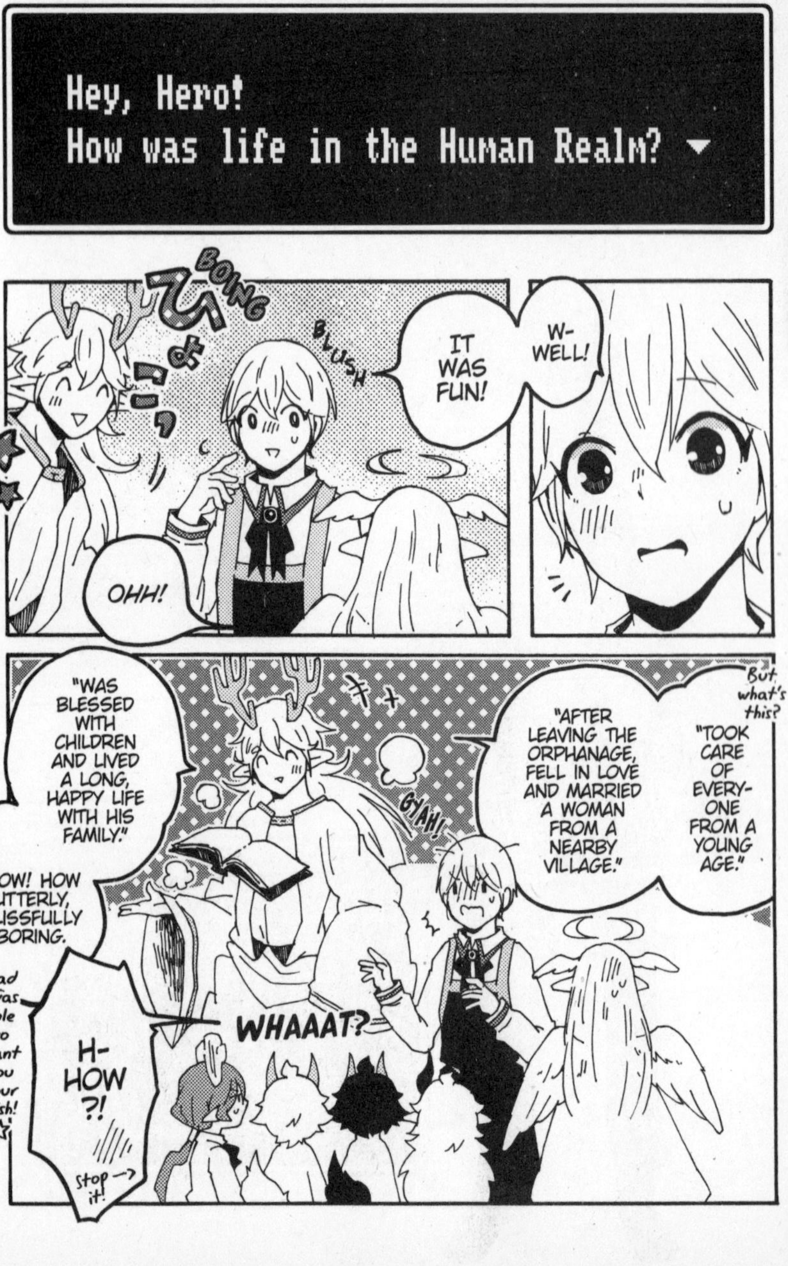
Hey, Hero!
How was life in the Human Realm?
W-WELL!
IT WAS FUN!
BLUSH
BOING
OHH!
But what's this?
"TOOK CARE OF EVERY-ONE FROM A YOUNG AGE."
"AFTER LEAVING THE ORPHANAGE, FELL IN LOVE AND MARRIED A WOMAN FROM A NEARBY VILLAGE."
GYAH!
"WAS BLESSED WITH CHILDREN AND LIVED A LONG, HAPPY LIFE WITH HIS FAMILY."
WOW! HOW UTTERLY, BLISSFULLY BORING.
WHAAAT?
H-HOW?!
Glad I was able to grant you your wish! ☆
stop it!

AFTERWORD

Uuumi

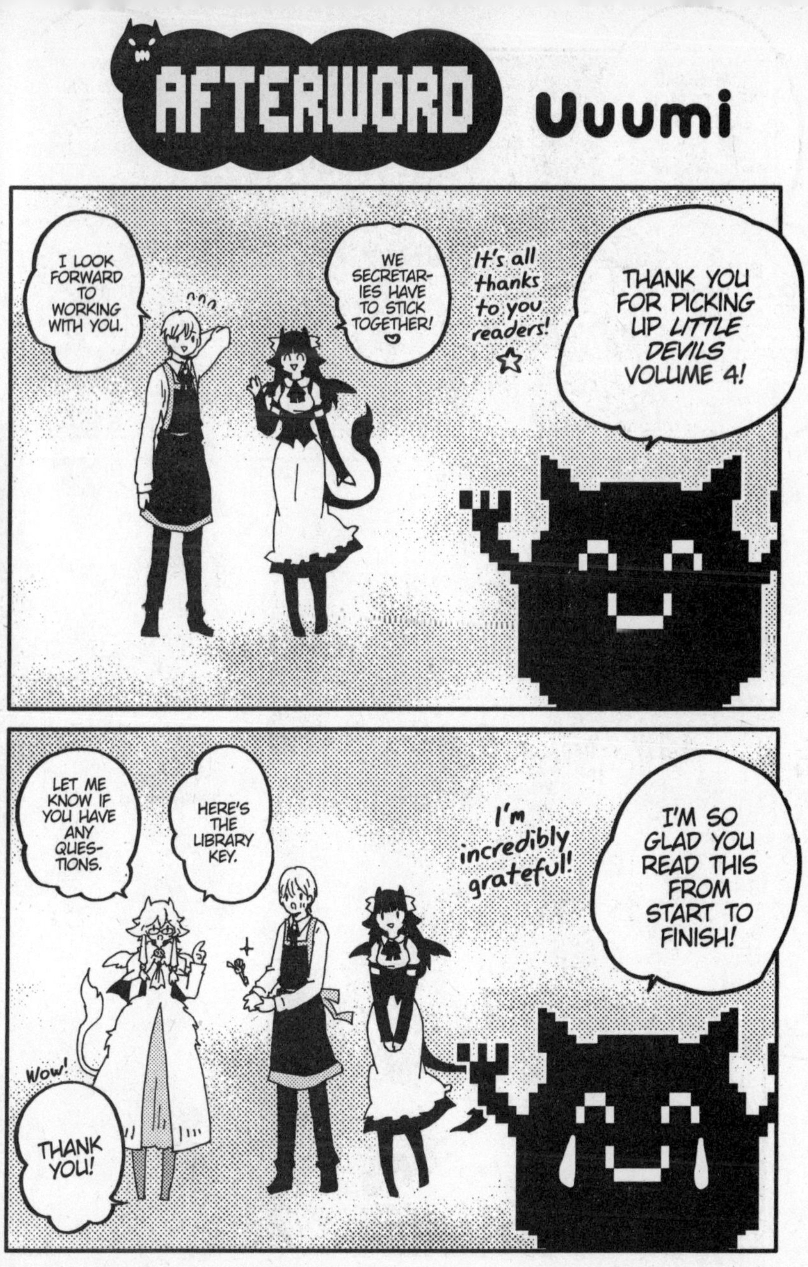
THANK YOU FOR PICKING UP *LITTLE DEVILS* VOLUME 4!
It's all thanks to you readers!
WE SECRETARIES HAVE TO STICK TOGETHER!
I LOOK FORWARD TO WORKING WITH YOU.
I'M SO GLAD YOU READ THIS FROM START TO FINISH!
I'm incredibly grateful!
HERE'S THE LIBRARY KEY.
LET ME KNOW IF YOU HAVE ANY QUESTIONS.
Wow!
THANK YOU!

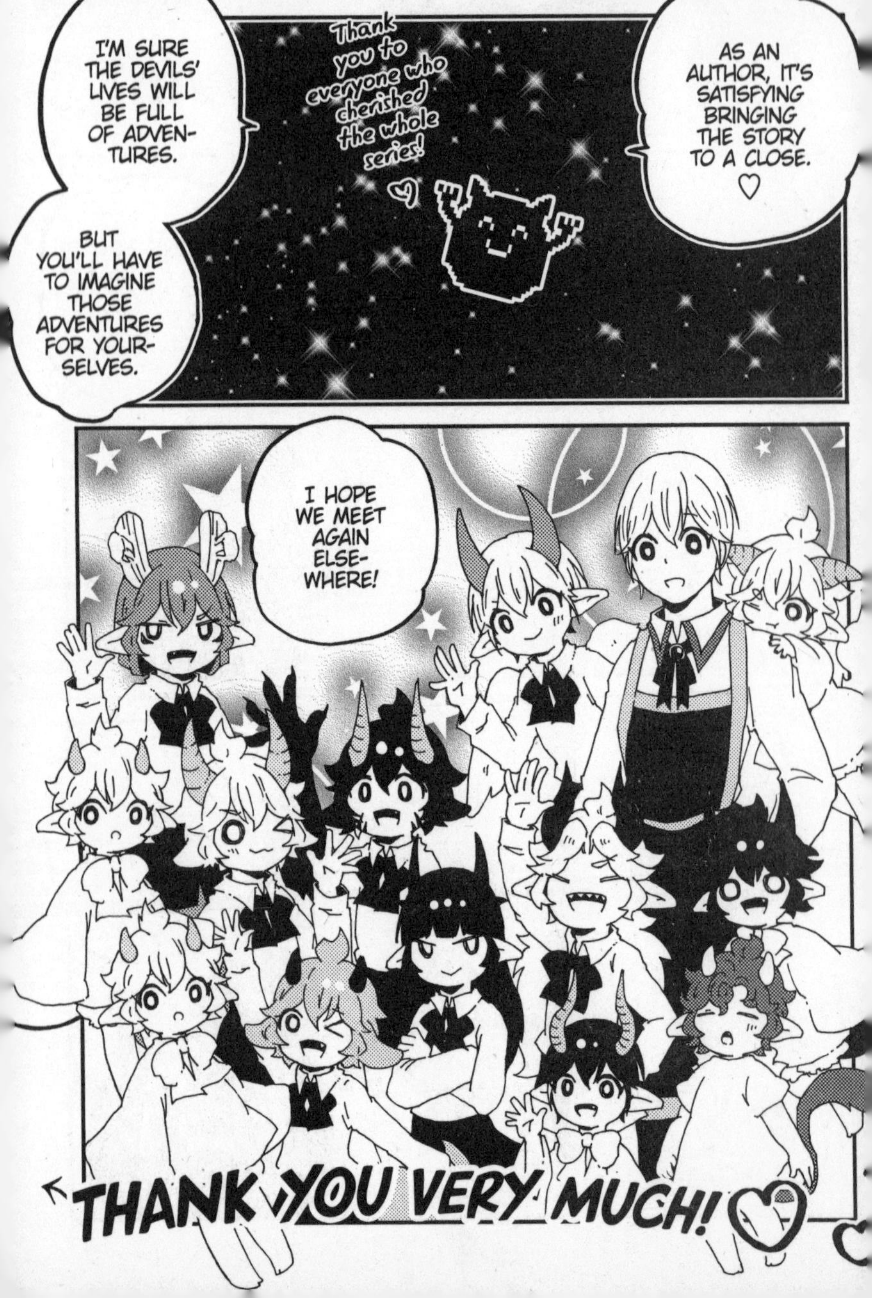
AS AN AUTHOR, IT'S SATISFYING BRINGING THE STORY TO A CLOSE. ♡
Thank you to everyone who cherished the whole series! ♡
I'M SURE THE DEVILS' LIVES WILL BE FULL OF ADVENTURES.
BUT YOU'LL HAVE TO IMAGINE THOSE ADVENTURES FOR YOURSELVES.
I HOPE WE MEET AGAIN ELSEWHERE!
THANK YOU VERY MUCH! ♡

☆ Special Thanks ☆

I'm grateful to
my editor Ikai-san
for taking care
of the series! ♡

Thank you so much!

Uuumi

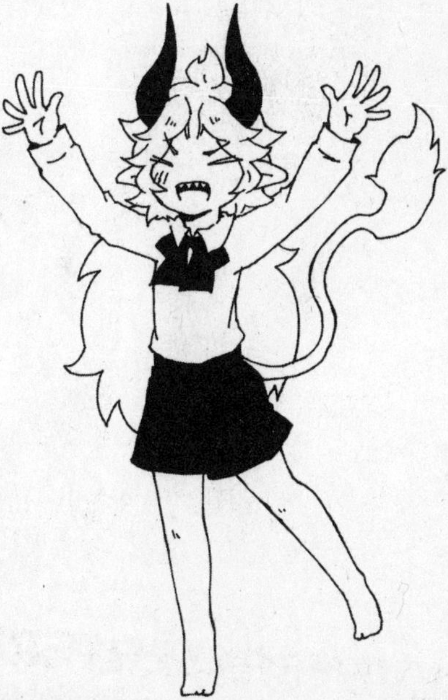

SEVEN SEAS ENTERTA...

LITTLE

story and art by UUUMI

VOLUME 4

TRANSLATION
Jennifer and Wesley O'Donnell

ADAPTATION
Casey Lucas

LETTERING AND RETOUCH
Ochie Caraan

COVER DESIGN
Nicky Lim

PROOFREADER
B. Lana Guggenheim

EDITOR
Shannon Fay

PRODUCTION MANAGER
Lissa Pattillo

MANAGING EDITOR
Julie Davis

ASSOCIATE PUBLISHER
Adam Arnold

PUBLISHER
Jason DeAngelis

MAOU KYOUDAI VOLUME 4
© UUUMI 2019
Originally published in Japan in 2019 by TOKUMA SHOTEN PUBLISHING
CO., LTD., Tokyo. English translation rights arranged with TOKUMA SHOTEN
PUBLISHING CO., LTD., Tokyo, through TOHAN CORPORATION, Tokyo.

Seven Seas press and purchase enquiries can be sent to Marketing Manager
Lianne Sentar at press@gomanga.com. Information regarding the distribution
and purchase of digital editions is available from Digital Manager CK Russell
at digital@gomanga.com.

Seven Seas and the Seven Seas logo are trademarks of
Seven Seas Entertainment. All rights reserved.

ISBN: 978-1-64505-476-4

Printed in Canada

First Printing: July 2020

10 9 8 7 6 5 4 3 2 1

FOLLOW US ONLINE: **www.sevenseasentertainment.com**

READING DIRECTIONS

This book reads from *right to left*, Japanese style.
If this is your first...
reading from the to...
take it from there.
numbered diagram...
first, but you'll get the hang of it! Have fun!!

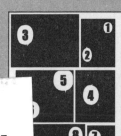

Coy Public Library of
Shippensburg
73 West King Street
Shippensburg, PA 17257